Thorsten Büring

Zoomable User Interfaces on Small Screens

I0009514

Thorsten Büring

Zoomable User Interfaces on Small Screens

Presentation and Interaction Design for Pen-operated Mobile Devices

VDM Verlag Dr. Müller

Imprint

Bibliographic information by the German National Library: The German National Library lists this publication at the German National Bibliography; detailed bibliographic information is available on the Internet at http://dnb.d-nb.de.

Cover image: www.purestockx.com

Publisher:
VDM Verlag Dr. Müller Aktiengesellschaft & Co. KG , Dudweiler Landstr. 125 a, 66123 Saarbrücken, Germany,
Phone +49 681 9100-698, Fax +49 681 9100-988,
Email: info@vdm-verlag.de

Zugl.: Konstanz, Universität Konstanz, Diss., 2007

Produced in USA and UK by:
Lightning Source Inc., La Vergne, Tennessee, USA
Lightning Source UK Ltd., Milton Keynes, UK
BookSurge LLC, 5341 Dorchester Road, Suite 16, North Charleston, SC 29418, USA

ISBN: 978-3-8364-6166-5

Meinen Eltern und meiner Schwester, die mich stets unterstützt und ermutigt haben.

Für Christiane, für die schöne gemeinsame Zeit und für die vielen Dinge, die ich von dir gelernt habe.

iv

Acknowledgements

There are several people who contributed to the research presented in this thesis. Firstly, I have to thank my advisor Prof. Dr. Harald Reiterer for giving me the opportunity to work in his *Mensch-Computer Interaktion* group. His guidance, comments, and suggestions throughout the last three years have been most valuable to me. Among the group members, special thanks are due to my colleague Jens Gerken with whom I worked on almost all projects, and who supported me with his expertise in HCI evaluation. Another person who spent many hours testing the various interfaces developed is Dominik Morbitzer. Moreover, I would like to thank my second advisor Prof. Dr. Daniel Keim for his interest and input, and Prof. Dr. Ronald Hübner for agreeing to be on my committee.

A key factor in enabling me to undertake a Ph.D. program in the first place was the support of the Deutsche Forschungsgemeinschaft, who provided me with a stipend for three years. Thanks to Prof. Dr. Dietmar Saupe, Dr. Giuseppe Di Fatta, all the advisors, doctorate students, associated students and administrators (especially Jens Schulze) of the Graduiertenkolleg *"Explorative Analysis and Visualization of Large Information Spaces"*, who supported and inspired me in many ways.

Abstract

Due to continuous and rapid advances in mobile hardware and wireless technology, devices such as smartphones and personal digital assistants (PDAs) are becoming a truly mobile alternative to bulky and heavy notebooks, allowing the users to access, search and explore remote data while on the road. Application fields that benefit from increased staff mobility are business consultants, mechanical engineers, and doctors in hospitals, for instance. However, a drawback that impedes this development is that the form factor of mobile devices requires a small-sized screen. Hence, given a large data set, only a fraction of it can be displayed. To identify important data the users are typically forced to linearly navigate the off-screen space via scrolling. For large information spaces, this is tedious, error-prone, and particularly slow. In contrast, the concept of zoomable user interfaces (ZUIs) has been found to improve the user performance for a variety of retrieval and exploration scenarios. While ZUIs have been investigated mainly in desktop environments, the objective of this work is to analyze the usability potentials of zooming and panning in a mobile context given the constraints of a small screen and pen-input.

Based on a comprehensive review of related work, the reported research is structured in two parts. First, we focus on the development of mobile starfield displays. Starfield displays are complex retrieval interfaces that encode and compress abstract data in a zoomable scatterplot visualization. To better adapt the interface to the requirements of a small screen, we merged the starfield approach with semantic zooming, providing a consistent and fluent transition from overview to detail information inside the scatterplot. While the participants in an informal study gave positive feedback regarding this type of data access, they also showed difficulties in orienting themselves in the information space. We further investigated this issue by implementing a zoomable overview+detail starfield display. Thus, while navigating the detail view, the users could keep track of their current position and scale via an additional overview window. In a controlled experiment with 24 participants, we compared the usability of this approach with a detail-only starfield and found that the separate overview window was not able to improve user satisfaction. Moreover, due to the smaller size of the detail view and the time needed for visual switching, it worsened task-completion times. This result led us to implement a rectangular fisheye view for starfield displays. The interface has the advantage that it displays both detail and context in a single view without requiring visual switching between separate windows. Another usability evaluation with 24 participants was conducted to compare the focus+context solution with an improved detail-only ZUI. While task-completion times were similar between the interfaces, the fisheye was strongly preferred by the users. This result may encourage interface designers to employ distortion strategies when displaying abstract information spaces on small screens. Our research also indicates that zoomable starfield displays provide an elegant and effective solution for data retrieval on devices such as smartphones and PDAs.

The second part of the research deals with map-based ZUIs, for which we investigated different approaches for improving the interaction design. Maps are currently the most common application domain for ZUIs. Standard interfaces for controlling such interfaces on pen-operated devices usually rely on sequential interaction, i.e. the users can either zoom or pan. A more advanced technique is speed-dependent automatic zooming (SDAZ), which combines rate-based panning and zooming into a single operation and thus enables concurrent interaction. Yet another navigation strategy is to allow for concurrent, but separate, zooming and panning. However, due to the limitations of stylus input, this feature requires the pen-operated device to be enhanced with additional input dimensions. We propose one unimanual approach based on pen pressure, and one bimanual approach in which users pan the view with the pen while manipulating the scale by tilting the device. In total, we developed four interfaces (standard, SDAZ, pressure, and tilting) and compared them in a usability study with 32 participants. The results show that SDAZ performed well for both simple speed tasks and more complex navigation scenarios, but that the coupled interaction led to much user frustration. In a preference vote, the participants strongly rejected the interface and stated that they found it difficult and irksome to control. In contrast, the novel pressure and tilt interfaces were much appreciated. However, in solving the test tasks the participants took hardly any advantage of parallel interaction. For a map view of 600x600 pixels, this resulted in task-completion times comparable to those for the standard interface. For a smaller 300x300 pixels view, the standard interface was actually significantly faster than the two novel techniques. This ratio is also reflected in the preference votes. While for the larger 600x600 pixels view the tilt interface was the most popular, the standard interface was rated highest for the 300x300 pixels view. Hence, on a smaller display, precise interaction may have an increased impact on the interface usability.

Zusammenfassung

Aufgrund des stetigen und rasanten Fortschritts in den Bereichen mobiler Hardware und Datenfunk ist bereits abzusehen, dass tragbare Endgeräte wie Smartphones und Personal Digital Assistants (PDA) in Kürze eine echte mobile Alternative zu unhandlichen und schweren Notebooks darstellen werden. Dies gilt insbesondere für den mobilen Zugriff auf Datenbanken, beispielsweise für Unternehmensberater, Maschinenbauingenieure und Ärzte im Krankenhaus. Ein Hemmschuh für diese Entwicklung ist jedoch der bei tragbaren Geräten implizit kleine Bildschirm, auf welchem oftmals nur ein Bruchteil der Daten angezeigt werden kann. Um alle wichtigen Informationen zu identifizieren, ist der Nutzer in der Regel gezwungen, den nicht sichtbaren Bereich mittels einer linearen Navigation über Bildlaufleisten zu durchsuchen. Für grosse Datenräume ist diese Strategie anstrengend, fehleranfällig und vor allen Dingen langsam. Eine Alternative bieten Zoombare Benutzeroberflächen (ZUIs), welche für eine Vielzahl von Such- und Explorationsszenarien eine höhere Leistungsfähigkeit versprechen. Während die bisherige Forschung ZUIs insbesondere in Bezug auf Desktop-Anwendungen betrachtete, ist es das Ziel dieser Arbeit die Benutzungsqualität von Zoomen und Pannen in einem mobilen Kontext mit Hinblick auf kleine Bildschirme und Stifteingabe zu untersuchen.

Ausgehend von einem umfangreichen Überblick über den bisherigen Forschungsstand, gliedert sich die vorliegende Arbeit in zwei Schwerpunkte. Zunächst wird über die Entwicklung von mobilen Starfield Benutzeroberflächen berichtet. Starfields sind komplexe Suchprogramme, die abstrakte Daten mittels eines Punktdiagramms darstellen und visuell komprimieren. Um diese Benutzeroberflächen besser an die Anforderungen kleiner Bildschirme anzupassen, haben wir Starfields mit einer semantischen Zoomfunktion erweitert. Diese erlaubt einen flüssigen und konsistenten Übergang von Übersichts- zu Detailinformation im Punktdiagramm. Ein entsprechend entwickelter Prototyp stiess in einer informalen Nutzerstudie auf positive Resonanz. Es zeigte sich jedoch auch, dass die Probanden Schwierigkeiten mit der Orientierung im Datenraum hatten. Um diesen Umstand näher zu untersuchen, entwickelten wir eine Overview+Detail Benutzeroberfläche für Starfield Applikationen. Diese erlaubte es den Nutzern während der Navigation in einer Detailansicht, die Position und die Skalierung des momentan sichtbaren Datenausschnitts in einem zusätzlichen Übersichtsfenster abzulesen. In einer Nutzerstudie über Bedienungsqualität mit 24 Teilnehmern verglichen wir den Overview+Detail Ansatz mit einer ursprünglichen Variante der Oberfläche, welche lediglich eine Detailansicht bot. Wir fanden heraus, dass das Übersichtsfenster die Nutzerzufriedenheit nicht steigern konnte. Zudem führte die kleinere Detailansicht und das stetige visuelle Hin- und Herwechseln zwischen den zwei Fenstern zu einer signifikanten Zeiteinbusse bei der Bewältigung von Testaufgaben. Auf-

grund dieses Ergebnisses wurde in einem weiteren Projekt eine rechtwinklige Fischaugenverzerrung für Starfields entwickelt. Diese Oberfläche hat den Vorteil, dass Detail- und
Kontextinformationen in einer integrierten Ansicht dargestellt werden können, und sich der
Benutzer somit während der Navigation auf ein einzelnes Fenster konzentrieren kann. Eine
weitere Nutzerstudie mit 24 Probanden wurde durchgeführt, um die Fischaugenverzerrung
mit einer weiterentwickelten Variante des semantischen Zooms zu vergleichen. Während
es keinen Zeitunterschied bei der Bewältigung der Testaufgaben zwischen den Oberflächen
gab, wurde die Fischaugenoberfläche von den Probanden stark präferiert. Dieses Ergebnis
ermutigt Designer, in Zukunft verstärkt Verzerrungstechniken für die Visualisierung von
abstrakten Daten auf kleinen Bildschirmen einzusetzen. Unsere Forschung deutet auch
darauf hin, dass Starfield Applikationen eine elegante und effektive Oberflächenlösung für
die mobile Datensuche mit Smartphones und PDAs bieten.

Der zweite Teil der Arbeit befasst sich mit kartenbasierten ZUIs, für welche ein verbessertes
Interaktionsdesign entwickelt werden soll. Karten sind der momentan häufigste Anwen-
dungsbereich für ZUIs. Der Standardansatz zur Bedienung derartiger Applikationen auf
Geräten mit Stifteingabe beruht zumeist auf sequentieller Interaktion, d.h. die Nutzer
können entweder Zoomen oder Pannen. Eine demgegenüber fortgeschrittene Technik
ist Speed-Dependent Automatic Zooming (SDAZ), welches kontinuierliches Pannen mit
Zoomen in eine einzelne Nutzereingabe bündelt und daher eine simultane Navigationsin-
teraktion ermöglicht. Wiederum ein anderer Ansatz ist es, dem Nutzer eine simultane
aber zusätzlich auch separate Kontrolle von Zoomen und Pannen anzubieten. Eine der-
artige Funktionalität erfordert jedoch, dass die ansonsten zu begrenzte Stifteingabe mit
weiteren Eingabedimensionen erweitert wird. Diesbezüglich stellen wir eine einhändig zu
bedienende Technik basierend auf Stiftdruck vor, und eine zweihändige Variante, bei der
der Nutzer den Kartenausschnitt mit dem Stift horizontal und vertikal navigiert, während
die Skalierung der Ansicht über das Kippen des Geräts gesteuert wird. Entsprechend
haben wir vier Benutzeroberflächen entwickelt (Standard, SDAZ, Stiftdruck und Kippen)
und diese in einer Nutzerstudie mit 32 Probanden getestet. Die Ergebnisse zeigen, dass
SDAZ eine effektive Bearbeitung von simplen Schnelligkeitsaufgaben als auch von kom-
plexeren Navigationsszenarien ermöglichte, jedoch das Koppeln von Zoomen und Pannen
dennoch zu einer hohen Nutzerfrustration führte. In einer Präferenzbefragung bezüglich
der getesteten Benutzeroberflächen zeigten die Probanden eine starke Ablehnung gegen
SDAZ und erklärten, dass sie die Oberfläche schwer und umständlich zu bedienen fanden.
Im Vergleich dazu wurden die neuartigen Interaktionvarianten Stiftdruck und Kippen aus-
gesprochen gut angenommen. Allerdings machten die Probanden während des Tests kaum
Gebrauch von der angebotenen parallelen Interaktion. Dies führte bei einem 600x600 pixel
grossen Sichtfenster zu ähnlichen Lösungszeiten wie für die Standardbenutzeroberfläche.
Letztere stellte sich für ein 300x300 pixel grosses Sichtfenster sogar als die signifikant
schnellere Variante heraus. Dieses Verhältnis wird auch durch die Präferenzwahl widerge-
spiegelt. Während für das grössere Sichtfenster die Kippvariante die bevorzugte Technik
war, erhielt für das kleinere Sichtfenster die Standardvariante die meisten Stimmen. Wir
vermuten daher, dass auf einem kleineren Bildschirm, präzise Interaktion einen relativ
höheren Einfluss verglichen mit dynamischer Interaktion auf die Nutzungsqualität hat.

Parts of this thesis were published in:

1. Thorsten Büring. *Handbook of Research on User Interface Design and Evaluation for Mobile Technology*, chapter Navigation support for exploring starfield displays on personal digital assistants. Information Science Reference, 2007 (in press).

2. Thorsten Büring, Jens Gerken, and Harald Reiterer. Interaction design for zooming maps on pen-operated devices. *International Journal of Human-Computer Studies*, 2007 (submitted).

3. Thorsten Büring, Jens Gerken, and Harald Reiterer. Dynamic text filtering for improving the usability of alphasliders on small screens. *In IV '07: Proceedings of the Eleventh International Conference on Information Visualisation*, Zuerich, Switzerland, 2007 (in press). IEEE Computer Society.

4. Thorsten Büring, Jens Gerken, and Harald Reiterer. User interaction with scatterplots on small screens - a comparative evaluation of geometric-semantic zoom and fisheye distortion. *IEEE Transactions on Visualization and Computer Graphics (Proceedings Visualization / Information Visualization 2006)*, 12(5):829–836, September-October 2006.

5. Thorsten Büring, Jens Gerken, and Harald Reiterer. Usability of overview-supported zooming on small screens with regard to individual differences in spatial ability. In *AVI '06: Proceedings of the working conference on Advanced visual interfaces*, pages 233–240, New York, NY, USA, 2006. ACM Press.

6. Thorsten Büring. Interaktionsstrategien für Punktdiagramm-Visualisierungen auf kleinen Bildschirmen. *i-com, Zeitschrift für interaktive und kooperative Medien*, 5(2):32–37, 2006.

7. Thorsten Büring and Harald Reiterer. Zuiscat: querying and visualizing information spaces on personal digital assistants. In *MobileHCI '05: Proceedings of the 7th international conference on Human computer interaction with mobile devices & services*, pages 129–136, New York, NY, USA, 2005. ACM Press.

Contents

List of Figures

List of Tables

Chapter 1

Introduction

Contents

1.1 Mobile User Interfaces

Mobile devices such as Personal Digital Assistants (PDAs) and smartphones have become a dominant information system in many people's everyday life. Originally, those handhelds were designed to support users in managing personal information data such as dates and contacts. However, continuous advances in hardware technology and the ubiquitous availability of wireless networks led to novel application domains for mobile software. People now use their devices to download, share, and play music, to record and watch movies in DVD-like quality, to play 3D games, navigate via GPS, to receive and send emails, and to edit presentations and spreadsheets. Furthermore, there is a growing palette of business software available for handhelds. Major companies such as SAP[1] and Oracle[2] provide their customers with a variety of mobile applications to access, administer and edit remote business data. Target groups are mobile sales professionals, field service engineers, and managers, for instance. Another growing market for mobile applications is the health sector, which benefits from increased staff mobility. Doctors use PDAs to facilitate patient handovers at hospitals and to browse and search pharmaceutical information while on the ward. Further application domains for mobile devices exist in areas such as mechanical engineering and logistics.

The examples mentioned above illustrate that many tasks today scale from desktop computers to mobile devices. Most user interfaces do not, however. One reason for this is

---

[1] www.sap.com/solutions/xapps/mobilebusiness/index.epx
[2] www.oracle.com/applications/sales/sales_handhelds.html

that PDAs and smartphones are considerably less powerful in terms of CPU, memory, and graphics hardware. Mobile programming frameworks such as Java ME and the .NET compact framework are also limited to a small core of classes and methods to achieve a minimal footprint. Due to the limited hardware resources and low-level drawing APIs, the porting of complex user interfaces to mobile devices often proves difficult.

While hardware and software development issues may soon be overcome by technological progress, other problems are of a more lasting nature. When targeting mobile devices such as shown in Figure 1.1, the most apparent difference compared to desktop computers is the small screen size. PDAs and smartphones usually feature a 2.5 to 4 inch display with a resolution ranging from 240 x 240 pixels (e.g. Palm Treo 700w) to 480 x 640 pixels (e.g. HP iPAQ hx4705). This is only about 5% of the display size available on a regular 19-inch desktop screen. In addition, fewer colors (65k) are supported.

(a)   (b)   (c)

Figure 1.1: A collection of mobile devices: (a) Personal Digital Assistant (PDA) (www.hp.com), (b) smartphone (www.palm.com), (c) PDA Phone (www.hp.com).

The problem that arises from a limited screen real estate is that most information spaces such as documents and images are considerably larger than the display. This leads to a tension between showing detail information and showing context information [212]. One workaround for this problem may be to equip handhelds with a projector tool so that a large screen can be created on any surface [51]. However, this technique is still in an early experimental phase and also touches on additional questions such as privacy issues and outdoor feasibility. A currently more applicable approach for mobile interfaces is to utilize presentation techniques that were originally developed to ease the detail-context tension on desktop interfaces [138]. The most widely adopted one is the scrolling interface, but it has the drawback that its usability decreases with a growing information space. Since the viewport only visualizes a small fraction of the data, users are forced to apply a tedious and error-prone manual search to explore the contents of the off-screen area [175].

An alternative to scroll bars is the concept of a zoomable user interface (ZUI). ZUIs are based on a spatial metaphor and assume that data objects are organized in space and scale. Users gain an overview of the entire information space by zooming out, and access details by zooming in. ZUIs for desktop-based systems have been extensively studied during the past fifteen years and were found to improve the user performance and satisfaction for a variety of domains and task scenarios. More recently, they are also becoming well known to a wider audience, due to popular zoom applications such as Google Earth[3] and NASA World Wind[4]. ZUIs have the benefit of making more efficient use of limited screen real estate, and thus are considered to have a great potential on small-sized mobile devices [17]. However, work in this field is still in its early stages, with no comprehensive overview of concepts or design guidelines being available. With regards to the next generation of mobile applications that will handle and present large amounts of data, we think there is a strong research need to investigate how the full potential of ZUIs can be exploited for devices such as PDAs and smartphones.

1.2 Research Objectives: ZUI Presentation Design

The first contribution of this work is to report on three research projects we carried out to improve the usability of ZUIs in the context of PDA starfield displays. Starfield displays are complex search interfaces that visualize data as abstract representations inside a scatterplot. Due to the compact representation, large numbers of items can be displayed on a small screen. However, this technique cannot prevent overlappings. To prune visual clutter and to explore the information space, the starfield enables the users to zoom and pan the scatterplot. Our research objectives focused on the following issues:

- *Space and focus-preserving transitions*
  At some point, users of starfield displays want to switch from the scatterplot overview to the textual information of data objects. Interfaces on desktop computers usually meet this requirement by presenting details in a separate frame. However, on a small screen an additional window decreases the space available for the scatterplot and thus increases data clutter. Pop-ups are another common approach, but they carry the drawback of blocking the users' view on the scatterplot. This can hamper rapid data access by forcing the users to frequently re-locate their previous scatterplot focus after closing the pop-up. As an alternative solution we examined a multiscale interface approach with semantic zooming to provide a smooth and intuitive transition from overview to detail information inside the scatterplot control.

- *Orientation support for starfield ZUIs.*
  Another common drawback with ZUIs is that users may easily become disoriented once they have zoomed into the information space [52] [120]. This is due to the clipping of orientation cues, an aspect that becomes increasingly significant as less display real estate is available. To preserve context, previous research has proposed

---

[3]http://earth.google.com/
[4]http://worldwind.arc.nasa.gov/

three approaches: smooth zooming [207] [17] [208], overview+detail [175], and focus+context [213] interfaces. We applied these presentation techniques to PDA starfield displays and evaluated their usability in three user studies.

- *Interaction design for pen-based touchscreens*
  PDAs and smartphones usually feature a touchscreen in conjunction with a stylus. This kind of interaction has been found easy for novice users to learn, but on the other hand primary input commands are limited to a small set of states and events. While high-end devices are likely to be equipped with more advanced input technologies, for current standard devices the ZUI designer still needs to map zooming, panning, and selection to no more than pen-down, pen-move, and pen-up events. Given these constraints, we developed and investigated different designs to allow for precise and fast navigation for traveling short and long distances in the information space.

1.3   Research Objectives: ZUI Interaction Design

The second contribution of this work is to research interaction design in a wider context, i.e. considering advanced zooming and panning strategies and non-standard input technologies for mobile devices. The issue was motivated by analyzing an interaction technique called speed-dependent automatic zooming [123], which in previous research has been found to outperform manual zooming approaches on desktop computers [66] [202]. SDAZ couples rate-based scrolling and zooming into a single drag gesture with a pointing device, and thus can be easily implemented for pen-operated devices. We carried out a usability evaluation in which we compared SDAZ to three alternative interfaces for navigating a zoomable map. One of the interfaces featured solely sequential interaction, which is standard for current pen-operated software, one used a pressure-sensitive pen to control zooming and panning independently, and the last one used a bimanual approach combining pen input with device tilting. Two other objectives of the project were to measure the effect that task types of different navigation complexity and different view sizes would have on the usability of the techniques.

1.4   Methodology

This work presents various experimental interfaces that have been developed in an iterative design and prototyping process. The applications were implemented in Adobe Flash, the .NET compact framework, the full .NET framework, and managed DirectX. We tested our prototypes in several controlled user experiments using PDAs, a Wacom display, and a Tablet PC as test devices. Apart from logging performance data, we used screen and video recordings to document the user interaction. To measure user satisfaction and subjective workload, we employed questionnaires such as AttrakDiff[5] and the NASA Task Load Index[6]. For hypotheses testing we used common inferential statistical tests.

---

[5]http://www.attrakdiff.de/
[6]http://www.nrl.navy.mil/aic/ide/NASATLX.php

The overall objective of this research was to improve the usability of mobile ZUIs. The term usability is defined by the International Organization for Standardization as *"the extent to which a product can be used by specified users to achieve specified goals with effectiveness, efficiency and satisfaction in a specified context of use."* [7] Usability aspects within the scope of this work were task-completion time, mental workload, satisfaction, interface preference and errors.

1.5 Outline

Having explained the research motivation and objectives in the introduction, the second chapter then provides an overview of presentation techniques for visualizing information spaces larger than the screen and of how these techniques may be utilized for mobile devices. It starts with the scrolling interface as the most conventional solution and then presents the concept of zoomable user interfaces. Different design considerations and existing mobile ZUIs are discussed. As mentioned before, one of the main challenges with ZUIs is to preserve overview information. The chapter highlights two presentation techniques that can reduce this problem, namely overview+detail and focus+context interfaces.

The third chapter introduces the scientific domain of Information Visualization along with starfield displays as complex search interfaces. Apart from the development history, we present and discuss implementations of starfields for both desktop computers and mobile devices.

Chapter 4 is based on three research projects that we have conducted to improve the usability of starfield displays for pen-operated mobile devices. The chapter proposes several design alternatives and reports the results of one informal and two quantitative user evaluations. Eventually, an outlook is given on how starfield ZUIs on mobile devices could be further improved.

In Chapter 5 we examine the usability of different interaction designs and input technologies for zooming and panning on pen-operated devices. We present several experimental interfaces that were developed to navigate a Munich city-map. We also report the settings and results of a comprehensive usability study in which we compared the various approaches to one another.

The work concludes with Chapter 6, which sums up the main results of the research conducted.

---

[7]ISO 9241-11 (1998) Guidance on Usability

Chapter 2

Presentation Techniques

Contents

2.1 Scrolling Interfaces

Scrolling interfaces provide a common solution for accessing information spaces that are larger than the display size. For example, the PDA application shown in Figure 2.1 visualizes a portion of a city-map. To view the content that is currently off-screen, users can shift the viewport by operating scrollbars. Such a scrollbar typically consists of the following components.

- Two arrow buttons, one for each direction in the given dimension. Users tap, or tap and hold, the buttons to move the viewport incrementally.

- The scroll thumb. Its size corresponds to the ratio of the viewport size and the size of the information space. By dragging the thumb, users can shift the viewport in a direct-manipulative fashion.

- The scrollbar track on which the thumb runs. Tapping the track outside the area occupied by the thumb causes the viewport to jump to the indicated position.

Scrollbars have the advantage that most users are familiar with them, but they also have several drawbacks. Firstly, navigation with scrollbars is limited to horizontal and vertical shifts. To move diagonally, users must therefore perform time-consuming sequential actions. Secondly, the spatial cues provided by the location and size of the scroll thumbs are rather abstract and do not convey any information about the content in the off-screen region [212]. Searching in a reasonably large information space for an object not currently

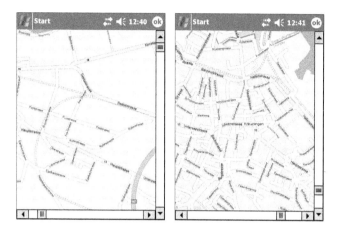

Figure 2.1: A PDA scrolling interface showing a map.

visible forces users to scroll incrementally until the object eventually enters the viewport. Thus, scrolling is often experienced as a slow and tedious way of navigating [167]. Moreover, it also hampers the recall of the spatial locations of information - knowledge which can, for instance, improve users' comprehension while reading, and help to speed up search and retrieval tasks [168].

The drawbacks of scrollbars are exacerbated on mobile devices, where a smaller viewport increases the need for scrolling [168]. Two-dimensional scrolling can be particularly cumbersome - an example is reading text, when users have to scroll each line horizontally. Systems such as Adobe Reader try to avoid this problem by reformatting content such that users only need to scroll vertically. The same strategy can also be applied to web browsers. The Opera browser for mobile devices[1] uses a proxy server to reformat web pages into a single column to fit inside the screen width. While this may improve the browsing experience when compared to two-dimensional scrolling, usability studies have revealed that applying a new layout to the logical structure and grouping of a web page can also lead to significant irritations. Users may not recognize familiar web pages, and content such as timetables, which relies on a two-dimensional layout, is broken down into successive vertical parts and thus becomes almost unreadable. With a big screen, moreover, the user's attention is typically focused on the center of the monitor. With a small screen, the highest priority is given to the topmost information, which, on a commercial site, is typically a banner ad. To reach the actual content of the web page, users first have to scroll down [198] [96].

A general problem with scrolling is scalability. Scrollbars have been found effective for rather small information spaces, in which users may only move in a single direction by small increments [175]. As the size of the information space grows, the usability deteri-

---

[1]http://www.opera.com/products/mobile/smallscreen

orates. Not only does the manual search process for locating off-screen objects increase, but the handling of the scrollbars also becomes more difficult. First of all, there is a limit to how small a thumb can be scaled so that it still remains easily tappable. For .NET Windows controls, for instance, the minimum size for a thumb in a vertical scrollbar is defined as half the height of the vertical scrollbar button. From that point on, the thumb no longer provides true feedback on the ratio of the viewport and information space sizes. Furthermore, the control sensitivity increases. Each pixel that the thumb is dragged results in coarse jumps of the viewport, with no overlapping area. In that situation, precise navigation is no longer feasible. Another aspect is that of the costs in terms of screen real estate. Since scrollbars require a visual representation for interaction, they thus reduce the display size available for the viewport. This is usually not a problem on desktop monitors, but it can be a significant constraint for applications running on small screens.

If a scrollbar cannot be avoided, we can enhance its functionality by turning the control into an abstract overview. As will be discussed in detail in Chapter 2.3, encodings can, for instance, highlight the position of information objects in the off-screen space [50]. An example of this approach is shown in Figure 2.2. It assumes that users previously define some kind of filter to identify objects of interest. In some cases, e.g. when reading a multi-column document, scroll paths may also be automatically adjusted by the system [126]. Other concepts to enhance the functionality of scrollbars have been proposed in [113] [61] [105].

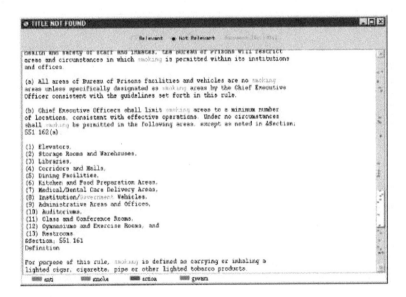

Figure 2.2: Enhancing scrollbars with additional overview information [50].

2.2   Zoomable User Interfaces

ZUIs facilitate data presentation on small screens by exploiting users' innate spatial ability [17]. They are based on the assumption that *"navigation in information spaces is best supported by tapping into our natural spatial and geographic ways of thinking"* [172]. In order to implement this approach on a computer screen, data objects must be organized in space and scale. Users can manipulate which part of the information space is shown, and at what scale, by performing panning and zooming operations. Panning is a movement of the viewport over the information space at a constant scale. Zooming means altering the scale of the viewport such that it shows a decreasing fraction of the information space with an increasing magnification [212].

A method of illustrating ZUI properties is that of space-scale diagrams [92]. Figure 2.3 models a ZUI in which the 2D information space is shown at different magnification levels and aligned by the vertical axis representing scale. The white rectangle represents the viewport, i.e. the portion of the information space that is visible. The outer gray area is the off-screen space. In the diagrammatic example, users are searching for the target object that is off-screen (top-most scale level). Instead of panning the view around, as in the scrolling interface, users zoom out until the target object enters the viewport. In a second step, they can then access the object's details by zooming back in.

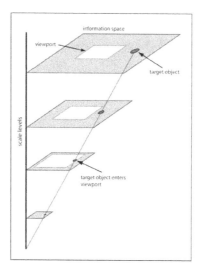

Figure 2.3: Space-scale diagram visualizing a zoom-out operation to locate a target object.

In contrast to scrolling interfaces, which are only effective for small spaces, ZUIs develop their full potential as the size of the information space grows. Even if users know the precise location of an off-screen target, in most cases a pan operation would still be a slow way of navigating. Panning only covers distance at a constant pace, while zooming allows users to view off-screen content in a non-linear fashion. This advantage is due to the special properties of multiscale interfaces, in which the shortest path between two points is usually not a straight line, but a combination of zoom and pan operations [92].

Previous research indicates that, on desktop computers, ZUIs reliably outperform scrolling interfaces in terms of performance and preference [136] [75]. Similar effects can be observed for small screens. One study, in which different interfaces were tested on a simulated hand-held display, found that a two-level zoom was significantly faster for accomplishing editing and monitoring tasks than a scrolling interface. Even in cases where users failed to achieve optimal performance with the two-level zoom, they preferred it to the other experimental interfaces [104].

2.2.1 Development History

The first application to use zooming as a fundamental interface approach was the Spatial Data Management System (SDMS) [74] in 1978 (see Figure 2.4). The SDMS system relied heavily on custom hardware, including an octophonic sound system and an instrumented chair equipped with pressure-sensitive joysticks, two touch-sensitive Tablets and a digital lapboard. The data was presented via a rear-projected color television display. SDMS enabled users to manage and zoom into a visual database representation consisting of alphanumeric, graphical, and filmic information.

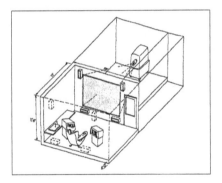 

Figure 2.4: The media room running the Spatial Data Management System [74].

In 1993, the first multiscale interface was developed and was called Pad [172]. It introduced several fundamental design concepts that, in total, serve as an alternative to the Windows paradigm. The system visualizes an infinite two dimensional information plane populated by objects that users can interact with. Such Pad objects could, for instance, be text files, a clock program, or a personal calendar. Each of these entities occupies a well-defined region on the Pad surface and they are visualized by means of graphics and portals. Portals are used for navigation; they show portions of the Pad surface at different scales, and may also look recursively at other portals. One way to use a portal, for instance, would be to show a miniature overview of a large Pad object. Users can manipulate the view's scale by semantic zooming, which allows objects to change their appearance dependent on the current scale. Another important concept is portal filters that transform data into other complex views, e.g. present tabular data as a bar chart.

Pad was designed to run on inexpensive hardware (Sun 3 computers). It only supported two colors (black on white) and was entirely based on bitmaps. When magnifying objects, drawing and text became pixelated. While the developers recognized the importance of a continuous smooth zoom, the hardware resources were too limited to support a sufficiently high frame rate. The interface only allowed users to zoom in and out by the powers of two [17].

Only one year later, the successor to Pad, Pad++ [25] [18] [19] [26] [17], was presented, a system that also constituted the first ZUI toolkit. Pad++ was aimed to serve as *"the basis for exploration of novel interfaces for information visualization and browsing in a number of complex information-intensive domains"* [25]. It is important to note that Pad++ itself is not an application - it is a framework for simplifying and extending the creation of multiscale applications such as Pad. Pad++ is implemented as a Tcl/Tk widget, which has the advantage that application developers do not have to write C code, but can use the simple Tcl scripting language.

Pad++ introduces some, mostly technical, enhancements over the original Pad implementation. Much effort has been devoted to realizing smooth semantic zooming (see Chapter 2.2.5.2), even with hundreds of thousands of objects loaded into the information space. To achieve this, the rendering is implemented in C++ and follows a 'parallel lazy loading' strategy, i.e. only the portion of the database that is currently visible is loaded. One initial design objective of Pad++ was to support a wide range of platforms ranging from high-end workstations to PDAs and Set-top boxes. This indicates that the developers judged the ZUI approach to be highly scalable for different screen sizes and tasks. However, an increased level of platform independency was only achieved by later ZUI toolkits such as Jazz (2000) [28] and Piccolo (2004) [24].

Both Jazz and Piccolo were developed in the HCI lab at the University of Maryland. While Jazz is no longer maintained, its easier-to-use replacement Piccolo offers editions for Java, the .NET framework and the compact framework. Thus, ZUI developers can also target mobile devices such as PDAs and smartphones. Apart from switching to more modern and popular programming languages, another improvement compared to Pad++ is that Piccolo is based on a scalable scene graph architecture, which facilitates the generation of efficient, reusable and object-oriented code. Piccolo is under BSD license and has been used for the implementation of various experimental ZUI interfaces such as, for instance, PhotoMesa (see Figure 2.5).

Since the original Pad was presented 14 years ago, numerous systems have utilized the idea of multiscale interfaces for various application domains, including web [27], image [21], document [32] and database [169] browsers, browsing history widgets [112], slide show programs [94], thought organizers [95], 3D character animation controls [173], and

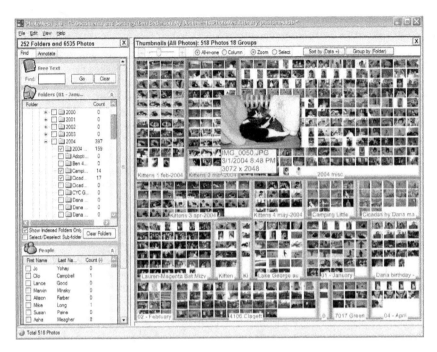

Figure   2.5:   PhotoMesa   ZUI   for   browsing   image   collections
(http://www.windsorinterfaces.com/ photomesa.shtml). The interface was implemented
using the Piccolo.NET framework.

novel desktop systems [87] [185].

2.2.2   2D, 2.5D and 3D

ZUIs present objects in a 2D space on multiple scales, but they are not 3D applications.
Some people actually refer to them as 2.5 dimensional interfaces. The reasons for not
using 3D are twofold. Firstly, the developers of seminal ZUI applications such as Pad++
wanted to make the software available to a wide range of people and one of their aims
was thus to avoid any special hardware requirements. Today, however, this constraint is
scarcely valid any longer. Off-the-shelf desktop computers and even high-end PDAs are
equipped with sufficient graphics power to render complex 3D scenes. The other aspect,
which still remains valid, is simplicity. 3D systems are usually hard to navigate using
current display and pointer technologies, and thus the extra degree of freedom can lead to
confusion and complications [56].

Despite the current usability difficulties, it is believed that the evolving 3D technology will
eventually lead to a fundamental change in interface design. Previous research has shown
that the efficient use of graphical user interfaces strongly depends on human capabilities
for spatial cognition [78] [79] [72] [222]. Applications such as the Data Mountain [192] or

the Task Gallery [193] aim to exploit such capabilities by enabling users to arrange data representations freely in 3D space. Initial evaluations seem to confirm that such interfaces provide a better support for spatial memory. The Data Mountain, for instance, is an inclined plane tilted at 65 degrees to serve as a $3D^2$ document management system. Using a 2D interaction technique, users can place document representations anywhere on the mountain. The results of a user study showed that users were faster at retrieving individually arranged web page thumbnails from the Data Mountain than from a hierarchical tree user interface. However, there is also evidence that 3D may have fewer advantages than a 2D spatial layout. In an experiment in which a 2.5D ZUI image browser was compared to a scrolling interface and two 3D image browsers (landscape and carousel metaphors), the researchers found that the non-3D browsers were more effective at locating target items in a larger set of images [68]. Also, in a later study [64] on the Data Mountain, which compared the interface to a 2D version, no significant differences in performance were found. Users significantly preferred the 3D application. In a follow-up evaluation [65], the authors investigated the effectiveness of spatial memory for both virtual and real-world physical Data Mountains with the dimensionality factors: 2D, 2.5D and 3D (see Figure 2.6). For the real-world apparatus, fishing lines were used to hold the web page printouts in place. The results indicated that the participants' ability to quickly locate the web page images deteriorated as their freedom to use the third dimension increased. Moreover, user comments suggested that the participants found the 3D interfaces more cluttered and less efficient.

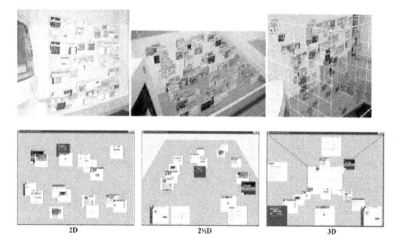

Figure 2.6: Set of physical and virtual Data Mountain systems with different dimensionality factors [65].

Another review of a 3D experiment lead to a similar change in interpretation. In 2001, a study [216] had investigated the effectiveness of spatial memory on interface interaction.

---

[2] Actually, the Data Mountain perspective is 2.5D, since the y coordinate of objects cannot be manipulated

During the test the participants were asked to recall the location of letters of the alphabet represented by non-labeled cards arranged in hierarchical 2D and 3D displays. The authors found an improved performance for the 3D interface and concluded that a realistic 3D display better supports a spatial memory task such as learning the place of an object. However, some people queried the validity of the experiment, since the layout of the two interfaces included differences that were not enforced by the difference in dimensionality and may have penalized the 2D interface. Thus, in 2004, an experiment [63] with similar settings to the 2001 study was conducted, but with an improved 2D layout. The results contradicted the findings of the earlier study and strongly indicated that the 3D perspective had no effect on the effectiveness of spatial memory in monocular static displays. The authors pointed out, though, that these results do not imply that there exists no difference in spatial memory when dealing with real-world 2D and 3D spaces. Too little is known as yet about such mechanisms to predict the positive or negative effects of 'perfect' virtual 3D on spatial memory [63].

2.2.3 Orientation in ZUIs

A common problem with ZUIs is the lack of context. Even after a short period of navigation, users lose their overview due to the continuous clipping of orientation cues during zooming [177] [52] [120] [56]. In this situation, *"users no longer know where they are in the information space nor where to find the information they are looking for"* [178].

How much context is needed in a given situation is hard to predict. It depends on variables such as the type and ordering of the information space, the users' familiarity with it, and the task that users want to accomplish. Given, for instance, a map-based ZUI in which users have drilled down to the highest magnification level, a displayed street label may provide city residents with sufficient context to orient themselves. On the other hand, if the street name is not unique or the people are less familiar with the map, they would have to zoom out to identify, for example, the closest high street. Tourists who are new to the city may even need to zoom out until the name of the quarter becomes visible, or until they can locate the quarter within the context of the entire city. Overall, the only way for a system to guarantee orientation, is to allow the users to freely adjust the level of context information provided.

As illustrated by the aforementioned example, the most straightforward way to rediscover context in ZUIs is to zoom out [17]. While this approach may help users to generate or refresh their internal model of the information space [212], it also implies frequent interaction that, after some time, users are likely to find tedious. Especially so in cases in which they have to zoom out extensively to regain context. While this problem seems to be inherent to ZUIs, a strategy that at least reduces the burden of frequent zooming is to provide a fast and precise interaction design. The less time-consuming and cognitively demanding the zooming is, the less it will annoy users. With respect to this, some developers have proposed automatic zoom features such as a rocket view, in which users trigger a pre-defined zoom-out-zoom-in operation. However, since the system cannot detect the degree of context needed (i.e. the value in the Z dimension to which it must zoom out), this feature is only useful for small information spaces in which a full zoom-out-zoom-in can be achieved in an acceptable time and speed.

A more severe type of orientation problem that cannot be solved solely by interaction has been termed desert fog [134]. Desert fog describes a condition in which users zoom into the white space between objects up to the point where the viewport goes completely blank. On the one hand, the empty screen could be indicating that there are no objects to be found in that direction, in which case users need to zoom out. Another possibility, though, is that there are indeed objects, but they are still too far away to be visible. In this case, users need to zoom in further to approach these objects.

One solution for providing navigational assistance in desert-fog conditions is to generate multiscale residues for all objects in view. Such landmarks are drawn across scale and indicate that a particular object exists in that direction. If no residues are seen, the users know that they have to zoom out to find other objects. To avoid visual clutter, navigational information should be clustered [134].

2.2.4 High-Level Interaction

ZUI interaction means that users must be able to zoom in and zoom out, to pan in four or more directions and, in most cases, to also perform a selection operation of some kind, e.g. given a map visualization, users may click on hotel icons to receive more detailed information. Depending on the application domain, the input device and the type of ZUI, different mappings of input events and actions are required.

Earlier systems were often limited to centralized zooming. Users click a device (or on-screen) button to increase the scale and another button to decrease it. Since the view is only scaled and not translated, this approach implies that for targeting information objects in space, users first have to move the object to the center of the screen. Furthermore, for large information spaces, users may frequently have to interrupt the scaling operation to readjust the focus [37].

A more elegant and effective scaling technique is point-directed zooming, which allows users to magnify and center information objects at the same time. One example is the default event handler in Jazz [28], and now in the Piccolo framework [24]. While pressing the right mouse button, users scale the view by dragging the mouse right or left to zoom in or out, respectively [28]. The zoom speed increases with the distance the mouse is dragged, and vice versa. During the operation, the point that the cursor was over when the dragging started moves to the center.

Often interfaces support zooming by visual mediators such as seen in Figure 2.7a. A slider widget has the advantage that the user is provided with additional visual feedback. The position of the slider thumb reveals the current zoom level of the view in relation to the range of scale factors available. Users can drag the control to increase or decrease the zoom level. Another example of a visual mediator is zoom bars (Figure 2.7c) [130]. Equipped with three thumbs, a zoom bar is a slider that controls the range boundaries of an axis dimension. Moving the two extreme thumbs, users can increase or decrease the upper and lower range boundary, causing a zoom in or a zoom out by changing the scale on the corresponding display axis. That way, any rectangular region can be enlarged to full diagram size. This is also the reason why zoom bars are usually limited to abstract information spaces, in which the two dimensions do not require a fixed aspect ratio. While their similarity to a regular scrollbar may support first-time users in operating the widget, a drawback is that the usability of a zoom bar deteriorates with a decreasing ratio of the physical slider size and the attribute range of the related scatterplot dimension. When visualizing large-scale data on small screens, the increased thumb sensitivity may render a precise zoom operation difficult if not impossible. Moreover, zooming in on a region of interest means having to subsequently modify up to four thumbs, which makes navigation rather tedious.

Overall, ZUI widgets may provide important information to the users and facilitate navigation, but at the same time they suffer from the drawback that they take away screen space from the view. Thus, widgets are often not appropriate for small screens.

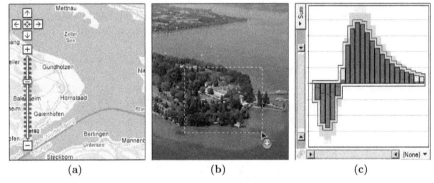

(a)   (b)   (c)

Figure 2.7: Visual mediators: (a) zoom slider (http://maps.google.com), (b) bounding-box zooming, (c) zoom bar (http://www.spotfire.com).

A similar zoom effect as with zoom bars, but without occluding the view, can be achieved with a bounding-box tool (see Figure 2.7b). Users drag the pointing device over the view and a focus rectangle is drawn that takes the drag starting point as a corner location and the drag distance as a diagonal. When the users release the pointing device, the defined region is magnified to fit the full size of the view. In cases such as images and text, in which a constant aspect ratio is desired, the focus region is only scaled but not distorted. A bounding-box is a visual mediator that does not require permanent display space.

Next to scrollbars, the most common implementation of panning is drag&drop. By dragging the pointing device users push the information space in the same direction as the drag movement. This approach has also been found superior both in performance and preference for touch-controlled interfaces, when compared to either pushing the viewport or touching the window border [131]. Scrolling and panning may also be accelerated to cover large distances in less time [115]. One implementation that has also been incorporated in standard software such as Internet browsers is rate-based scrolling, in which the displacement of an input device is mapped to the scrolling velocity [240]. A similar technique has also been proposed for PDAs [156], but no performance difference to conventional drag&drop was found in either stationary or mobile conditions. However, the information space used for the evaluation was rather small (800 x 1040 pixel). A need to travel larger distances may have shown an advantage for rate-based scrolling, since it does not require time-consuming clutching, i.e. lifting the pen to relocate it.

While techniques such as point-directed or bounding-box zooming may also be implemented on mobile devices, there remains the difficulty of how to map limited input events to multiple actions. Compared to a computer mouse, a PDA or smartphone stylus offers far fewer input states. This makes the interaction design particularly challenging [114]. A common workaround is to offer a tool palette, as shown in Figure 2.8. Depending on which palette icon the users have previously tapped, input events are interpreted as zoom-in, zoom-out, pan or selection actions. However, this approach reduces not only the screen space available for the view on the information space (in this case a PDF document), but it also hampers interaction by forcing the users to frequently switch between modes. This problem, and how it may be eased with enhanced input technologies, will be discussed in Chapter 5.

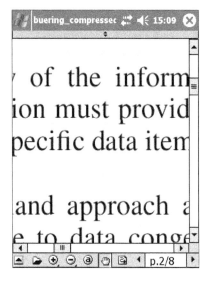

Figure 2.8: PDF reader with tool palette at the bottom of the interface.

2.2.5   Advanced ZUI Designs

Apart from the basic interaction design for a variety of applications that include zooming as part of their interface options (e.g. image editors and PDF readers), more advanced ZUI mechanisms have been developed to improve Pad-like multiscale interfaces. These will be introduced in the following paragraphs.

2.2.5.1   Smooth and Animated Zooming

The most basic ZUI is the two-level zoom. It lets users switch between a single overview and a single detail zoom level, and thus only works for small information spaces. To manage larger data sets, several intermediate zoom levels between the minimum and maximum scale must be introduced. In older systems such as, for instance, Pad [172], navigation between the levels is accomplished by discrete jumps. While this approach is easy to implement and computationally very effective, it hampers the usability of the system. Coarse jumps can irritate and disorient the users and thus may hinder the cognitive and perceptual processing required for navigation [25] [175] [17]. Accordingly, a lot of effort has been put into equipping multiscale interfaces with smooth continuous zooming.

Another important concept for ZUIs is animated transitions. Users may, for instance, click on a hyperlink to automatically move the viewport to a remote location. Or they initiate a scale manipulation via a bounding-box. In both cases the viewport needs to be adjusted. The transition between these interface states can either be instantaneous, which is fastest, or it can be animated by showing intermediate frames. The benefit of smooth and animated transitions is that they help users to maintain relations between application states [173]. Users are not required to consciously make connections between the change of interface content and thus they can stay focused on the task [22]. One system to employ this effect is Cone Trees [195]. Cone Trees visualize hierarchies in 3D by representing nodes as index cards positioned in space. Child nodes are linked by lines and arranged in interactive cones. On clicking an element, the system highlights it as well as each node in the path up to the root, and brings them to the front by rotating the cones. This transition is implemented as a smooth animation, which should shift some of the users' cognitive load to the human perceptual system. The developers state that: *"The perceptual phenomenon of object constancy enables the user to track substructure relationships without thinking about it. When the animation is completed, no time is needed for reassimilation."* [195].

Smooth transitions were also found to have a positive effect on the users' ability to build a mental map of the information space. In a study [23], users were asked to navigate a virtual family tree, in which each node showed a picture of a family member and hyperlinks to connected nodes. Only one or two nodes could be seen at a time. To move the viewport, users clicked on the hyperlinks. The authors discovered that animated transitions of one second improved the users' ability to reconstruct the information space, with no penalty on task performance time. To determine the optimal trajectory between two locations in a multiscale interface, some prior research has investigated how to calculate the shortest path with zooming and panning [92], or the path that specifically supports smooth animations [221].

An often-neglected benefit of gradual transitions is an increased user satisfaction [173]. Smooth zooming, for instance, gives the users the feeling of flying through space [130] and may not only help users to preserve their sense of position and context [207], but also improve the *hedonic* [133] qualities of the application.

Attention must be paid to how to design appropriate transitions. In an experiment that involved different window navigation techniques for browsing file icons, a two-level zoom was compared with and without animation [75]. The results showed no significant effect for employing animation. However, the interface was limited to a single in-between frame, which seems to be insufficient to give the users the impression of a smooth transition. Another design aspect is the zoom duration. For animated transitions this has been recommended to be approximately 1 second [53].

2.2.5.2 Semantic Zoom

Two different kinds of zooming can be distinguished. Most common is geometric zoom, in which objects are simply magnified. Zooming in, the object's size increases, and vice versa. This approach is found in many standard software applications such as PDF readers or image editors. Semantic zooming, in contrast, is a more sophisticated concept, in which objects change their appearance as the amount of screen real estate available to them changes [172]. In the directory browser shown in Figure 2.9, for instance, subfolders and files are first represented by small-sized icons that only show the name of the object. Increasing the scale, the icons change their appearance to present some more detailed information, e.g. the number of images in a folder, or the structure and amount of text contained in a document. Zooming in further, images become visible and text is magnified to a readable size. At this level, users may also be provided with additional functionality to manipulate the object in focus. Overall, the goal of semantic zooming can be summarized as providing the users with the most meaningful object representation at each magnification level. The difficulty with this approach is that the appropriate representations for all scale levels must be determined in advance by an expert user. However, for complex objects, several representations may be suitable for a given portion of display size. In this case, it is hard to reliably predict the users' requirements. Systems such as DataSplash [169] try to overcome this problem by enabling users to visually program how objects behave during zooming [234].

2.2.5.3 Clutter and Constant Information Density

A problem with many interfaces that display high information loads is that it is almost impossible to avoid visual clutter. Overlapping items may not only have negative effects on the visual appeal of the interface, but may also decrease the user performance. Studies showed that reducing visual clutter speeds up item retrieval [214] and improves map reading performance [174]. Moreover, clutter can lead to overplotting, which means that some objects are completely overlapped by others and thus are not visible. Overplotting gives

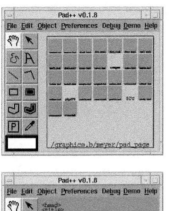

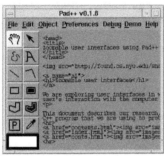
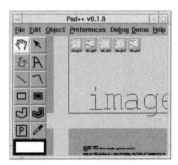

Figure 2.9: A simple directory browser implemented with Pad++. Users use smooth semantic zooming to move the viewport from the overview into directories or text and image files (htp://www.cs.umd.edu./hcil/pad++).

the users a false impression of data distribution and hampers the detection of patterns. This drawback applies especially to scatterplot-like applications.

Numerous techniques have been proposed to reduce the problem of clutter in visualizations. A rather simple but effective technique is to enhance representations with preattentive encodings [218] [110] such as hue and intensity to improve the users' notion of the amount of overplotting [82]. Other techniques include:

- clustering [227] [124] and sampling [30] [31] [80] algorithms to reduce the number of items on the display

- point displacement where overlapping points are moved to adjacent, free positions [139] [141] [140] [219]

- dynamic queries to filter data by direct manipulation [4] [93].

A clutter-reduction approach that specifically targets semantic ZUIs is constant information density [231] [230]. The approach is based on a design principle drawn from cartography and aims to keep the number of information objects constant as users scale and translate the view [88]. As demonstrated by the VIDA system in Figure 2.10b, objects that are located in areas with high information density are displayed using small-sized, low-detail representations, and objects in areas with sparse density are shown larger and with more detail. In this way, the display space can be utilized more effectively. To determine the optimal presentation parameters, the users may choose from different density metrics such as number of vertices, number of objects, or data density [220].

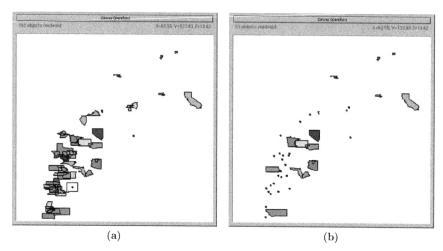

(a)   (b)

Figure 2.10: The Visual Information Density Adjuster (VIDA) system visualizing states of the USA positioned by housing cost (X axis) and income (Y axis): (a) cluttered default view in which all icons are displayed on the same representation level, (b) a view applying constant information density i.e. different representations are chosen for different objects based on local density [230].

2.2.5.4 Goal-Directed Zoom

With semantic zooming, users zoom until the target object shows the desired representation. An alternative is goal-directed zoom [232] [233], which means that users choose a representation of an object, and the change in scale and translation is performed automatically by the system.

An example is given by Figure 2.11, which again shows the VIDA system. This time it visualizes the Fortune 500 data where the X axis represents profit growth and the Y axis number of employees. Each company has three representations: (1) a dot, (2) an icon depicting the category of industry to which the company belongs, and (3) an icon revealing more specific information about the type of industry. Users interact with the interface by first clicking on a company they are interested in. The system responds by displaying a pop-up menu that holds all possible representations of that company (Figure 2.11a). In this case, the factory icon (middle one) indicates that the company is part of the heavy industry sector, and the benzene ring below gives the more detailed information

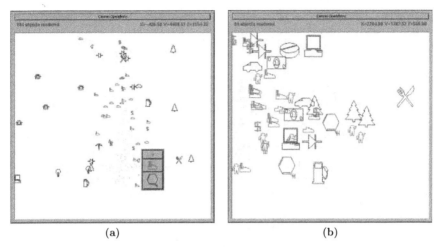

(a)   (b)

Figure 2.11: The VIDA system combining constant information density with goal-directed zooming to visualize the Fortune 500 data: (a) zoomed-out view with pop-up menu showing available representations, (b) zoomed-in view [232].

that it is a chemical company. In the example, the users select the benzene ring as the most detailed representation. The system automatically zooms and pans such that the selected company is centered in the viewport and the benzene ring becomes visible (Figure 2.11b). Surrounding items are also zoomed, but their current representations are based on the principle of constant information density (see Chapter 2.2.5.3). Thus, items are shown at different levels of detail depending on the display space available to them.

2.2.6 Mobile Applications

A ZUI makes more effective use of limited screen real estate, and thus it is considered to have a great potential on small screens [25] [17] [142] [208]. Moreover, current ZUI frameworks such as Piccolo [24] offer convenient extensions for mobile development. The following chapters present state-of-the-art implementations of experimental ZUI applications running on mobile devices.

2.2.6.1 Summary Thumbnails

A popular research topic in the context of mobile devices is how to display and interact with web pages on small screens (see for instance [49] [229] [228]). Web pages are usually designed to be viewed on desktop monitors and often feature a preformatted page width. Thus, when rendered on a small screen, the viewport only shows a subset of the data. To navigate inside the document, users must scroll in two dimensions, which is particularly tedious. While recent commercial systems use single-column reformatting to avoid horizontal scrolling, an alternative may be provided by semantic zooming approaches such as summary thumbnails [145].

The objective of summary thumbnails is to provide readable overviews of web pages, while at the same time the original layout of the document is preserved. If web pages are just scaled to fit the small screen, text usually becomes unreadable. Zooming in and out, the users must apply a trial-and-error strategy to identify the content they are interested in. With summary thumbnails, the original text of the scaled-down web page is replaced with readable fragments of text assembled by a proxy server (see Figure 2.12). Preserving the layout has the advantage that the overall page structure can help users to recognize previously visited pages and to orient in web pages that are familiar from browsing on desktop computers. Moreover, the aesthetic appeal of the screen design is better conveyed than it is by single-column reformatting. A drawback may be that the usability of summary thumbnails strongly depends on the quality of the generated summaries.

Figure 2.12: A scaled down web page with unreadable text (left) compared to a summary thumbnails view (right) [145].

To view the original web page content, a simple two-level zoom is provided. Users click on an area to view the unabbreviated page in full-size, centered around the approximate region denoted in the summary thumbnail. It is not reported how users can return to the overview. The results of a usability evaluation showed that with summary thumbnails users could locate content faster than with a single-column interface, and zoomed significantly less than when they used unabbreviated thumbnails. Nine of the eleven participants also preferred the summary approach over the other two interfaces [145]. A thing to note, though, is that the prototype ran on a desktop computer mimicking a PDA interface and the participants interacted with the application via a computer mouse and a keyboard.

2.2.6.2 Collapse-to-Zoom

A more sophisticated ZUI approach for browsing web pages on small screen is collapse-to-zoom [15]. Apart from zooming into areas of interest, this concept also allows the users to remove content identified as irrelevant, i.e. this may for instance be banner ads or navigation menus. Removed content collapses and is replaced by thin placeholders. The additional screen space is used to enlarge the remaining content, which in turn increases the chances of identifying relevant content. Different expand and collapse commands can be executed via pen gestures.

Figure 2.13: Removing a column in the collapse-to-zoom concept to view the remaining content in more detail [15].

2.2.6.3 ZoneZoom

ZoneZoom [191] is an input technique that facilitates zooming in discrete steps on smartphones using the number keypad of the device. Given, for instance, a map information space as in Figure 2.14, users press the '#' key to split the view into nine subregions, which are outlined as a grid superimposed on the display. Each cell corresponds to a number key. The assignments are also indicated by semi-transparent labels. On pressing a number key, the view zooms smoothly into the corresponding sector of the display. Users can zoom out to the parent sector by pressing the same number again, or they can pan the view to a sibling sector at the same zoom level by pressing the other numbers keys. Zooming works iteratively. At each scale level, users can press the '#' key, which causes the system to segment the display and redefine the current view to be the parent view.

ZoneZoom offers different visual and interactive features to support the users' orientation when navigating the information space. First, each child view possesses a rudimentary overview, implemented as a small rectangle outline in the upper right corner of the display (see, for instance, bottom left image in Figure 2.14). A smaller filled rectangle is drawn within the rectangle outline and denotes the location and size of the child view in the context of the parent view. Moreover, a gradation margin is drawn around the parent view. Zooming into a child view, the existence or absence of a border gives a further indication of the relative position of the child view. Users can also gain contextual information by initiating temporary view movements. This is achieved by pressing and holding the number keys. The view still zooms or pans as expected, but on release of the key, the view returns to the initial parent or sibling sector. However, all these approaches are limited to easing orientation between the previous and the current zoom step. No global overview is given.

An obvious shortcoming of the grid-navigation is that zoom and pan foci are static. If, for instance, an information object such as a street or lake runs across two or more sectors, users cannot adjust the view to fully contain or center the object. The authors describe how distortion could be employed to devote more screen space to important, previously defined, information objects, but it is unclear how this approach could be enhanced to allow the authoring at run-time. Another problem with distortion is that it may degrade the readability of the map [175]. ZoneZoom is currently implemented as a Flash prototype running on desktop computers. A stripped-down version of the zoom (only two zoom-levels) has been integrated into a traffic monitoring software for smartphones using the Microsoft Smartphone 2002 SDK.

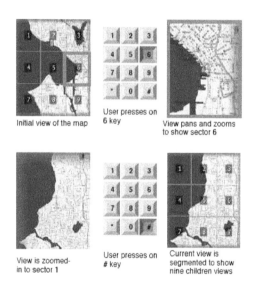

Figure 2.14: View segmentation and zooming in the ZoneZoom prototype [191].

2.2.6.4 Pocket PhotoMesa

Pocket PhotoMesa [142] employs a ZUI approach with discrete but animated zoom steps to facilitate the browsing of a photo collection on PDAs. The application is a port of the desktop PhotoMesa system [21] (see Figure 2.5), which has been tailored to better match the requirements of mobile devices. Pocket PhotoMesa is available as a commercial application, but a trial version can be also downloaded.

Pocket PhotoMesa aims to avoid scrollbars by displaying all images as interactive thumbnails on a single PDA screen (see Figure 2.15). For efficient file and directory-hierarchy layout, quantum strip treemaps are used to group items and reduce the amount of white space between them. Users can zoom into an image group by tapping into a white space inside the group or the group's name. Tapping a thumbnail enlarges the image, so that more details can be identified. To view the photo at full size, the image must be tapped again. Users can pan the full-resolution image by dragging it with the stylus, or zoom into a portion of the image by first tapping the icon with the magnifying glass and the plus sign, and then drawing a bounding-box. If zoomed in, tapping the white space in a view lets the users return to the next higher (zoomed-out) scale level. All zoom transitions are animated to support the users' comprehension of the interface changes.

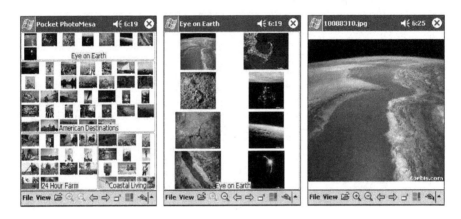

Figure 2.15: Zoom steps with Pocket PhotoMesa [142].

In a usability study, the developers compared Pocket PhotoMesa to another commercial image browser called Pocket ACDSee. The latter features a more conventional interface design with a split-window approach. The upper view shows a tree visualization of directories from which users can choose image folders. Having selected a folder, the images are presented as fixed-size thumbnails on a scrollable pane in the bottom view. Pocket PhotoMesa was tested in two versions - with and without animated zooming. During the experiment, 15 participants had to use all three applications running on a PDA to locate images via a written textual description or a printed color version of the image. No significant differences were found for task performance time. Informal feedback about the usefulness of animated transitions was mixed. Users appreciated the support of maintaining the context during navigation, but also felt that the animation slightly increased the time it took them to find the target image. Considering the positive effects of fluent transitions observed in desktop studies (e.g. [195] [23]), this result may indicate that the usefulness of smooth animations is rather limited for small data sets, but increases with growing complexity and size of the information space. However, the lack of scalability is a general limitation of the Pocket PhotoMesa. In a pilot experiment the authors found that, given the small PDA screen, an image count of only 100 already caused the thumbnails to be rendered at a size too small to be easily identified. Hence, the number of images used in the usability study was reduced to 75.

2.2.6.5   LaunchTile

LaunchTile is a single-handed interaction ZUI for visualizing, and providing access to, at most 36 applications. The system has been developed as a partly functional prototype, which runs on both smartphone and PDA devices. In the case of PDAs, the single-handed interaction design is based on thumb gestures.

LaunchTile features three zoom levels and transitions between the levels are animated. In the world view (Figure 2.16a), users can monitor active icons for all 36 applications at the same time. The display is partitioned by blue onscreen buttons into 9 zones, where each zone consists of 4 application tiles. Users can zoom into a zone by tapping it with the thumb. If the device has only a numeric keypad and no touch-sensitive screen, zooming is triggered by pressing the corresponding number key (1 - 9) mapped to each blue button. The selected zone expands such that its four application tiles cover the entire screen (Figure 2.16b). Users can pan the view by dragging the thumb on the display. To keep the interaction design consistent for the directional joysticks featured in many smartphones, only vertical and horizontal movements are supported. A panning operation always ends with a zone being automatically centered on the display. To zoom out, users tap the blue button or press the 5 key.

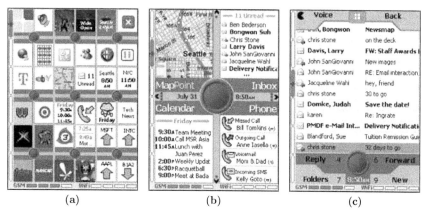

| (a) | (b) | (c) |

Figure 2.16: Zoom steps with LaunchTile: (a) world view, (b) zone view and (c) application view [137]. In a real-world scenario the 36 application tiles would actively visualize application-specific information appropriate for the amount of screen space allocated to them at each zoom level.

Having focused on a zone view, users can zoom into one of the four application tiles by tapping it with the thumb. On a smartphone, they may press a number key: 1 for top-left, 3 for top-right, 7 for bottom-left or 9 for bottom-right, the remaining number keys are used as an alternative to pan the view. The selected application is magnified to full size. Additional functionalities and onscreen buttons are provided to manage global as well as application-specific interaction. To return to the zone view, users hit the 'back' button in the upper right corner (Figure 2.16c). Panning in the application zoom-level seems not to be supported.

As in the ZoneZoom application, LaunchTile features some overview cues to aid navigation. A simple feedback is provided by the black arrows in the zone view. If no arrow is drawn for a particular direction, then the users know that, in the given direction, the view is adjacent to the border of the information space. Additional context information is given by the blue dots located next to the arrows. The number of dots indicates the number of off-screen zones in that direction. A third feedback mechanism is the small scale on the left side of the application, which visualizes the current zoom level. Unlike the arrows and the dots that are limited to the zone view, the zoom scale is visible on all three zoom levels.

2.3   Overview+Detail Interfaces

An overview+detail (o+d) interface as shown in Figure 2.17 is characterized by a multi-window layout, where one window is used to present details while another, typically smaller, window shows an overview of the information space [16] [175]. Such overview windows are usually enhanced with a visual cue such as a field-of-view box to indicate the portion of the information space currently visible in the detail view.

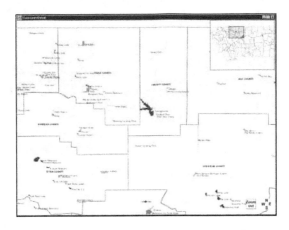

Figure 2.17: Overview+detail interface visualizing a map information space [120].

O+d concepts have a long tradition in graphical user interfaces with one of the earliest being the SDMS system [74] previously mentioned in Chapter 2.2.1. As can be seen in Figure 2.4 (right), users were provided with a separate *world view monitor* located on their right. It showed a global data view together with a field-of-view box. Apart from orienting, users could use the overview to navigate the large detail screen by pointing at the desired position on the touch sensitive monitor. Current examples of overview-enhanced applications are commercial programs such as Adobe Photoshop and Acrobat Reader.

Most overview windows present a miniature of the detail view, but abstract overviews as in [166] are also a common solution. Unlike images that lose much of their detail information when being compressed to a smaller size, abstract views can use the limited screen real estate more effectively and may even contain extra information not present in the detail view. Figure 2.18 shows an abstract overview that visualizes an entire text document. Mapping each text line to a row in the overview would require far more pixels in the vertical dimension than available. Instead the position of each character in the file is scaled into the overview and the resulting density of characters is mapped to the intensity scale. In addition, color coding is used to highlight different sections in the document [129]. Another example of abstract overviews is that of CAD systems for chip design that display both the logical structure and the actual geometry of the integrated circuit [9].

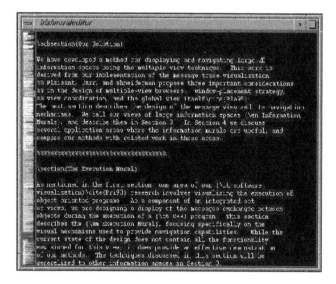

Figure 2.18: An abstract overview of a Latex file where density is preserved via intensity scale [129].

O+d interfaces aid orientation by giving the users direct and constant feedback on their current position in the information space [175]. Moreover, navigation in the overview can significantly improve the interface performance. Users may directly access details that would otherwise require them to perform several zooming and panning operations in the detail view [175]. This effect was also observed in [16] where the authors compared the usability of three different o+d interfaces: the first allowed for bounding box zooming on both the overview and the detail view, the second only supported panning in the overview, and the third was controlled by scrolling the detail view in two dimensions. Both zooming and panning in the overview proved to be superior to operating the scrollbars for navigating and searching a balanced binary tree structure of 280 words. Another part of the study compared the interfaces to a set of no-overview interfaces that featured the same interaction techniques. The authors found that the participants were significantly faster using the overview enhanced interfaces.

A major drawback for multiple windows is the cost of visual switching. Breaking down information into two or more windows can degrade performance due to the time it takes to mentally relate the views, which may also strain the users' memory [52]. For instance [120] compared ZUIs with and without overview for map navigation tasks and found that the participants were significantly faster without an overview widget when searching a map with multiple levels (semantic zooming). The authors assumed that the decreased performance was at least partially due to the time it took users to visually and actively (moving the mouse) switch between the two views. A positive correlation measured between the number of view transitions and task completion time supported this hypothesis. It also corresponds to the findings of an earlier study [11] in which visual switching, as recorded by an eye-tracker, led to a decreased performance and an increased error rate for routing and context monitoring tasks.

The performance degrade due to visual switching may in some cases still be preferable to the time it takes to navigate back and forth in a single view. One study [176] found that for multiscale spaces a detail-only ZUI was superior for comparing small sets of objects, while a multi-window layout was faster for comparing larger sets. The authors concluded that extra windows may be used *"when visual comparisons must be made involving patterns of a greater complexity than can be held in visual working memory"* [176]. They admit, though, that the exact capacity of visual working memory is unknown. It is estimated to hold about two or three quite simple visual components.

An interesting result across previous studies is that users in most cases preferred an o+d interface over other interfaces, even if it leads to a decreased performance (e.g. [13] [120] [122]). In [120] the participants stated that they particularly appreciated the orientation and navigation features of the overview widget. These may give users the feeling of being in control. An exception to this pattern is [11], in which participants clearly preferred the more effective alternative of a focus+context screen, i.e. a wall-size low-resolution display with a small high-resolution screen embedded.

Some comprehensive taxonomies [175] and guidelines [9] on when and how to use multiple windows exist. The main difficulty with o+d interfaces seems to be that they require the developer to balance a complex set of design tradeoffs [9]. Important interface parameters are window coordination, scale factors and view layout. These will be discussed in the following two sections.

2.3.1 View Coordination and Navigation

The most basic type of overview displays a static image of the information space. Users must identify their current position by comparing the visual cues in the detail view with the compressed cues in the overview. Depending on the type of data presented, this may be hard or even impossible to accomplish. To aid orientation, current systems usually include a field-of-view box that denotes the clipping area of the detail view. This feature implies an essential design principle for o+d interfaces, namely that the windows should be coordinated. Coordination, also termed tight coupling [4], means that an update in one view leads to an immediate update of the other view. Hence when navigating in the detail view, the field-of-view box moves correspondingly in the overview. Another example would be the simultaneous selection or highlighting of objects among the views. The effectiveness of coordination has been shown in an experiment, in which a detail-only interface was compared to a coordinated o+d interface, and to an o+d interface with two independent views [166]. For accessing textual Census data, the coordinated views were found to be 30% to 50% faster than the other two interfaces.

Coordination between windows can be non-existent, unidirectional, or bidirectional [175]. In a unidirectional o+d interface, only one view is interactive, while a bidirectional co-ordination supports user input in both views. Figure 2.19 illustrates different types of overview interaction. With the Google Maps widget, users can pan the detail view by dragging the field-of-view box or jump to distant locations by clicking outside the box. The rectangle immediately centers the new position and the detail view is updated. Panning is also implemented in the overview of the Photoshop image editor, but in addition it supports centralized zooming. Dragging the slider to the right decreases the size of the field-of-view box and thus also decreases the size of the clipping shown in the detail view. Alternatively, a scale percentage can be directly entered into the text field. To zoom in the overview of the Acrobat Reader, users must resize the box by dragging one of its four handles. The box always keeps a fixed aspect ratio, which is determined by the size of the dimensions of the detail view. Another feature of the widget is that users can switch between the pages of the PDF document by clicking the arrow buttons.

2.3.2 View Layout and Scale Factors

A major problem with overview windows on mobile devices is that they take up a signifi-cant amount of space on the screen. Given a basic side-by-side layout as featured in [129] [166], for instance, the designer has to partition the available display real estate between the detail view and the overview. However, for both views the usability increases with growing size, i.e. more information can be displayed, and navigation in the window be-comes easier and more accurate. There can be no general solution for this space tradeoff, since it is highly task-dependent. According to [175], an open-ended exploration or draw-ing task would be best supported by a large detail view, while tasks such as monitoring require a larger overview. Some interfaces also allow for manually adjusting the ratio between the windows.

The second balancing tradeoff is the zooming factor, which is the level of magnification

 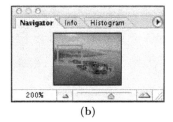 

(a) (b) (c)

Figure 2.19: Interactive overview windows: (a) Google Maps, (b) Adobe Photoshop, (c) Acrobat Reader.

between the detail view and the overview. This has been recommended to be less than 20 [175], or between 3 and 30 [208]. Larger zoom factors may require intermediate views. As noted by [120], it is unclear whether the recommended factors are affected by different ratios of the window sizes.

Apart from the common side-by-side layout, a more customizable design is that of overview windows that overlap the detail view. Such widgets are shown in Figure 2.19b and c. They can be freely positioned, and even scaled, by dragging the bottom right corner. If currently not needed, the users can close the overview. This approach offers great flexibility, but managing windows manually takes time and attention and thus adds considerable extra complexity to the interface [176]. An alternative approach is to allow the system to decide when to display the overview window. Overview visibility could, for instance, be triggered by extensive zooming or panning. However, this feature may not only be distracting, but in situations in which occlusion is obstructive, it may be highly annoying and hinder the interface performance. Such malfunction is very probable since the system's decision can only be based on the level of interaction and not on the users' actual need for an overview.

A special case of dynamic overviews is magnification lenses (pixel magnifier). Here, the overview fills the screen, while the smaller detail view is a movable display region that magnifies the underlying content. Figure 2.20a shows a variation of this concept in a PDF reader, in which a field-of-view box is dragged around and the magnified portion is shown in the small detail view window. Next to magnification, the lens metaphor may provide the basis for more complex interaction and visualization applications. For instance, magic lenses as presented in [33] are movable filters that provide a modified view of the underlying data to reveal hidden information, to enhance objects of interest, or to suppress distracting information (Figure 2.20b).

A space-preserving solution for overview windows is transparency [69]. One such example is the macroscope interface, which uses translucent overview layers so that detail and

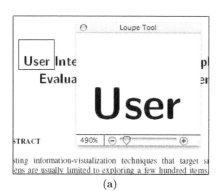
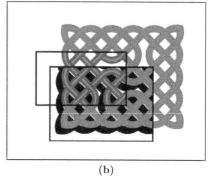

(a)   (b)

Figure 2.20: Lenses: (a) magnification lens with movable field-of-view box in the Adobe Acrobat Reader, (b) two magic lenses with an achromatic and a drop shadow filter positioned over a knotwork [33].

overview share the same physical screen [152] [151]. The overlaid detail view is controlled via a movable and resizable field-of-view box. A similar approach called context layers is used to aid navigation in ZUIs [178]. Context layers are transparent overviews that the users can display on-demand to orient themselves and to re-position the focus with respect to the global context. General problems of transparent widgets are increased visual clutter and a deteriorated readability of both overview and detail view content. One way to reduce these problems may be to use advanced blending techniques as, for instance, proposed in [12].

2.3.3 Mobile Applications

Due to the space tradeoff, most attempts to utilize the o+d concept for mobile interfaces comprise automatic or on-demand overviews. There are also a growing number of applications that employ translucency effects, but since this requires a considerable degree of graphics power, only recent devices can run the software with an acceptable performance. The following sections present examples of commercial and experimental o+d implementations.

2.3.3.1 O+d Document Readers

Reading a paper document has the advantage of supporting the awareness of spatial location of information. This not only speeds up search processes, but improves the users' comprehension of the document structure and the recall of content. However, interfaces that require extensive scrolling, which is enforced by small screens in particular, may undermine the ability of spatial awareness. As a solution [168] propose an o+d approach, where a small detail view presents a single sentence at a readable size while a large overview window shows a thumbnail image of the entire document page. Within the thumbnail, the sentence currently viewed in the detail view is highlighted. The users use buttons to move to the next or the previous sentence of the document.

In a usability test with 20 participants, the o+d document reader (Figure 2.21a) was compared to a standard scrolling interface in Microsoft Word. Both interfaces were scaled to a 3x5 inch window to mimic a mobile device. During the test, participants had to read a 5 page document and subsequently recall the locations of text extracts given to them. The results indicate that the o+d approach can significantly improve the incidental memory for spatial location of information on small screens.

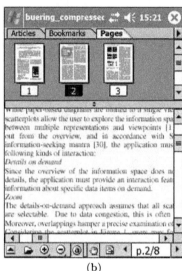

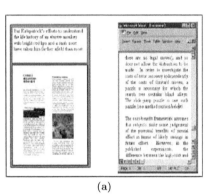

(a)   (b)

Figure 2.21: Overview+detail interfaces to support reading: (a) experimental o+d document reader to improve the spatial recall of information versus a conventional single-view document reader [168], (b) Adobe Acrobat Reader for Pocket PC.

The same o+d principle has also been incorporated into the Adobe Acrobat PDF reader for Pocket PC. The users can switch from the conventional detail-only view to a resizable o+d interface (Figure 2.21b). The views are synchronized via a bidirectional coordination, i.e. scrolling or zooming in the detail view will update the position and size of the field-of-view box in the overview, while manipulating the field-of-view box updates the detail view. The overview supports scaling by redrawing the field-of-view box, and jumping by double-tapping a desired location outside the field-of-view box. Panning by dragging the box is not supported. The overview is fixed to a scale level at which the document structure and different content types can be roughly distinguished. To better highlight the small red box, the pages are rendered in grayscale. If the document contains more than 3 pages, the overview no longer covers the entire information space. To enable the users to position the overview over different chunks of pages, the system provides vertical scrollbars.

2.3.3.2   Automatic Overviews

Two applications that make use of automatically displayed overviews are the Pocket PC
image browser HP Image Zone and the Nokia Internet browser for S60 3rd Edition Sym-
bian devices [96]. Hence, in the default state, both applications can devote the entire
screen space to the detail view.

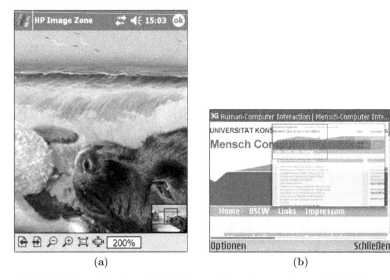

(a)   (b)

Figure 2.22: Mobile applications that feature automatic overviews: (a) HP Image Zone,
(b) Nokia web browser for S60 3rd Edition devices.

The HP image browser (Figure 2.22a) displays an overview each time the users complete a
zoom or pan operation in the detail view. However, the widget is displayed at a very small
scale, which makes it hard to identify smaller portions of the image in the overview and
also hampers a precise navigation by dragging the field-of-view box. If not actively used
by the users, the system hides the window after 2 seconds. No zooming in the overview is
supported.

The Nokia application (Figure 2.22b) is based on open-source libraries such as WebCore
and JavaScriptCore and contains several features to improve Internet browsing on small
screens [199] [96]. Users scroll web pages on a smartphone by pushing the 5-way joystick,
and if the operation lasts for more than 2 seconds, the system automatically displays an
overview window that superimposes almost half of the detail view. The overview is fixed
to a scale at which content can be discriminated. During scrolling, the field-of-view box
is centered while the viewport of the underlying overview is continuously moving. Once
the joystick is released, the overview disappears after a time threshold of 2 seconds. Another thing to note is that the overview is rendered as a transparent layer. Thus, during
scrolling the users may still observe, though in a very limited way, the content displayed

in the obscured portion of detail view. Apart from the automatic overview, the browser also features a simple two-level zoom.

As described, the mechanism for displaying the overview in the Nokia browser uses a timer event. This can be annoying in situations in which the users either need the widget immediately, or not at all. An alternative design could be based on rate-based scrolling, i.e. the users can pan the detail view at different speed levels. If the overview were to be displayed above a certain speed threshold, this would mean that the users could control the display moment more directly. However, rate-based scrolling requires a non-binary input device such as an isometric joystick or a touch screen, which is not featured by all devices. Another issue is the limited readability of small-sized overviews as found for instance in the HP Image Zone. For images, this problem may be eased by rendering the overview as a contour- or edge-map. This technique can reduce the clutter in highly scaled images [196].

2.3.3.3   Hanmer

Hanmer is a PDA interface that visualizes time-based multimedia data such as records of meetings, consisting of linked audio speech segments and text notes [155]. As shown in Figure 2.23, the interface presents the users with an abstract o+d interface, where the lower windows show an overview of activity intervals along a time line for both text and audio contributions of two persons who participated in a meeting. The scrollable upper window initially displays a detail view that lists all text segments, and usually serves as the starting point for data exploration. Users select text segments that refer to subjects they are interested in. The system responds by replacing the text-based detail view with a magnified portion of the abstract overview. Within the new detail view, all intervals in the temporal neighborhood of the selected subject are highlighted. The enlarged sections can now be examined in more detail.

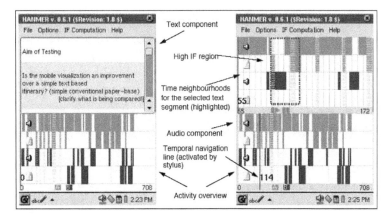

Figure 2.23: Abstract o+d interface to visualize multimedia recordings on a PDA [155].

2.3.3.4 Grid-Based Overview

The application shown in Figure 2.24 uses a fully transparent overview to navigate large images on small screens [197]. The overview consists of a simple grid that is displayed on demand and superimposes the detail view. While the grid shows the proportions of the entire image, each of the grid cells represents an image region, which, given the current scale level, could be displayed on a single PDA screen. A highlighted field-of-view box with the same dimensions as the grid cells indicates the current image portion shown in the detail view. Users can either pan cell-wise by tapping a cell in the grid-overview or they can pan pixel-wise using the rocker-button of the PDA. To zoom out, the users drag the pen over multiple cells, which are instantly highlighted (Figure 2.24b). Lifting the pen, the viewport is scaled and positioned to cover the corresponding portion of the image (Figure 2.24c). Also, the grid is updated such that each cell now has the size of the previously selected cell range. To zoom into a portion of a cell, the users divide it into four sub-cells by first tapping the cell and then holding the pen down on it. After a delay, the cell splits and the sub-portion can be selected.

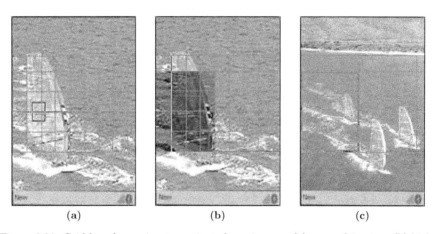

(a)   (b)   (c)

Figure 2.24: Grid-based overview to navigate large images: (a) zoomed-in view, (b) highlighting multiple cells to zoom out, (c) zoomed-out view [197].

While the grid-based zoom & pan technique may provide an effective way of navigating, the level of overview information conveyed does not exceed the one provided by scrollbars: the grid visualizes spatial information, i.e. the relative size and position of the viewport for a given zoom level with respect to the entire image, but no content information is given. Thus, if the widget is not enhanced by additional encodings, users are still forced to find regions or objects of interest via a time-consuming trial-and-error strategy.

2.4   Focus+Context Interfaces

Focus+context (f+c) means a presentation technique where both detail and overview information are integrated into a single view by employing distortion [212]. A popular example of this approach is fisheye views as introduced by Furnas in 1981 [90]. A fisheye visualization is based on the metaphor of a wide-angle lens that presents the local focus in great detail and the global context in progressively less detail. An interesting aspect of this design is that it appears naturally in a human context, e.g. in the way we categorize information in our mind. Furnas formalized fisheye views by defining a generalized degree of interest (DOI) function [89] [91]. Each element of an information structure is assigned an *a priori* importance, which is traded off against the element's distance from the current focus element. To construct a view, a minimum threshold is defined, such that only elements with a larger DOI than the threshold are displayed. In Figure 2.25a, this technique is applied to the tree-structure of programming code. Given the current focus line denoted by arrows, less important lines are pruned for the benefit of more important ones. In this case, the distance of an item is defined as its path length to the focus line, and *a priori* importance is the distance to the root. A derivation of this editor interface with an adjusted importance definition was found superior for understanding and navigating source code when compared to a linear interface [128]. Another study investigated the usability of the Furnas fisheye view for the reading and writing of electronic documents [121]. The results indicate that participants were fastest with the fisheye when reading, but received higher grades for essays written using an o+d interface. The participants significantly preferred the o+d interface.

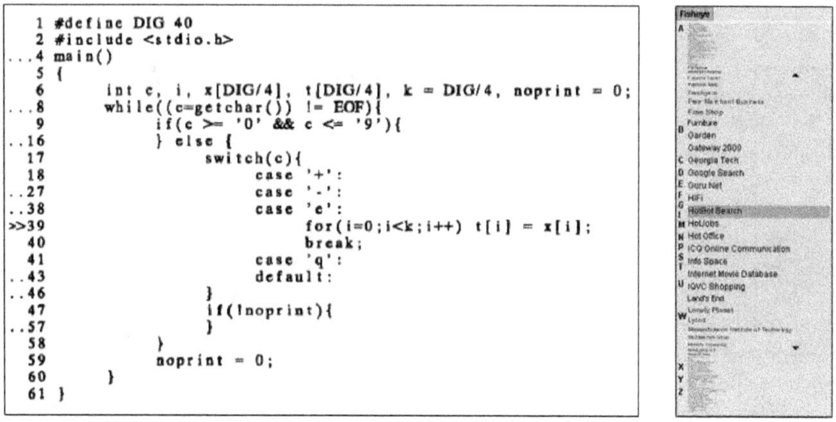

Figure 2.25: Two types of fisheye views: (a) logical fisheye view applied to programming code [89], (b) graphical fisheye view for browsing a collection of menu items [20].

2.4.1 Graphical Fisheye View

There also exist a wide range of graphical interpretations of the fisheye metaphor. These have, for instance, been used to visualize graph structures [200] or to make a large collection of menu items more manageable [20] (Figure 2.25b). An early distortion approach is the bifocal display [213] (Figure 2.26a). It was designed to support professionals in an office environment to visually search large volumes of electronic data. Information objects are positioned on a horizontal strip and viewed through the viewport of a computer monitor. To increase the number of objects that can be presented on a limited screen real estate, a central region of the display is defined as a focus area in which the objects are shown at full size. The context regions to the left and right side of the focus present objects in a low-resolution representation of a reduced width. An example would be a week-object of a calendar that is shown with each day visible in the focus region while adjacent weeks are accumulated to month-objects in the context regions. Users can horizontally scroll objects into the focus region to see them at full size. This change of object appearance is closely related to semantic zooming as described in Chapter 2.2.5.2.

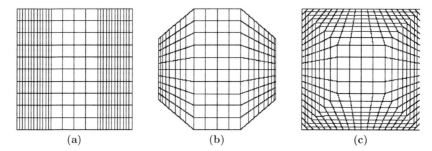

Figure 2.26: Distortion patterns: (a) bifocal, (b) perspective wall, (c) document lens [54].

A 3D descendent of the bifocal display is the concept of the perspective wall as developed by [158]. The objective is to provide a more intuitive integration of linear detail and context information by folding the 2D information space into a 3D layout. This results in the wall-like structure shown in Figure 2.26b. The panel in the center presents details and the two perspective panels on either side represent the context. Instead of semantic zooming, the objects in the context regions are reduced by the distortion inherent in perspective, i.e. the more distant an object is to the focus panel, the smaller it will appear in the context, and vice versa. As with the bifocal display, users can interactively adjust the wall. Changes in the view are eased by smooth animations. A related distortion technique is the document lens [194]. The latter is a rectangular magnification lens where the surrounding parts are pulled towards the focus panel to form a truncated pyramid (Figure 2.26c). It was designed to facilitate the browsing of a rectangular array of text documents. Users move the mouse to change the XY position of the focus, while the keyboard is used to move the lens back and forward in the Z dimension. A taxonomy of distortion-oriented presentation techniques can be found in [149].

In contrast to an o+d interface, f+c approaches do not require the users to switch between separated views. Also, due to the integration of local and global information, less display space is needed. A common aspect of o+d interfaces and fisheye views is that the performance seems to be strongly task-dependent. [106] found that, for large steering tasks, each of three different fisheye lenses was faster than two undistorted views. However, the distortion of f+c interfaces has a negative effect on the perception of proportions, angles, and distances and thus hampers tasks that require precise targeting [103] [102], or the recall of spatial locations [210]. Moreover, these problems may become increasingly troublesome with a growing zoom factor [210]. One study [209], for instance, investigated the participants' ability to memorize the location of nodes within a distorted graph. The performance deteriorated significantly as the distortion factor increased up to a scale factor of 5 - the maximum factor as recommended by [208]. However, even with a low zoom factor, users constantly have to reorient. Overall, f+c interfaces can be inappropriate for visualizing domains such as maps, where a high fidelity to the standard layout is important. Instead, and as recommended by [175], the approach should preferably be used for abstract information spaces.

There have been a number of studies comparing the usability of f+c approaches to ZUIs and o+d interfaces on desktop computers. In [203], researchers applied a multi-focus fisheye zoom to a hierarchically clustered network and compared the technique's usability to a ZUI application. Users were quicker to complete a monitoring and rerouting task when using the fisheye. The interface also allowed them to make fewer unnecessary navigational steps through the hierarchy. Although the participants appreciated the preservation of context, expert comments seem to suggest that in a real-life scenario (operating a telephone network) the distortion of the familiar grid structure would make them feel rather unconfident. Another study [165] compared a ZUI to a rectangular fisheye zoom based on the rubber sheet metaphor [201]. Both interfaces were tested with and without an overview window for navigating a large binary tree structure and judging the path length between highlighted nodes. The participants were faster using the bounding-box ZUI and needed fewer navigational actions. The presence of an overview had no significant effect on the performance, but users still perceived them as more enjoyable and less physically demanding than their detail-only counterparts. In [13], a fisheye approach was used to display large websites on a single screen by vertically compressing content that would otherwise be clipped. The application was enhanced with a mechanism to highlight search terms in both the focus and context regions. An evaluation comparing the interface to an o+d interface and a conventional linear browser revealed mixed results. The performance of the fisheye seemed to deteriorate for task types in which users were required to discriminate rows of text. For other task types, the f+c approach proved to be twice as fast than the other two interfaces. Regardless of the varying performance, there was a significant preference for the o+d interface.

2.4.2 Symbolic Representation of Context

As discussed in the previous section, f+c interfaces suffer from the drawback of being limited to small zoom factors. A way to allow for greater factors while still guaranteeing the readability of the context is to fuse graphical and symbolic content representations. A concept based on this approach is the table lens application [183][184], which is shown in Figure 2.27. The columns represent different attribute variables of a house data set (e.g. number of bedrooms, city) and each row is a record, consisting of values for each column variable (e.g. "3", "San Jose"). A table lens can visualize many more cells on a single screen than a conventional spreadsheet application by distorting the spatial layout. However, instead of simply compressing rows and columns that are not in focus, which would render the text values unreadable even at a small zoom factor, the application uses small-size symbolic encodings of context data. Not only does this preserve low-level content information, but users are provided with an effective overview of data, which facilitates tasks such as the detection of outliers or patterns. To view and compare text representation of records, users can set multiple focus areas.

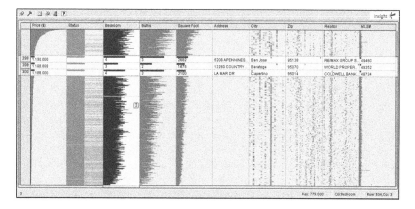

Figure 2.27: TableLens that visualizes a housing database (http://www.inxight.com/).

Recently, the table lens approach has also been used to visualize line graphs [143]. The context regions were created by encoding the Y-dimension of individual line graphs with color instead of space, and thus summarizing major common features and alignments of the data in a 1-pixel row.

Another application domain for symbolic representation in f+c interfaces is the visualization of off-screen objects. One such approach is shown in Figure 2.28 where a technique called city lights [238] [95] is used to provide peripheral awareness in a zoomable nested windows environment. The figure displays overview windows with a field-of-view box in a clipped detail view to indicate the position of off-screen objects. In Figure 2.28a, the city lights encodings are shown as colorings on the window borders and represent orthogonal projections of windows in the off-screen space. Further encodings are added to the corners of each window to indicate objects in the corner regions. Users can navigate to the next off-screen window in a direction by clicking the corresponding coloring. A problem with the proposed line projection is that it can easily lead to clutter if a growing number of objects are projected. A more space-conserving alternative is to use a point projection of the objects' centers as illustrated in Figure 2.28b. Figure 2.28c shows a variant employing radial projection, which treats orthogonal and corner regions more consistently. In addition, in this interface distance is encoded by color: projections of objects in close proximity are dark green while those of objects farther away are light green.

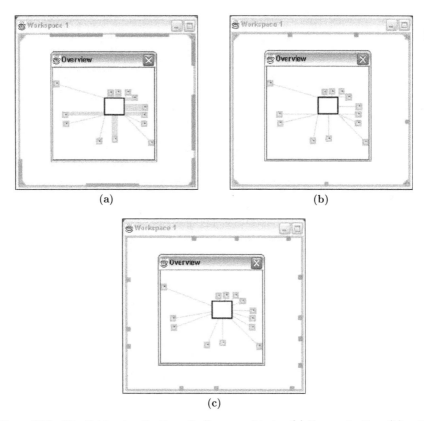

Figure 2.28: City lights visualization of off-screen objects: (a) line projection, (b) point projection, (c) radial projection (adapted from [95]; lines have been added to emphasize the different projection techniques).

2.4.3 Mobile Applications

On the one hand, f+c techniques make efficient use of limited screen real estate and thus may provide a powerful interface solution for mobile devices. On the other hand, given an information space of a reasonable size, the small display usually enforces a large zoom factor that may hinder the usability of the application. Hence the success of mobile f+c interfaces depends on how well designers can ease the tension between detail and overview information.

While previous research proposed a number of experimental PDA fisheye applications that will be discussed in the following sections, little is known about the usability differences between the three concepts of f+c, o+d and zoomable user interfaces on small-screen devices. One of the very few evaluations dealing with this topic is [104]. As already mentioned in Chapter 2.2, the study compared a two-level zoom to a flat-top pyramid fisheye and a panning system on a PC-simulated small screen. The fisheye interface proved to be significantly faster for web navigation and the two-level zoom for a monitoring task. The participants were slowest with the panning interface.

2.4.3.1   Graphical Fisheye

Based on the rubber-sheet metaphor [201], previous research proposed rectangular fisheye views to present images on small screens [187] [186]. The technique is illustrated in Figure 2.29, with the rectangular focus region always being displayed in the center and at a high level of detail. In Figure 2.29a, the context portion of the map is split into 8 cells that surround the focus region. Each cell is scaled in the X and Y dimensions to fit the remaining screen space. The smoothness of the focus integration into the context can be increased by arranging the context regions into an inner and an outer belt with a decreasing zoom factor (Figure 2.29b). Several belts could be used to further ease the transition. The maximum smoothness is achieved by non-uniform scaling (Figure 2.29c), in which the context scaling factor is decreasing continually with increasing distance from the focus boundary. In [187] some interaction functions to manipulate the rectangular fisheye are sketched, but no information is given on how these could be mapped to input on mobile devices. No further evaluations of the techniques were conducted.

We experimented with an algorithm similar to uniform scaling and found its scalability to be limited to a zoom factor of about 4. Also, computationally expensive filters for rescaling the image were needed to improve the readability of heavily distorted regions.

A more sophisticated approach for displaying images on small screens is to automatically detect the most important region in an image and then to crop it according to the potential focus (Figure 2.30a). A context-preserving variant of this solution has been proposed in [153]. The authors used fisheye view warps to emphasize some parts of an image while shrinking others (Figure 2.30b). While this approach can retain important information in an image, it may be less useful, for instance, when aesthetics in image composition is an issue. In an online poll with 45 responses, the participants showed no significant preference for either distorted or undistorted images. However, in the case of the distorted images, the results showed a high variance of user ratings.

As shown in Figure 2.31, another application domain for graphical fisheye views on mobile devices may be sketching. In [146], a PDA application is presented that provides users with a high resolution drawing area that is embedded into a compressed belt region showing the context of the sketch. The results of a user evaluation, in which 17 participants had to write a text passage and draw a UML diagram, indicate a preference for the fisheye view when compared to an undistorted but scrollable sketch pane. No information is given on whether the distortion had an effect on the quality of a drawing, or whether less schematic figures than UML diagrams may be more difficult to accomplish using the fisheye.

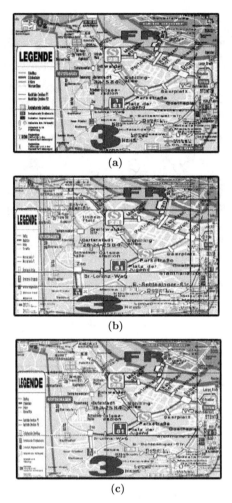

Figure 2.29: Rectangular fisheyes: (a) uniform, (b) belt-based, (c) non-uniform scaling [186].

2.4.3.2   PowerView

PowerView is a PDA application that provides structured access to four personal information management (PIM) tools: calendar, email, address book, and to-do list [36] [34]. Figure 2.32a shows the default state of the system. Each PIM domain is displayed as a small text box in an overview. By tapping a tile with the stylus, the box is highlighted and a more detailed representation of the domain is displayed in the larger detail view (Figure 2.32b). Another tap on the focus tile activates a full-screen navigation view of the hierarchically organized domain data, e.g. the contacts in the address book are grouped by

(a)   (b)

Figure 2.30: Automatic focus on the potential region of interest: (a) image cropping, (b) fisheye warp [153].

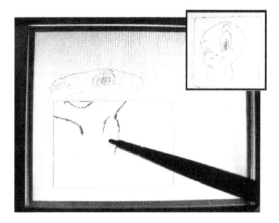

Figure 2.31: Employing fisheye distortion to allow for focus+context sketching on PDAs [146].

the initial letter of the surnames (Figure 2.32c). To present data on the small screen real estate of a PDA, PowerView uses a f+c approach called flip zooming [118]. Flip zooming is a concept where the information space is divided into several regular tiles that are laid out as thumbnails in a left-to-right, top-to-bottom order on the display. In the default view, all thumbnails are shown at the same small size. Upon selecting one, the system responds by enlarging the tile to a readable size, while all the surrounding thumbnails are shrunk and re-arranged to make space. In the address book example, the user has set the focus on contacts with the initial letter 'N'. The focus can be moved to different tiles using back and forward commands or by directly selecting an item. To improve the users' orientation, the sequential ordering of the tiles is always maintained. Moreover, the application allows filtering of the information given within the tiles. If, in the example, the user selects a person from the address book, PowerView creates a context view that uses a layout similar to the o+d default view but limits the information displayed across the PIM domains to the meetings, to-do-items, and emails associated with this particular person.

PowerView was evaluated in a usability study with 16 participants, in which the application was compared to the standard PIM applications shipped with Windows CE. The results indicate the users significantly preferred the PowerView application.

Another PDA application that makes use of the flip zooming technique is WEST, a terminal browser for small screens [35]. Web pages are chunked by a proxy server into tiles that are presented via flip zooming on the client device. Different tile dimensions can be selected including thumbnail, keyword, and hyperlink representations.

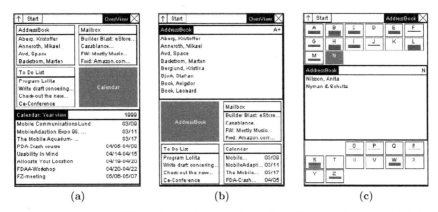

Figure 2.32: Managing PIM tools on a PDA with the PowerView application: (a) default view, (b) overview with focus on the calendar, (c) navigation view of the address book with focus on the letter 'N' [36].

2.4.3.3 Halos

Halo [14] is a variation of the f+c city lights approach (Chapter 2.4.2) to support map navigation on mobile devices. Instead of using line or point projections, peripheral awareness is achieved by surrounding each clipped object with an ellipse (halo) just large enough to reach into the viewport. Based on the curvature of a halo, users can judge not only the direction but also the distance of the corresponding off-screen object with respect to the current viewport (see Figure 2.33).

Figure 2.33: Halo visualization of off-screen objects in a map information space.

The developers carried out an evaluation in which the halo approach was compared to screen arrows labeled with a distance value. Both interfaces ran on a PC-simulated PDA interface showing a street map. During the test, 12 participants had to complete different task types requiring them to judge and compare the position of off-screen objects. The results show a significant performance benefit for the halo technique, while accuracy deteriorated slightly. Participants tended to underestimate distances when using the Halo interface [14]. In contrast, a similar study with 17 participants found that the subjects were faster and more accurate at ordering off-screen objects according to distance when using arrow signs that encoded distance by scale or length of the arrows. Halos were found better for tasks in which the correct location of off-screen objects had to be identified [39].

Just as with city lights, halos become easily cluttered even with a small number of objects. To make halos more scalable, the authors propose to cluster strongly overlapping arcs into a single multi-halo. This solution produces a smaller number of halos, but also reduces the approach's precision and consistency. Overall, halos may be more suitable for visualizing smaller numbers of objects [95].

2.4.3.4 DateLens

DateLens is a f+c calendar interface for PDAs that is strongly motivated by the bifocal display and the TableLens [24]. As illustrated in Figure 2.34a, in the default overview the dates are organized in a tabular display where each row represents one week, with seven columns representing the days of the week. Each cell is allocated the same amount of display space, and appointments are indicated by symbolic depictions with a white rectangle at the top of the day rectangle. Tapping on a cell causes it to expand and reveal more detailed information about the corresponding date (Figure 2.34b). Based on a fisheye algorithm, the other cells shrink accordingly. Only cells with sufficient screen space are equipped with symbolic representations, i.e. in the example, the cells that are orthogonal to the cell in focus. Within the focus cell, a textual list of appointments in order by time is shown, while the peripheral dates preserve some degree of the day's context. The users can further enlarge the cell to fill the entire screen by tapping on the background, or tapping on the cell's maximize button. The system switches to a conventional detail view of appointments familiar from the Microsoft Outlook calendar (Figure 2.34c). The appointments can be edited by tapping them with the stylus. In both the focus-view and the zoomed-in view, the users can return to the next-lower granularity view by tapping the focus cell's minimize button.

Apart from allocating display space according to the users' focus, DateLens also offers the option to manipulate the scope of the viewport. Users can use the range slider on the right side of the application to control how many weeks are visible at a time. Just as with zooming in on dates, all interface changes are animated.

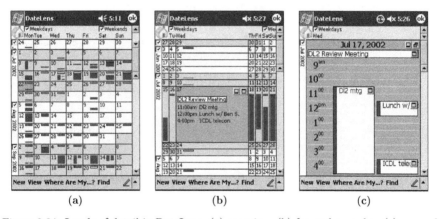

Figure 2.34: Levels of detail in DateLens: (a) overview, (b) focused on a day, (c) zoomed into a day [24].

Two evaluations were carried out to compare DateLens to the standard Microsoft Pocket PC 2002 calendar. In the first study, 11 participants used DateLens on a PC-simulated PDA interface controlled by a mouse and a keyboard. The participants performed complex tasks significantly faster with DateLens, while the standard application was faster for simple tasks. The same result was found in a second study with expert PDA users who used DateLens on their own devices. No significant differences in preference were found; satisfaction varied with different task types [24].

2.4.3.5 AppLens

AppLens [137] is as an alternative design to the ZUI-based LaunchTile concept discussed
in Chapter 2.2.6.5. Its tabular interface shown in Figure 2.35 is based on DateLens and
visualizes multiple application views. In the default overview state (Figure 2.35a), each of
the nine cells is of the same size and displays high level application-specific information.
Activating a cell enlarges it to about half of the display size, while the surrounding cells
shrink accordingly (Figure 2.35b). For each cell, the representation is changed to fit into
the allocated screen space. To avoid a visual overload of information, peripheral tiles are
displayed at 40% transparency. In the highest zoom level (Figure 2.35c), the view fills
the entire screen and provides the full set of the application's functionalities. AppLens
can be controlled by a single-hand. By using thumb (or stylus) gestures, users navigate a
cursor (orange rectangle outline) from cell to cell or switch between the three zoom levels
provided by the application.

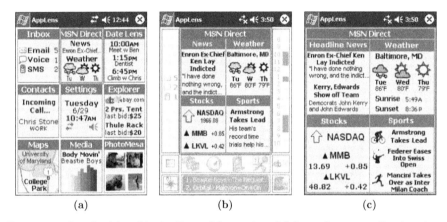

(a)   (b)   (c)

Figure 2.35: Levels of detail in AppLens: (a) overview, (b) focused on an application view,
(c) zoomed into an application view [137].

In an informal usability study run on an Hp Ipaq PDA, 10 participants used both AppLens
and LaunchTile. The participants seemed to prefer AppLens, but this result is influenced
by performance differences and the different amount of application views supported -
LaunchTile comprised 36 and AppLens only 9 items [137].

2.5 Summary

Chapter 2 has discussed presentation techniques for displaying large information spaces
on a limited screen real estate:

- Scrolling interfaces are the de-facto standard for desktop and mobile applications.
  Many users are familiar with them, but due to the linear presentation approach,
  scrolling is not suitable for navigating large data sets.

- ZUIs make use of a spatial metaphor to allow for non-linear data access. The users can rapidly navigate an information space by performing panning and zooming operations. An important concept is semantic zooming, which means that information objects change their representation according to the scale level or the amount of display space available to them.

- O+d interfaces show overview and detail information in separate views. This concept has been found successful for many desktop applications, but, due to space constraints, it is less frequently used for mobile devices. Existing approaches often feature automatic overviews that temporarily overlap the detail view. However, this approach suffers from the imprecision of having to estimate the moments when users may need overview information.

- F+c interfaces integrate both detail and overview information in a single view and thus make more efficient use of the display space. A drawback is that large zoom factors are difficult to achieve without rendering the context unreadable. One solution may be to incorporate small-sized symbolic representations of context items.

All the techniques presented were originally designed with the desktop monitor in mind, but may also provide an effective strategy for meeting the growing interface demands on small-screen mobile devices. While the majority of mobile interfaces still rely on scrolling interfaces, there also exist some examples of commercial and experimental applications utilizing ZUI, o+d, and f+c concepts. Mobile ZUIs in particular are often limited to basic zoom features, however, and thus do not exploit the concept's full potential, for instance, with regard to multiscale interfaces such as Pad++. Another aspect to note is that only a very small amount of research has been done to analyze the usability differences between ZUI, o+d, and f+c approaches on mobile devices. To support a successful migration of those techniques to portable platforms, more comparative evaluations must be conducted.

Chapter 3

Starfield Displays

Contents

3.1 Information Visualization

This chapter will present the concept of starfield displays. Starfield displays are complex search interfaces that, like many of the presentation techniques discussed in the previous chapter, have been developed in the scientific field of Information Visualization. With a history of about 15 years, Information Visualization is a relatively young research discipline. It aims to support users in understanding and analyzing data, and can be defined as: *"The use of computer-supported, interactive, visual representations of abstract data to amplify cognition"* [52]. Information Visualization draws from fields such as Human-Computer Interaction, Information Science, Computer Graphics, and Cognitive Psychology. A closely related discipline is Scientific Visualization, which deals with the presentation of physical or geometric objects (e.g. the human body, ozone concentration etc). In contrast, Information Visualization focuses on abstract information such as financial data and collections of documents.

Due to the ever-increasing amounts of data that are produced and need to be analyzed, Information Visualization is receiving more and more attention and has already begun to find its way into the everyday life of our information society. An interesting aspect of the development with respect to this work is a recently initiated reorientation of research objectives; since its founding, the discipline has largely concentrated on the creation of innovative computing techniques, while nowadays user-centered design and usability evaluation techniques are becoming more important [60] [57]. As put by [190]: *'Effective human computer interaction continues to be one of the top research and development goals*

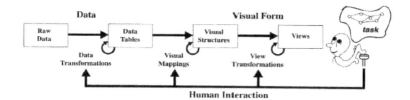

Figure 3.1: The reference model for visualization [52].

for both visualization and computer graphics."

As stated in the definition, Information Visualization aims to amplify cognition. This can be achieved through the following means [52]:

1. Increasing the memory and processing resources available to the users

2. Reducing the search for information

3. Using visual representations to enhance the detection of patterns

4. Enabling perceptual interference operations

5. Using perceptual attention mechanisms for monitoring

6. Encoding information in a manipulable medium

As indicated by the enumeration, the quality of a visualization strongly depends on the mapping of data to visual forms. This process is illustrated by the reference model for visualization shown in Figure 3.1. The model starts with acquiring the raw data, which is transformed and mapped into data tables. This step usually assumes some degree of preprocessing (e.g. cleaning, filtering) to handle errors and missing values in the data. Moreover, the information contained may also be enriched by derived values such as provided by statistical analysis. In the second step, the data tables are transformed to visual structures, i.e. the data is mapped to graphical properties. Mackinlay refers to this step as defining a sentence in a visual language that expresses relations in a data table [157]. The designer's task is now to find a balance between compressed data representations and the mental effort it will take the user to learn the language. A key factor in achieving this goal is making use of the innate human perceptual abilities via preattentive encodings, i.e. graphical properties that can be processed faster than 10 msec per item [225]. The most important encodings suitable for Information Visualization are: spatial position, color, shape, orientation, surface texture, motion, and blink coding. The encodings vary in the number of dimensions they can encode, i.e. how many expressions they provide that are easily distinguished. For instance, rapid preattentive processing requires that no more than eight colors and fewer than five orientation steps are used. Moreover, conjunctions of codes are considered to be non-preattentive, but there are exceptions to this rule, e.g. space or perceived convexity may be combined with color, or motion with target shape [225]. Many systems also allow the users to dynamically adjust the mapping of encodings.

In case of high-dimensionality data, however, the large variety of mapping compositions can lead to the problem of finding the relevant parameter settings that show interesting patterns. One approach to solving this problem is to let the computer perform an automatic preselection of potentially expressive settings [204].

The last step in the reference model for visualization is to apply view transformations to turn the visual structure into an interactive application that can be controlled by the users. Interactivity is essential since it allows the extraction of more information than can be gained from a static representation [73]. Examples of view transformation are discussed in Chapter 2 and include zooming and panning, and distortion approaches.

3.2 Scatterplot Interface & Dynamic Queries

Starfield displays were invented at the Human-Computer Interaction Laboratory at the University of Maryland during the early nineties. The objective was to provide a more powerful and user-friendly interface to support information seeking and browsing in large databases. Originally, such systems were (and in some cases still are) controlled by command line interfaces and query languages that are difficult for novice users to learn and error-prone in their use.

Being based on the principles of direct manipulation [206] [205], starfield displays are designed to support:

- rapid filtering to reduce result sets

- progressive refinement of search parameters

- continuous reformulation of goals

- visual scanning to identify results [4].

To achieve these goals, a starfield display consists of two major components: a visual database representation and an advanced filter mechanism called dynamic queries. Dynamic queries were developed to allow users to formulate queries with graphical widgets such as a slider. The control must be designed such that it provides visible limits on the query range, gives immediate feedback of the query result after every adjustment, and enables novice users to begin working with little training, but still provides expert users with powerful features [6]. Apart from the increased ease-of-use, another benefit over textual input is that no false values can be entered. Thus error messages due to invalid queries are avoided.

In an early example of the approach, dynamic queries were applied to an application showing the periodic table with chemical symbols (see Figure 3.2). The six sliders were used to set properties such as atomic number, atomic mass and electronegativity to highlight elements in the periodic table that fulfilled the given filter criteria. The coordination between the sliders and the table is an important design aspect (see Chapter 2.3.1), which ensures that display invariants are preserved and each output can be used as input for a

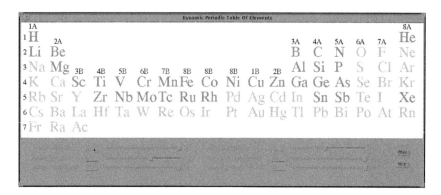

Figure 3.2: Dynamic query sliders applied to the periodic table of elements [6].

refined query [4].

A usability test was conducted, in which the interface was compared to two more conventional approaches: an interface with the same periodic table display but featuring form fill-in text fields instead of sliders, and an all-textual interface with not only text-input fields but also an output text box, which replaced the periodic table. After each query update a list of the remaining chemical elements was printed in the text box. During the test, 18 participants had to solve comparison and interpretation tasks by using the different filter mechanisms. For most task types, the dynamic query sliders were significantly faster than the two alternatives. Also, the comments of the users suggest that they preferred the sliders over text input [6].

A more advanced version of dynamic query widgets was developed for the HomeFinder application [226], which is shown in Figure 3.3. The application provides a graphical interface to a real-estate database by representing properties as points of lights on a map of Washington DC. The users can modify the result set by controlling the sliders and buttons on the right hand side to define search criteria. If the users are looking for a house with a garage, for instance, they toggle off the buttons for condominium ('Cnd') and apartment ('TH') and press the garage ('Grg') button. Upon each interaction event, the map display is rapidly updated, showing only the properties that satisfy the query. The constraints of the query are generated by ANDing all widget values.

Apart from the binary toggle buttons, the users can also use the slider widgets to set ranges of numerical data. By dragging the end points of the sliders, they may for instance define the minimum and maximum number of bedrooms the property must include, or the price range acceptable to them. Another important feature of the HomeFinder is that the visual database representation (the map) serves as an additional input area for formulating queries. By dragging two letter icons on the map, the users can define a spatial search radius, which is fine-tuned by manipulating the 'Dist to A' and 'Dist to B' sliders. The textual information about any house can be accessed by clicking the corresponding point on the map. The system responds by displaying a pop-up window, which lists the specific item data.

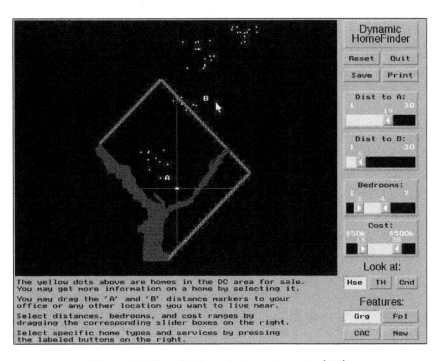

Figure 3.3: HomeFinder with dynamic queries [226].

The HomeFinder was evaluated by comparing it to a natural-language query system (Q&A) and a paper listing sorted by various fields. 18 participants were asked to find houses, and to identify trends and outliers in a property database with 944 items. For all but simple search tasks, the HomeFinder proved to be significantly faster and also scored significantly higher on a satisfaction questionnaire [226].

The spatial layout of items via longitude and latitude in the HomeFinder application was found to be very effective. Spatial encoding is the most dominant visual property [52] and can also be used in conjunction with color and shape without reducing its preattentivity [225]. Due to the small size of the representations, large quantities of data can be displayed on a single screen, and updates of items (hiding, displaying, changing color) are achieved very rapidly. However, for most abstract information spaces such as molecules or collections of books there is no natural map. For those cases a meaningful spatial display can be constructed by using a scatterplot diagram: two ordinal attributes are chosen as the axes and each item in the database is mapped to a spatial position inside the diagram based on its attribute value [4]. Paper-based scatterplots have been used to present abstract data since the early 1800s and are still one of the most common forms of data graphics in scientific literature [220]. They provide an overview of large data sets and clearly reveal characteristics of the distribution. A starfield display enhances this functionality with filter, zoom, and selection features to allow for interactive data exploration.

Figure 3.4 shows a starfield display called FilmFinder [5]. As indicated by the name, it visualizes a movie database. The X-axis represents the year of release and the Y-axis a measure of popularity. Each movie is mapped to a small rectangle positioned inside the diagram (e.g. movies that are very popular and were produced recently are located in the top-right corner). The rectangles are color-coded by genre type.

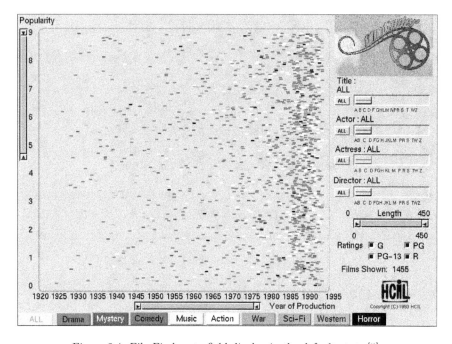

Figure 3.4: FilmFinder starfield display in the default state [5].

The design of FilmFinder follows the principle of Shneiderman's information-seeking mantra: *"Overview first, zoom and filter, then details-on-demand"* [207]. In the default state of the application (Figure 3.4), the users are provided with an overview of the entire information space. This can be very useful as a starting point for retrieval or browsing operations, or to analyze data patterns. However, as with many other visualizations, clutter and over-plotting cannot be avoided. FilmFinder provides two solutions to this problem. First, the users can prune items that are not of interest by adjusting the dynamic query widgets on the right hand side. Next to toggle buttons and range sliders, alphasliders [3] are also provided for setting textual filters (e.g. filter movies by actress or director). The second option to reduce clutter is to zoom into a portion of the diagram by operating the two zoom bars (see Chapter 2.2.4). Fewer items are displayed and the distribution of movies inside the visible area can be seen in more detail. During zooming the items become slightly larger to emphasize the zooming metaphor of flying in closer to the movies [4]. Once fewer than 25 items are displayed, the movies are labeled with their titles. To access movie details, the same approach as in the HomeFinder application is used: data is presented on-demand in a pop-up window (see Figure 3.5).

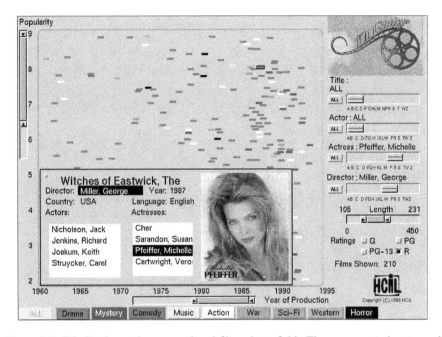

Figure 3.5: FilmFinder with a zoomed and filtered starfield. The pop-up window is used to display details on-demand [5].

Since FilmFinder, the concept of starfield displays has been implemented in many ways and for many application domains. One example of a commercial derivative is SpotFire[1] [2], which couples enhanced starfield displays with additional visualizations to support the work of business analysts and pharmaceutical scientists (see Figure 3.6). The company was founded by one of the initial developers of dynamic queries and FilmFinder. A more recent example of starfield displays designed for non-expert users is immo.search[2], a web-based interface to a Swiss housing database (see Figure 3.7).

3.3 Mobile Starfield Displays

Data retrieval on mobile devices is an emerging field in both research and business. All major search engines such as Google and Yahoo already offer optimized web sites and

---

[1]http://www.spotfire.com
[2]http://immo.search.ch

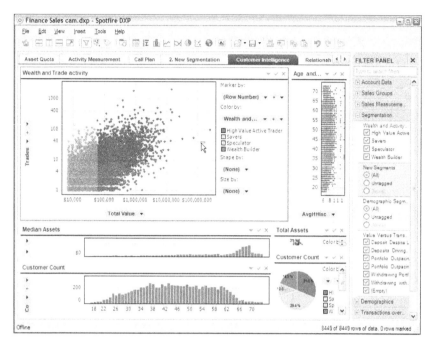

Figure 3.6: Visual analytics platform SpotFire.

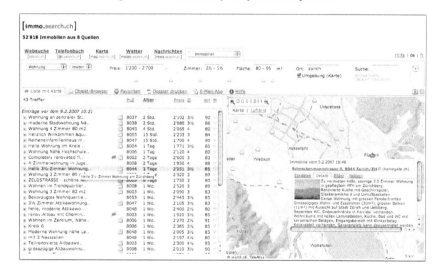

Figure 3.7: immo.search.ch: a web-based derivative of the HomeFinder design.

stand-alone applications for mobile phones and PDAs. However, a bottleneck that impedes this development is that current mobile interfaces still present data as scrollable lists and tables. For rather small data sets such as a contact list, this approach may be sufficient, but the increasingly powerful mobile hardware and fast wireless connections enable searches in large, remote databases that may return thousands of hits. For such a scenario a starfield display is a promising solution, since the compact visualization coupled with zooming makes more effective use of the small screen real estate. However, as was found with other desktop applications (see for instance [29]), starfield displays cannot be ported one to one, but must be carefully redesigned and enhanced to meet the requirements of mobile devices.

3.3.1 PalmMovieFinder

The first attempt to implement a starfield display on a PDA platform was the Palm-MovieFinder [76] [77]. As shown in Figure 3.8, the application provides access to a collection of 71 movies by spatially mapping them as 8x8 pixels icons to the static axes of year of release (X) and popularity rating (Y). The users query the database by marking and unmarking checkboxes for movie genre and film classification. Tapping the filter checkboxes results in immediate updating of the scatterplot, showing only those movies (icons) that satisfy the filter requirements. Exploration is limited to a simple two-level zoom in which a quarter of the display is magnified. To view a data object's content, the user taps on an icon and the movie details are presented on a new screen.

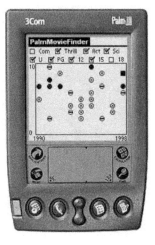

Figure 3.8: PalmMovieFinder: a PDA-based starfield display [76].

An interesting functionality of the PalmMovieFinder is that it visualizes multiple-data-points (MDPs), i.e. in a scatterplot it is very likely that icons are not only overplotted due to the limited diagram space but that they are completely overlapped by other items that feature the same values for the attributes of the scatterplot axes. The original FilmFinder design did not explicitly handle this issue. In the PDA-based version, an MDP is indicated by a fully black icon (all other icons depict different movie genres). Accordingly, tapping such an icon causes the system to display the information about all the movies in the cell.

In a usability test, 16 participants were significantly faster solving query tasks with the PalmMovieFinder than with SQL. Furthermore, according to the results of the NASA Task Load Index questionnaire, the participants found the starfield display significantly less demanding.

3.3.2 Liquid Browsing

In the PalmMovieFinder the axes units were chosen such that icons would not intersect. However, displaying larger information spaces automatically means producing visual clutter. In the FilmFinder, overlapping items could be dissolved by zooming in. An alternative for pressure-sensitive devices operated by a pen is the design concept known as Liquid Browsing [224] (see Figure 3.9). Scatterplot items behave as if floating in oil or liquid and tapping a cluster with the stylus causes a nuzzle effect: representations that originally overlapped are spread out, making it easier to isolate and select single items. A drawback of this approach is its imprecision and that it only works for a very limited point density. Moreover, the distortion, which affects the items in proximity to the pen but not the axes labels, may give a false impression about the attribute values of these items.

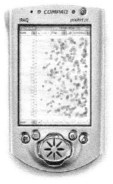

Figure 3.9: Liquid browsing: using pressure to scatter overlapping items [224].

3.3.3 Geographic Points-of-Interest

The HomeFinder system's strategy of visualizing spatial information objects as points-of-interest on a map has become quite common in mobile navigation and local search applications. Two examples of such systems are shown in Figure 3.10. They feature basic zoom, pan, and filter capabilities; textual details are presented as tooltips or pop-up windows. In the case of Mobile Google Maps[3] (a), extensive clutter of points-of-interest is avoided by limiting the number of items concurrently displayed to 9. This maximum is also convenient for mapping each point to a number key to allow for a quick details-on-demand mechanism on mobile phones. Other points that are also located on the same map clipping have to be displayed sequentially. The application smart2go[4] (b) shows points-of-interest such as parking lots and service stations as icons. The users must navigate the cursor over an icon to receive detail information.

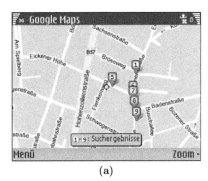 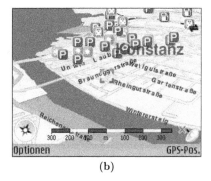

(a) (b)

Figure 3.10: Map-based starfield displays visualizing points-of-interest: (a) Google Maps Mobile showing restaurants, (b) smart2go with points-of-interest depicted as icons.

3.4 Summary

Starfield displays are powerful search and visualization interfaces that are based on a zoomable, two-dimensional scatterplot enhanced with dynamic queries. Due to the overview provided by the diagram, the users can discover at a glance which sections are sparsely or densely populated; they can locate clusters, exceptions, gaps, outliers, and trends in the data. Filtering lets them investigate data distribution in detail, test variables for correlations, and reduce the result set to contain only items satisfying specific search criteria. In comparison to query languages, users can playfully explore a database in less time and with fewer errors.

The ability to display large data sets on a limited screen real estate makes starfield displays a promising interface option for searching data on mobile devices. Map-based approaches are already a common solution, but using a starfield display for visualizing abstract data on PDAs and smartphones has hardly been investigated yet. The few experimental applications that exist are very limited in their functionality and do not work for larger information spaces.

---

[3]http://www.google.de/gmm
[4]http://smart2go.com

Chapter 4

Designing Mobile Starfield Displays

Contents

4.1 Design Iteration I: Smooth Semantic Zooming

Starfield displays, as discussed in the previous chapter, may have a great potential to reduce the small-screen problem for mobile data retrieval, but in order to exploit that potential, the interface approach must be fundamentally enhanced to cope with the special requirements of mobile devices. Our solution is to merge the starfield design with the advanced presentation techniques reviewed in Chapter 2. Based on that idea we carried out three research projects ([45] [42] [43] [40] [41]), in which we developed and user-tested various prototypes of zoomable starfield displays for PDAs. The first project discussed in [45] aims to employ smooth semantic zooming.

4.1.1 Interface Objectives

Based on the review of previous implementations, we formulated several interface objectives and requirements that we think are fundamental for successfully leveraging the starfield approach on mobile devices. Some of these objectives refer solely to properties of starfield displays; others are more general design considerations for targeting mobile devices.

- *Scalability*
  A key requirement for using mobile starfield displays in real-world scenarios is scalability. The visualization and interaction design must work for potentially large data sets.

- *Pen input*
  The application should target PDAs that are operated using a small set of hardware buttons and a stylus. Pen input provides far fewer states than a conventional computer mouse, which means a significant constraint for the interaction design. Chapter 5 discusses alternative interaction mechanisms to extend pen input.

- *Fast and orientation-preserving transition from overview to detail*
  While a scatterplot visualization is an effective tool for generating an overview of a large data set on limited screen real estate, it fails to provide detail information. In desktop applications, such information is often presented on-demand in a separate frame, but on mobile devices the screen real estate is too limited to reserve permanent space for a widget that is only temporarily of interest to the users. Another solution, as featured in the FilmFinder, is to use pop-ups, but this technique drags the user's attention away from the diagram. On closing pop-ups, users need time to re-orient inside the scatterplot. A novel approach is needed to support fast and fluent exploration of scatterplot items.

- *Orientation support*
  One of the most important functionalities of starfield displays for exploring data and for pruning visual clutter is zooming. The problem of overlapping items is even more significant on small screens than on desktop monitors, and thus the users must be equipped with effective zoom techniques. However, as discussed in Chapter 2.2.3, extensive zooming can also cause disorientation. Appropriate mechanisms must be found to preserve the users' sense of position and context.

- *MDP representation*
  Another problem that scatterplot visualizations often face is caused by multiple-data-points (MDPs) [2]. Given a reasonably large information space, there is a high probability that some data objects have similar attribute values and thus also share the same spatial position for the scatterplot visualization. MDPs were not handled in the original FilmFinder design. In the PalmMovieFinder, such points were indicated by a symbol and presented on-demand as text. The prototype should support a more advanced visual representation of MDPs, one that allows an exploration of each MDP-contained item inside the scatterplot.

- *History and bookmark functionality*
  The FilmFinder design lacks some useful functionality that is standard in most search systems. One is a history of actions, so that users are able to retrace their steps [207]. Another feature that we consider essential is a bookmarking mechanism to store items of interest for further consideration. For the prototype, we aim to present both the history and bookmarks in a way that integrates with the scatterplot as the main interface concept.

4.1.2 Design Approach

Based on the objectives, we developed the prototype shown in Figure 4.1. The application provides access to a DVD movie database. To start the retrieval process, the users enter keywords in the text field in the start interface and then hit the *go* button. As with the original FilmFinder, search results are represented by small rectangles, which are positioned according to the scatterplot dimensions (Figure 4.1b). By default, the dimensions are set to the variables of year of release (X) and lending frequency (Y). Each of the axes is mapped by label coloring to a combo box in the top toolbar. The user can change an axis assignment by selecting another variable from the corresponding combo box. The variables available next to the default ones are: popularity rating, section, and language. Changing an axis assignment causes the scatterplot visualization to update its labeling and to redistribute items.

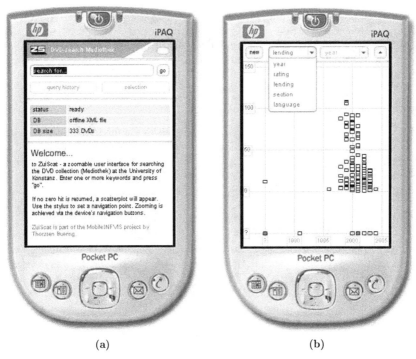

(a)   (b)

Figure 4.1: Mobile starfield display: (a) start screen. (b) scatterplot visualization with 335 items and opened combo box for selecting an attribute variable for the Y-dimension.

As indicated by the axes variables, the prototype encodes both quantitative (e.g. rating) and nominal values (e.g. section) by spatial position. On the one hand, this approach may in some cases cause irritations: nominal values do not possess a meaningful order and thus the positioning may give the users the false impression that such a relation does exist [52]. On the other hand, the approach can reveal important information about the data that would otherwise be hard to impart [160]. However, this assumes that the set of nominal values is rather small and that the scatterplot labels can thus be displayed without overlapping each other. For larger data sets, some kind of clustering mechanism is needed.

Meta-information about the search can be accessed by tapping the arrow button on the top right hand side. A small window unfolds from the toolbar showing the current query keywords and the number of hits achieved. Displaying this information on-demand saves screen real estate for the benefit of the scatterplot. Moreover, there is no actual need to display meta-information continuously: users will usually remember the current query executed and a direct, though rough, visual feedback about the amount of retrieval results is already given by the visualization. Tapping anywhere on the screen closes the meta-information window.

One thing to note about the prototype is that it focuses solely on the scatterplot design, and thus no dynamic queries were implemented. However, the latter may be easily integrated with the interface using an additional toolbar window. Another example of how to lay out a scatterplot and dynamic queries on a small screen is given by a later prototype discussed in Chapter 4.3.

4.1.2.1 Geometric & Semantic Zoom

The main design solution of the prototype with regard to the interface objectives stated in Chapter 4.1.1 is to turn the starfield into a multiscale interface in the tradition of Pad and Pad++ (see Chapter 2.2.1). Users can explore data items in a 2.5D information space via semantic zooming. One difference to the previous applications is that the information objects are positioned in space according to a scatterplot layout.

Zooming and panning in the mobile starfield is based on both pen and button input, and aims to encourage free exploration of the scatterplot. In contrast to the PalmMovieFinder, which only supports a two-level zoom with fixed focus points, users can continuously move without restrictions to any point in the information space at any scale. We also avoid zoom bars as featured in the FilmFinder, as these widgets may require up to four sequential actions for a single scale operation and their precision decreases with a growing information space (see Chapter 2.2.4). Another reason is that the sliders would take away valuable screen space from the starfield.

The prototype's zoom mechanism is illustrated by Figure 4.2. The users first set a focus point by tapping the screen with the stylus. A blue cross-hair appears at the selected position. If the cross-hair is positioned over a rectangle, additional scatterplot labels are displayed to show the exact attribute values of the focus item (e.g. the movie targeted in the example was produced in 1998 and has a lending frequency of 4). By continuously pressing the upper part of the four-way rocker switch button of the PDA, the scatterplot is magnified and the area denoted by the focus point moves to the center of the screen. As shown by the screenshots, the rectangles grow in size during zooming. This geometric zoom is used to prune visual clutter, i.e. having zoomed in, the users can accurately tap the item of interest, even if most of the representation is covered by another item. Zooming out is achieved by pressing the lower part of the rocker switch button. If not previously stopped, the operation automatically comes to a halt when the visualization is back to the default scale. It is important to note that, unlike previous mobile starfields, the prototype supports smooth continuous zooming, which was suggested in previous research to help users to maintain relations between application states, to stay focused on the task and to build a mental model of the information space (see Chapter 2.2.5.1). Apart from zooming, the users can also pan the scatterplot by dragging the surface with the stylus.

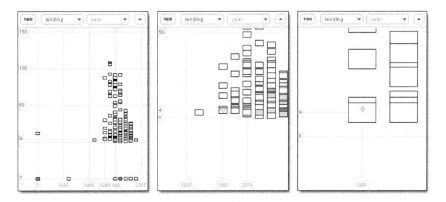

Figure 4.2: Geometric zoom in the prototype to resolve overlappings of items with different scatterplot values.

Having focused on an item of interest, the user wants to switch from abstract representation of data to a content view. One design objective was to avoid coarse and disorienting interface transitions such as those caused by pop-up windows. To achieve this, the prototype employs semantic zooming: at a certain scale level the application switches from geometric to semantic zoom, using the magnified rectangle as a display area for the content it represents. This transition is illustrated by Figure 4.3. In the first screenshot the users have zoomed in on an item that turns into a record card showing the movie title 'John Grisham's The rainmaker'. Further information about the DVD can be accessed by tapping one of the subcontent units of the record card labeled *description*, *details*, *poster*, and *trailer*. The information for the unit selected is displayed on demand. Dependent on the current scale, the user may need to perform another zoom-in operation to magnify text or pictures to a readable size. Units for which there is no data available are marked gray (disabled).

In the example shown in Figure 4.3, by repositioning the cross-hair with the stylus the users move the focus to a second scatterplot item that is partly overlapped by the first one. As indicated by the now-visible record card, the title of the movie is 'Batman'. The users tap the subcontent unit labeled *description* and subsequently magnify the text displayed. Then they become interested in the movie poster, which can be accessed by first zooming out and then back in with the focus on the corresponding *poster* unit. Overall, the users never actually leave the scatterplot, which means that no orientation disruptions are caused. Zooming in and out, the users can rapidly gain insight into the data objects of the underlying information space. The different types of content units emphasize that the multiscale starfield approach can be utilized for a wide variety of multimedia data.

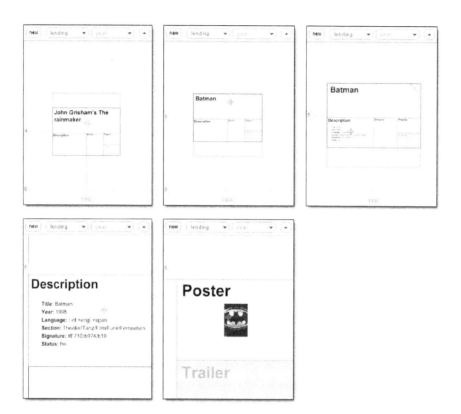

Figure 4.3: Semantic zoom in the prototype to display content information inside the scatterplot. The users switch from *'John Grisham's The rainmaker'* to the partly overlapped *'Batman'* record card (in the first screenshot indicated by the light gray outline). Then they zoom in on the item to receive further detail information.

4.1.2.2 Multiple-Data-Points

A starfield is likely to contain a number of MDPs, e.g. in the movie database there exist several films that have a lending frequency of 4 and were released in 2003. These rectangles share the same position inside the scatterplot, and accordingly they are represented by a single rectangle. To indicate the accumulation of data at this point, the prototype uses a small preattentive set of gray scales (white, light gray, dark gray, black). The darker a rectangle, the more data objects it holds. Although this technique is not precise, it provides a rather intuitive way of improving the overview of item distribution. Other techniques to indicate overplotting of items were mentioned in Chapter 2.2.5.3 and include point displacement and drawing MDPs with an increased color intensity.

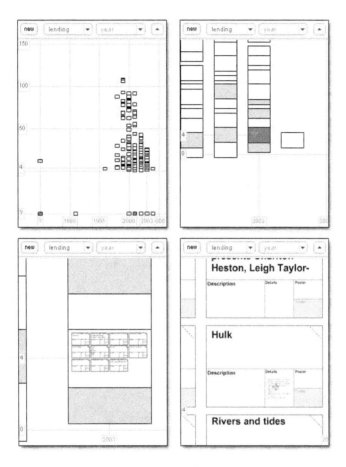

Figure 4.4: Multiple-data-point visualization (zoom animation goes from top-left to bottom-right).

To make each item of an MDP equally accessible, while at the same time preserving the spatial layout consistency, the prototype makes use of the design principle of closure (part of the Gestalt laws [144]) as an auxiliary tool to support comprehension. In Figure 4.4, the users zoom in on a rectangle with the attribute values year of release 2003 and lending frequency 4. The rectangle is encoded with a dark gray scale, which indicates that the item represents not one but several movies in the database. When the application switches to semantic zoom, all items of the multiple-data-point are displayed as separate record cards but grouped together by the outline of the initial rectangle. That way, the users intuitively know that the DVDs presented belong together, i.e. share the same value pair for the given scatterplot dimensions. In order to fit several record cards into a single rectangle, they must be drawn at a smaller scale, but due to the ZUI this aspect is not crucial. For displaying larger numbers of items inside an MDP, some kind of sorting or ordering criteria may prove helpful to reduce search times.

4.1.2.3   User-Generated Information Spaces

In submitting queries, and by bookmarking movies, the users generate two additional information spaces, namely a query history and a selection. Both spaces are again visualized in a zoomable scatterplot, which means that users only have to learn a single interface for viewing and interacting with different data sets.

To bookmark items, users fold the edge of the corresponding record card by tapping it with the stylus. This is shown in Figure 4.5a. Another feature indicated by the screen shot is keyword highlighting, i.e. the query in the example was 'Hitchcock' and thus the term is colored red on the record card. To retrieve previously bookmarked items, the users tap the selection button on the start screen (see Figure 4.1a). This loads a scatterplot, in which each rectangle represents a selected DVD. Since the selection is a subset of the original DVD search space, the same variables (year, lending frequency, rating, section and language) can be used for spatial positioning. Further variables that could be included are the time of bookmarking and a reference to the query by which the DVD was returned.

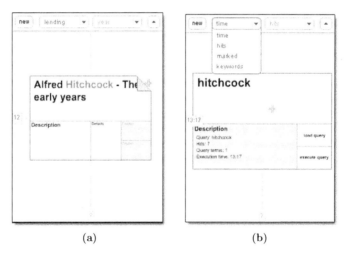

(a)   (b)

Figure 4.5: Custom information spaces: (a) bookmarking a scatterplot item, (b) query history.

The prototype stores each executed query in a query history and assigns meta-information to it. Tapping the query history button brings up a scatterplot in which each item represents a previous search. The users can trace and identify specific queries by adjusting the scatterplot dimensions. Dimension variables available in the query history are: time of query execution, number of keywords, number of hits, and number of items bookmarked. Zooming in on an item, the query text appears along with the meta-information stored for that particular search (see Figure 4.5b). The users are also provided with buttons to either load the query keywords into the search field on the start screen or to re-execute the query directly.

4.1.3 Implementation

The prototype was implemented with the Adobe (formerly Macromedia) Flash MX 2004 authoring environment using ActionScript 2.0. ActionScript is a scripting language based on ECMAScript and supports object-oriented programming. Programs in Flash are compiled to a Shockwave file format (swf) and executed by a Flash player. Flash players are available as a browser plugin or as a stand-alone player for a variety of platforms, and with 'Flash Lite' for cell phones and 'Flash player for Pocket PC' mobile devices are also supported. However, in order to minimize the footprint, these applications only implement a subset of the functionality offered by their desktop counterparts. The prototype was compiled for Flash player 6, which can be installed as a browser plugin for the PPC Internet Explorer on PDAs running Windows Pocket PC 2003[1]. We used FlashAssist Pro 1.3 together with Microsoft eMbedded Visual C++ 3.0 to make the prototype run full screen in the browser, and to receive button events from the PDA rocker switch via an XML event server.

The prototype consists of 40 ActionScript classes with in total about 3,600 lines of code. Upon startup, the application checks whether a network connection is available. If so, the movie data is loaded from a postgreSQL database using AMFPHP, an open-source Flash Remoting gateway for PHP. The gateway automatically handles the serialization and deserialization of data exchanged between the flash movie and the backend. If no network connection exists, a local XML file with 335 movies is loaded into memory. For navigating and searching the XML file, we used an ActionScript implementation of XPath 1.0 provided by XFactor Studio. We modified parts of the code to support features such as case insensitivity for keyword search.

The scatterplot GUI of the prototype consists of a set of nested movie clips. The movie clip class is at the core of each visual element in Flash. An object of this type can be manipulated to listen to events, to change its position, rotation, scale, and transparency, and it can be used as a canvas for various drawing procedures. Each movie clip may also contain a timeline with multiple frames that can be navigated programmatically. In the prototype, one movie clip serves as the container for the scatterplot viewport. All items are drawn on separate movie clips and are then attached directly or indirectly to the container. In that way, all the clipping is done automatically by the Flash player. Moreover, zooming and panning can be easily implemented by manipulating the scale and translation properties of the nested movie clips.

---

[1]By the time of writing, Flash player 7 for Pocket PC has become available. This runs on both Pocket PC 2003 and Windows Mobile 5 devices. Moreover, Adobe is about to release the Flash 9 authoring environment, the second generation after Flash MX 2004.

The main elements for storing and managing scatterplot items are:

- The *DataPoint* class
  Represents a rectangle in the scatterplot and holds at least one object implementing the *Document* interface.

- The *Document* interface
  Defines method declarations for the object to draw itself as a record card to a parent movie clip, to check for a hit given a stylus position, and to display and remove subcontent units. The *Document* interface is implemented by a set of classes representing the different types of information objects in the prototype: a *DVD*, a *Query*, and a *Bookmark* class.

After a query has been executed, the retrieved database items are loaded into *DVD* objects that are assigned to *DataPoint* objects using a custom implementation of a map data type. For each *DVD*, the map checks if the key (the combination of the values for the two scatterplot dimensions) already exists. If not, a new *DataPoint* object is created, and this object stores a reference to the *DVD* object. If the key is not unique, the *DVD* is added to the existing *DataPoint*, which then becomes an MDP. The assignment of *DVDs* to *DataPoints* is updated each time the users change the axes variables of the scatterplot. In case the users want to display the query history, the assignment procedure is applied to the *Query* objects that have been previously added to a *QueryHistory* collection.

For each *DataPoint*, the position inside the scatterplot is calculated based on the current dimension variables. For nominal and ordinal levels of measurement, the DataPoint always lies on one of the labeled grid lines, for which the positions have been pre-calculated. Thus, a simple search of the item value retrieves the position. For data that is a minimum of interval type, the position is calculated relative to the device coordinates of the minimum and maximum axis values. When the scatterplot is displayed for the first time, or the axes settings have been altered, each *DataPoint* attaches its movie clip as a drawing canvas to the scatterplot. Initially, the drawing canvas only shows a black rectangle outline. If the users tap an item, and the minimum scale for semantic zoom has been reached, the *Data-Point* calls its *Documents* to draw themselves to the screen. This is done by adding each *Document's* content to a predefined record card template (based on movie clip), which is then attached to the drawing canvas of the calling *DataPoint*. If the *DataPoint* is an MDP (containing more than one *DVD* or *query*), the items are scaled and positioned to the nested layout shown in Figure 4.4.

Flash is a very effective and popular tool for web development and prototyping custom front ends, but when targeting mobile devices a number of issues arise. First, the limited performance of the Flash player 6 on the Pocket PC has influenced several design decisions. For instance, to improve the frame rate for zooming and panning operations, the content of scatterplot items is only displayed on demand, and, during animation, the scatterplot labels are temporarily hidden. Furthermore, although interface components such as buttons and combo boxes were specifically designed for use on the Pocket PC, they show a very slow response time. For example, opening a combo box with five items may take two or three seconds. To overcome this problem, we developed light-weight replacements for these components. Overall, and due to the high abstraction level of ActionScript 2.0 and Flash, there is little potential for optimizing the drawing procedure, e.g. no manual double buffering or clipping is supported. The second major issue is precision, which we found to decrease for positioning scaled, nested movie clips.

4.1.4 Informal User Evaluation

We conducted a qualitative user evaluation to gain some initial feedback on the prototype's usability. We were specifically interested in the effort the users would need to make to understand the visualization and interaction strategies used. The evaluation was based on observation and interviews.

For the experiment, the prototype was installed along with the Mobile Flash Player 6 on a Hewlett-Packard iPAQ hx4700 Pocket PC running Windows Mobile 2003. The device featured a 624 MHz processor, 64 MB SDRAM, and a 64K color VGA touchscreen. The test database contained 335 movies. We recruited 6 participants (2 male and 4 female) to solve retrieval tasks using the PDA under stationary conditions. The user group consisted of a journalist, a project manager in business development, and 4 students of non-IT-related university courses. Ages ranged from 21 to 33 years. Only one user had previous experience of using a PDA, but all of them had basic computer skills such as using a word processor, browsing and searching the Internet, and writing emails.

After being given a short introduction on how to use a PDA, the participants were first asked to try out the scatterplot interface on their own while thinking aloud. Support was provided as required. Subsequently, the participants had to solve a set of retrieval tasks that involved an increasing effort in scatterplot adjustment and zoom operations (see Appendix A). Finally, they were asked to give their overall impression of the software and to add any additional comments or observations they felt were pertinent to the improvement of the software.

4.1.5 Results

The user test showed that once participants understood the basic principles of the visualization, they were able to solve all retrieval tasks quickly with only a minimum of support. Moreover, the concept of using semantic zoom to display data content inside the scatterplot proved to be intuitive and easy to grasp. Users appreciated the concise design of the interface and that it was not overloaded with information.

A negative result of the evaluation was that the separation of steering and zoom interaction, which had been intended to simplify the navigation, proved a failure. Users found the sequential procedure tedious and slow and would clearly prefer a one-step and purely pen-based zoom interaction. Zooming in on an item, users also experienced difficulties in accurately achieving the right magnification scale for reading text. With regard to this, it may be useful to introduce a more bounded or guided way of zooming. For example, in his book, Raskin suggests using predefined zoom ratios at which zooming slows down or briefly stops, making it easier to get characters to standard sizes [185]. Another zoom problem was that the participants found it increasingly difficult to orient with a growing magnification of the scatterplot. Accordingly, we observed rather undirected and unsuccessful panning operations frequently followed by zooming out to the default scale. Two participants also zoomed into the empty space between items. This kind of problem is quite common for ZUIs and was discussed in Chapter 2.2.3.

While not having a problem with the spatial mapping of both quantitative and nominal data, users got confused with the gray scale encoding for multiple-data-points. This effect is likely to be due to the small size of the scatterplot items, which made it hard to distinguish between different shades of the filling color. User feedback concerning the experimental bookmarking mechanism turned out to be rather ambiguous. Being asked to bookmark a DVD, users did not recognize the edge of the record card as a tappable area but instead kept looking for a check box. Once explained, the edge-folding-metaphor was found appealing and clear. Users also appreciated the concept of a visual query history. Though powerful, this feature is more demanding than a simple back-button approach and thus needs explanation. Considering the screen design, a better visual differentiation between query history and retrieval scatterplot was suggested to avoid confusion of modes. Also, some participants failed to recognize the color coding of combo boxes to scatterplot axes. Hence the mapping should be emphasized by additional visual cues.

4.2 Design Iteration II: Overview+Detail

Providing scalability despite the small screen is the key requirement for mobile applications to cope with real-world retrieval scenarios. In the first prototype we had attempted to meet this requirement by merging a starfield display with a multiscale zooming approach. While the positive feedback that was gained through an initial user evaluation encouraged us to further pursue the design concept, we had also observed that, even for the small data set used, some users got lost in the information space. This problem is known from previous research and is due to the continuous clipping of context during zooming. Hence our second project (see [42]) focused on how user orientation in mobile starfield ZUIs could be improved. For this purpose we conducted another usability evaluation in which we compared the initial scatterplot ZUI with a context-preserving overview+detail (o+d) approach. As discussed in Chapter 2.3, o+d interfaces provide a constant visual feedback of the user's position inside the information space and thus they put less pressure on the user's memory. A drawback of the o+d approach, which is particularly significant for small screens, is the increased demand for display space.

4.2.1 Spatial Ability

An additional research objective of the second evaluation was to analyze the user performance with regard to individual differences in spatial ability. Spatial ability, which can be defined as the ability to generate, retain, retrieve, and transform well-structured visual images [154], is often cited as being one of the best predictors of human-computer performance [78] [79] [72]. One study, for example, examined individual differences among users of a hierarchical file system and found that high-spatial users completed tasks more quickly than low-spatial users, who tended to become lost in the file structure [223]. A later study showed that the differences between individuals could be eliminated when a hierarchical one-layer-view navigation was replaced by a visual mediator such as, in this case, an overview of the complete navigation hierarchy with no hidden layers [215]. The authors argued that the more visual interface compensated for the inability of low-spatial users to construct a mental model of the information space. The same cognitive mechanism may apply to ZUIs. While users zoom in, information objects move out of sight and thus fewer orientation cues are displayed. Without an overview, users are forced to either rely on their mental model of the information space or to perform repetitive and time consuming zoom-out operations to reorient themselves. Obviously, when it comes to task-completion time, such a system benefits high-spatial users. This hypothesis would also correspond with the results of another study that analyzed usability issues of 2.5D visual user interfaces [71]. It found that high spatial-ability users were significantly faster in initially navigating and finding search items in virtual reality systems that require a 'fly-through' with the mouse. The lower their spatial ability, the more users were likely to become lost and the fewer search tasks were completed [59].

While visual interfaces can improve the performance of low-spatial individuals, they may, on the other hand, hinder high-spatial users. A study that focused on spatial scanning and perceptual speed investigated the influence of spatial abilities on the interaction with digital library interfaces [7]. As it turned out, individuals with high spatial abilities performed worst when using a word map, i.e. a two-dimensional map of the 100 most frequent word roots reflecting the intrinsic structure of the bibliographic collection. Similar results were found for semantic search spaces: high-spatial users performed better in a plain, textual interface for a document collection than in a spatial user interface [58] [55]. While this effect has not been fully clarified, it may however give a hint as to why overview windows can, in some cases, degrade user performance.

Overall, the available literature indicates that it is difficult to predict the effect specific design features would have on users with different cognitive abilities [222] [59]. Hence, the need for further research into these issues is strongly indicated.

4.2.2 Interfaces

With regard to our research objectives, we implemented two experimental mobile starfield applications. Both are based on the semantic-zooming approach presented by the first prototype, but provide different levels of overview information. The detail-only interface relies on smooth continuous zooming in a single view, while the o+d interface features two coordinated views that present both overview and detail information.

4.2.2.1 Detail-only Starfield

The detail-only interface shows the already familiar scatterplot diagram in which each movie in the database is represented by a small rectangle and positioned according to the scatterplot axes of popularity rating (X) and year of release (Y) (Figure 4.6a). Based on the feedback and observations gained from the previous evaluation, we defined the following re-design objectives:

- *Simplify item selection*
  In the first prototype, to highlight and thus target an item as a zoom destination, users had to precisely tap the corresponding rectangle. Bearing in mind the small-size representations in the default scale and the rather imprecise nature of stylus input, this can be difficult to achieve. The users must be provided with a more intelligent mechanism that allows them to reliably select items even when they are on the move or in another condition in which they do not give the device their full attention (e.g. talking to somebody, etc.).

- *Reduce the likelihood of counterproductive operations*
  Multiscale interfaces provide users with complete freedom to roam to any point in the 2.5D space. As discussed, this freedom can lead to serious navigation and orientation problems such as desert fog. Even in the comparably simple setting of a zoomable starfield display, critical situations can arise when users, as observed in the first evaluation, zoom by accident into the empty space between items. For both problems, we propose to limit the user interaction to always focus on an information object.

- *Improve the effectiveness and ease-of-use of the zoom interaction*
  The first evaluation revealed that the users would prefer a zoom mechanism that controls both scale and translation in a single operation. Such a design may also allow a more rapid and fluent exploration of scatterplot items. Moreover, the operation should be controllable through the stylus.

With regard to the first objective, the re-designed detail-only starfield introduces a *selection-by-proximity* approach: to focus a movie in the scatterplot, the users do not have to hit an item directly; it is sufficient to tap in its vicinity. The system responds by highlighting the item that is closest to the pen position, i.e. the border of the rectangle is drawn red and enhanced with additional grid lines and data labels (Figure 4.6b). If the rectangle is overlapped by another item, it is moved to the foreground. Unlike the first prototype, no cursor exists. Instead, the currently highlighted item denotes the focus point.

The principle of selection-by-proximity also provides the key for achieving the second interface objective. Since the focus is always bound to a scatterplot item, it follows that each zoom operation targets an item. Hence no zooming into empty space is supported. The same strategy could also be used with respect to desert fog scenarios in unlimited multiscale interfaces (see Chapter 2.2.3): when there are no more objects in a given direction, zooming in would be simply disabled. If there are objects, these may be highlighted on demand; for instance, by multiscale residues as proposed by [134], and then the users can choose which one to target. Applying semi-automatic selection in this situation is especially useful when large distances in the Z dimension must be covered. As pointed out by [37], when zooming in on an object, the distance of the target from the expansion focus increases exponentially. This error in precision must usually be counterbalanced manually with panning. However, doing this in a continuous fashion while at the same time scaling the interface is already difficult and tedious when using a mouse. Given a stylus, it is even harder due to the partial occlusion of the display by the user's hand. If the system optimizes the location of the focus point by automatically shifting it to the center of the closest information object, frequent zoom interruptions to re-adjust the direction are avoided.

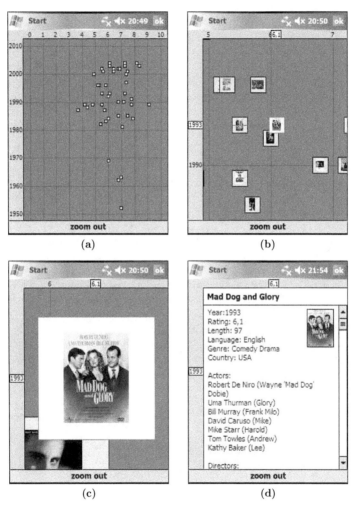

Figure 4.6: Detail-only starfield with 46 items on a PDA running Windows Mobile 5.0: (a) default scale, (b, c) fluent zoom, (d) content view.

To zoom in on the scatterplot items in the detail-only application, the users tap and hold the stylus on the display. A fluent zoom animation is triggered after an initial delay of

150 milliseconds. While zooming in, the highlighted item moves smoothly to the center of the screen and the magnified rectangles become display areas for the posters of the movies they represent (Figures 4.6b, c). Users can interrupt the zoom operation at any time by lifting the pen. If not interrupted, the animation continues until the highlighted rectangle fills the entire window space. At that point, the poster zooms back out (anti-zoom) and makes room for textual movie information to appear. The rectangle has changed its representation into a record card (Figure 4.6d).

To return to the diagram view and to zoom out, users press the button at the bottom of the screen. The record card grows smaller and changes its representation accordingly. Again, users can stop the operation by lifting the pen, otherwise the animation continues until the default scale of the diagram has been reached. Zooming in from the default scale to the maximum zoom level takes 1.8 seconds and magnifies the information space 40 times. Users can also pan the diagram by dragging it with the stylus. Panning is limited to the boundaries of the scatterplot diagram.

4.2.2.2   Overview+Detail Starfield

The o+d interface enhances the detail-only interface with a smaller overview window at the bottom of the screen (Figure 4.7a). We chose this approach of two non-overlapping windows because it is the most conventional and straightforward o+d solution. Due to their complexity, more sophisticated approaches such as transparent or on-demand views are likely to increase the variance of user performance and, with regard to our research objectives, they may have an unwanted effect on the dependent variables.

A difficult design question when dealing with a conventional o+d interface on small screens relates to the size ratio of the two windows. For both views, the usability increases with a larger size, since the presentation becomes less cluttered, and pen-interaction on the view is easier to perform. However, a larger detail view means a smaller overview, and vice versa. For the experimental prototype, we chose the size of the overview such that the same scatterplot units as in the detail view can be used, with the axes labels remaining legible. This results in a layout in which the detail view is 40 percent smaller than in the detail-only interface.

The coordination between the windows is bidirectional, i.e. performing an operation on one view immediately updates the other one. The overview features a field-of-view box (yellow rectangle) denoting the clipping currently presented in the detail view. Items that are highlighted on the detail view appear red on the overview (e.g. Figure 4.7b). Users can either pan on the overview by dragging the field-of-view box, or jump to another position by tapping the overview window outside the box. The field-of-view box then automatically moves to the pen position. If users have previously retrieved a movie's textual representation on the detail view (Figure 4.7c), panning or jumping on the overview changes the zoom level from 40 to 32 such that the detail window switches back to the diagram view. Zooming on the overview is achieved by first tapping on the *scale* button and then drawing a new field-of-view box on the overview. The box has a fixed aspect ratio that is determined by the ratio of the views. When zooming on the overview, it

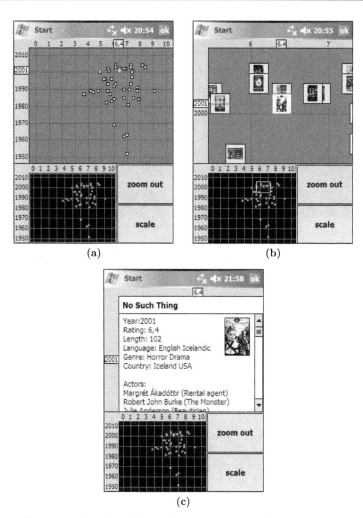

Figure 4.7: Overview+detail starfield with 46 items on a PDA running Windows Mobile 5.0: (a) default scale, (b) semantic zoom, (d) content view.

is not possible to achieve a scale level of over 32. Hence, to retrieve an item's textual representation, users have to zoom on the detail view. The detail view in the o+d starfield offers the same functionality as described for the detail-only interface. Figure 4.8 shows the anti-zoom animation that is automatically triggered when the user has zoomed into a rectangle. The poster zooms back out and the textual content is displayed on a scroll panel.

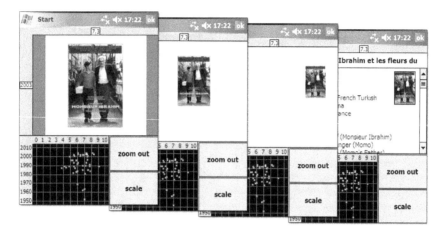

Figure 4.8: Animated transition from the poster to the full detail view.

4.2.3   Implementation

The experimental applications consist of about 4,000 lines of code and were developed from scratch using C# and the .NET compact framework (CF) 1.0. CF 1.0 is the smart device development extension that was shipped with Microsoft .NET framework 1.1. Similar to Java and the JVM, for instance, programs written for the .NET framework are first compiled to an intermediate byte-code and then executed by a virtual machine (Common Language Runtime). Native code can be accessed and executed from within the CF via *Platform Invoke*. As with other mobile libraries that are tuned for performance and size, a drawback of the CF is that it only implements a small subset of the corresponding desktop framework. During development we were therefore frequently forced to code around limitations. Nevertheless, we found the CF an efficient and fast technology for prototyping our experimental applications. Moreover, CF 2.0 is available by now, and this contains several helpful API enhancements. We ported our solutions to both the CF 2.0 to support Windows Mobile 5.0 and the full .NET framework 2.0 to run on regular desktop computers. For retrieving movie data from our postgreSQL database, a third-party data provider tool called PostgreSQLDirect .NET was used (the CF only supports SQL Server). Alternatively, the application can also read the data from a local XML file.

The starfield components are deployed as a library dll that can be loaded by other applications. The form that references the dll has access to all interface components (scatterplot, overview, buttons) and can position and resize them as desired. The buttons provided are a good example for the type of workarounds mobile developers frequently have to devise. Not only does the CF 1.0 fail to provide a toggle button, but the available *Button* class only implements a single *Click* event. This is not sufficient considering that we want a zoom out operation to continue as long as the corresponding button is tapped and held. Thus we implemented a custom *ExtButton*, which extends the *Control* class and implements the missing *MouseDown*, *MouseUp* and *MouseMove* events. The .NET *Control* class is fundamental to all components of the experimental prototypes. It provides the basic implementation for receiving input events and allows us to create an on-screen *Graphics* object, which can be used to draw to the screen.

The zoomable scatterplot control, which is used in both the detail-only and the o+d application, implements a lightweight 2.5D interface based on the limited 2D drawing API provided by the CF 1.0. As was illustrated by the space-scale diagram in Figure 2.3, a multiscale information space can be modeled as a 2D pane at different magnification levels. The viewport denotes the viewing rectangle, which is of a fixed size and can be moved to different locations. Scaling the interface means increasing (zooming in) or decreasing (zooming out) the scale of the information space by manipulating it with a scale factor. Panning is implemented as translating the position of the viewport rectangle. At the default scale level, the size of the viewport is equal to the size of the information space.

For each data record retrieved from the database an instance of type *Item* is created. The object contains an array of attribute values such as movie title, length, language, etc. Based on the axes units and the corresponding attribute values, the relative coordinates of each item in the information space are calculated and stored as two floating point values. A similar calculation is also performed for each grid line of the scatterplot. In order to increase the drawing performance and to avoid a flickering of the PDA screen, all drawing is implemented using double buffering. Double buffering means that the GUI is rendered completely as an off-screen bitmap in memory. Once all the drawing has been completed, the off-screen bitmap is copied in one quick operation to an on-screen *Graphics* object. The algorithm for updating the screen is described in Algorithm 1.

Algorithm 1 Update screen

  1: clear the off-screen bitmap with the scatterplot background color
  2: draw grid lines and labels to the off-screen bitmap
  3: draw items to the off-screen bitmap → *Algorithm 2*
  4: draw lines and labels for the *focus Item* to the off-screen bitmap
  5: copy the off-screen bitmap to the screen

Algorithm 2 shows the procedure for drawing items to the screen. To further increase the drawing speed when displaying scatterplot items, a clipping mechanism is used: only those items are drawn to the bitmap that are visible given the current scale of the information space and the position of the viewport. The default representation of an item is a white rectangle with a black outline (see Figure 4.6a). However, as previously described, at a certain scale level this representation changes to a rectangle displaying a movie poster. This is implemented by line 7 and 8, in which the code checks the current scale of the information space.

Interaction with the mobile starfield application is based on tapping and dragging the pen on the PDA screen. To receive those events, the *Scatterplot* class is derived from *Control* and adds event handlers to the mouse events (pen down, pen up, pen move). These event handlers contain the logic of how to interpret stylus input. The users can, for instance,

---

Algorithm 2 Draw items

1: **for** each item **do**
2:     calculate the position and size of the item rectangle in the information space
3:     **if** the *Item* rectangle overlaps with the viewport rectangle **then**
4:         translate the local coordinates of the item rectangle to global device coordinates
5:         draw the rectangle to the off-screen object
6:     **end if**
7:     **if** the current scale is greater than the minimum scale for semantic zoom **then**
8:         draw the item poster within the rectangle to the off-screen object
9:     **end if**
10: **end for**

---

start a zoom by tapping and holding the pen on the display for more than 150 ms without moving the pen for more than a distance threshold of 7 pixels. If the pen moves above that threshold within the time frame, the scatterplot pane becomes dragable (see Algorithms 3, 4 and 5).

Algorithm 3 Pen down event handler

1: set the focus item to be the item closest to the pen location
2: make the focus item the last item in the drawing queue
3: update screen → *Algorithm 1*
4: store the current pen location
5: set a timer that initiates a zoom animation after 150 ms

Algorithm 4 Pen move event handler

1: **if** the timer has been set **then**
2:     **if** the pen has been dragged more than 7 pixels away from the stored location **then**
3:         stop timer
4:         enable panning
5:     **end if**
6: **end if**
7: **if** panning is enabled **then**
8:     pan the view → *Algorithm 7*
9:     update screen → *Algorithm 1*
10: **end if**

We found these thresholds to work fairly intuitively for most users. However, some people tended to first set the pen on the screen and then think about their next move, a behavior that frequently triggered unwanted zoom-in operations. Zooming is controlled by a loop that works quite similarly to a game loop. During each iteration the navigation parameters in the multiscale model are updated and then the changes are drawn to the screen. For the number of items used in the evaluation, we achieved sufficiently smooth animations with 15 frames per second. Another step in the loop is to tell the system to process all events in the event queue. Otherwise the users would not be able to interrupt the animation by

---

Algorithm 5 Pen up event handler
1: **if** the timer has been set **then**
2:    stop timer
3: **end if**
4: **if** panning is enabled **then**
5:    disable panning
6: **end if**
7: **if** zoom animation is running **then**
8:    stop zoom animation
9: **end if**

---

lifting the pen. Algorithm 6 describes a zoom-in operation, which is triggered by a timer callback as indicated by line 5 in Algorithm 3. To make the focus item gradually move to the center of the viewport during zooming, the translation (line 9) is manipulated by an easing factor.

Algorithm 6 Zoom in
1: set the focus point for the zoom operation to be the center of the focus item
2: start the zoom animation
3: **while** zoom animation is running **do**
4:    **if** the maximum scale factor has not been reached **then**
5:       scale the information space by a fixed zoom-in factor
6:       **if** the current scale exceeds the maximum scale **then**
7:          set the scale of the information space to be the maximum scale
8:       **end if**
9:       translate the viewport rectangle to move in the direction of the focus point (easing)

10:       **if** the viewport rectangle is out of the boundaries of the information space **then**
11:          set the position of the viewport rectangle to the closest position within the information space
12:       **end if**
13:       screen update
14:    **else**
15:       stop the zoom animation
16:       start the detail view animation
17:    **end if**
18:    process pen events
19: **end while**

As described in line 16 of Algorithm 6, the detail view animation is initiated when the maximum scale factor has been reached, i.e. when the poster rectangle fills the entire screen. It is based on two additional custom controls: *TransitionView* and *DetailView*. First, *TransitionView* is displayed on top of the scatterplot. The control triggers an animation in which the poster of the focus item is scaled and translated in four drawing

iterations to the target position and size at the upper right corner (see Figure 4.8). After
the last step of the animation, *TransitionView* is replaced by the *DetailView* control.

DetailView reads in the movie data from the focus item and prints it to the screen (see
Figure 4.6d). Since the CF 1.0 does not provide ready-made controls that would allow
the display of formatted text along with images, *DetailView* implements this functionality
from scratch. As is the case with all animations in the application, the vertical scroll
pane is also based on double buffering to avoid a flickering of the screen while scrolling.
The users can return to the scatterplot visualization by tapping and holding the *zoom out*
button. Before the corresponding animation is started, *DetailView* is hidden to reveal the
scatterplot control.

Unlike zooming, which is controlled by an animation loop, panning is based on the pen
move event (see Algorithm 4). Each time the routine is called, the pen displacement is
used to shift the viewport rectangle in the direction opposite to the drag movement. The
view can only be panned within the bounds of the information space (see Algorithm 7).

Algorithm 7 Pan

  1: translate the viewport by the distance between the current and the previous pen
     position
  2: **if** the viewport rectangle is out of the boundaries of the information space **then**
  3:    set the position of the viewport rectangle to the closest position within the infor-
        mation space
  4: **end if**
  5: screen update

As discussed, the o+d interface adds a small overview window to the interface. The
overview control and the scatterplot are tightly coupled, i.e. both controls define custom
events for updating the multiscale model that the other control is registering with. When
such an event is fired, both controls are redrawn. In contrast to the scatterplot, the
background of the overview (items in the information space) does not change and thus the
off-screen bitmap only needs to be drawn once when the application is loaded. Redrawing
the on-screen overview means first copying the off-screen bitmap to the screen to erase the
previous image, and then drawing the highlighted focus item and the field-of-view box on
top of it. In a later version, the first step of the algorithm was improved by not copying the
entire bitmap to the screen, but only the portion of the overview that had changed (e.g.
the field-of-view box at its previous position). This resulted in a smoother performance
in particular for scaling the field-of-view box.

4.2.4 User Evaluation

We conducted a usability study to compare the two interfaces in terms of user performance,
preference and satisfaction. The participants had to perform several retrieval tasks using
both interfaces. To analyze the effect that individual differences in spatial ability would
have on the dependent variables, participants had to complete a psychometric test.

4.2.4.1 Participants

For the study we selected 24 participants, 12 males and 12 females. All of them were students at the University of Konstanz. Their fields of study varied greatly, however none of the participants studied computer science. The mean age was 24 years, ranging from 19 to 30 years. As revealed by the pre-test questionnaire, none of the participants owned a PDA, although eight had already used one and therefore knew about the general interaction concept. All of them were familiar with a PC and used it daily. We also asked our participants if they knew Google Earth. Twenty-one had at least heard of it and fourteen used it from time to time, but not regularly.

4.2.4.2 Hypotheses

Our hypotheses were as follows:

1. *Users would prefer the overview over the detail-only interface because of the additional orientation and navigation features provided.* This hypothesis was based on the previous research reviewed in Chapter 2.3. Across several studies ([13] [120] [122]), the participants were found to prefer an o+d approach to alternative interfaces, even if it decreased the user performance. We expected that the overview would give the users a feeling of control and thus compensate for the smaller size of the detail view, which, due to the space effectiveness of the ZUI, was still manageable for the users.

2. *Task-completion time would be better for the detail-only interface because of the rich orientation cues given by the scatterplot labels.* Previous research suggests that overview facilities can become a hindrance when the information space searched by users already provides extensive orientation cues [120]. Moreover, visual switching between the two windows may slow users down [11].

3. *Users with low spatial ability would have a longer task-completion time across interfaces than participants with higher spatial ability.* This hypothesis was based on the research findings discussed in section 4.2.1.

4. *The overview interface would reduce the performance difference between high and low-spatial participants.* We expected that users who were not able to build up a mental model of the information space would have to reorient themselves more frequently. Having an overview may eliminate the need for a mental model and hence support low-spatial users in catching up on task-completion times.

4.2.4.3 Evaluation Design

We used a counterbalanced within-subjects design, balancing the two interface types and task sets. This resulted in four different groups mirroring all possible variations of interface and task set order. We randomly assigned six participants to each group. For analysis, we mainly used repeated measures ANOVAs (RM-ANOVAs) and regression analysis. Our independent variables were *interface type* (overview and detail-only) and *spatial ability* (used as both LPS C-score and dichotomized group variable). The dependent variables were *task-completion time* (in seconds), *system-preference* (overview and detail-only), *user-satisfaction* (*Attrakdiff* PQ Scores), *error-rate* (number of incorrect answered tasks), and *navigation-actions* (panning and zooming attempts and distances).

4.2.4.4   Tasks

During the experiment, users had to solve a set of 12 tasks (see Appendix B) for each of the two interfaces. A task set comprised four questions for each of the three following task types:

- *Visual Scan*
  For example: how many movies in the collection were produced after the year 2000 and have a popularity rating greater than or equal to 6?

- *Information Access*
  Who is the director of the movie with a popularity rating of 4.4?

- *Comparison of information objects*
  Which of the two movies from 1990 with the popularity ratings 6.3 and 6 is longer?

The task questions were written in German, the participants' native language.

4.2.4.5   Materials

The study was run on a Hewlett-Packard iPAQ hx4700 Pocket PC with Windows Mobile 2003. The device featured a 624 MHz processor, 64 MB SDRAM and a 64K color VGA touchscreen. A digital video camera recorded the screen of the iPAQ; interactions such as zooming and panning were automatically logged on the device. To measure user satisfaction we used the *Attrakdiff* questionnaire [109]. It uses a 7-point semantic differential and has 28 items in total and 7 for each dimension. Since the dimensions appeal and hedonic quality (identity and stimulation) were of less interest, we only used the dimension pragmatic quality (PQ), which tries to measure the user satisfaction regarding functionality. As a psychometric test we used 5 subtests of the *Leistungsprüfsystem* (LPS) developed by Horn [119]. LPS is an intelligence test that measures the seven primary mental abilities as defined by Thurstone [217]. We used subtests 7-10 to measure the spatial ability and subtest 14 to measure perceptual speed. The latter was only used to test for unwanted correlations between spatial-ability scores and the perceptual speed. System preference and overview usage were obtained with post-test questionnaires; demographic information as well as PDA knowledge, computer experience, etc. with a pre-test questionnaire.

4.2.4.6   Procedure

Trials started with the participants answering the pre-test questionnaire. Next, they had to complete the spatial-ability test, which took about 20 minutes (14 minutes test time) for all 5 modules. After that a short break was offered. When the participants indicated that they were ready to proceed, the test administrator gave a short introduction on how to use a PDA and handed the device over to the participants. Once the first of the two applications had been loaded, a tutorial movie about the interface was shown. At certain points, the test administrator paused the movie and asked participants to reproduce operations on the PDA. Support was given as needed. When participants showed that they had understood the interface, each of the twelve task questions was presented to them successively as a printout. Participants read the question aloud and then pressed a button on the PDA screen to display the scatterplot interface, which they then navigated as necessary. When they felt they could answer the question, users tapped the cross button at the top-right corner of the interface. The scatterplot was then hidden and users answered aloud. During tasks sessions the test administrator was not allowed to provide any support. Having completed the first task set, participants answered the *Attrakdiff* questionnaire. Subsequently, the same procedure was repeated for the second interface and the second task set. The experiment ended with participants answering a preference questionnaire and receiving a movie theater voucher worth EUR 10. Experiment sessions lasted on average about one hour.

4.2.5   Results

The following section describes the results of our study. We will first focus on the four hypotheses and then present some additional analysis.

4.2.5.1   H1: Interface Preference

In our first hypothesis we assumed that users would prefer the overview interface over the detail-only interface. However, analysis revealed that only 10 participants preferred the overview interface compared to 13 favoring the detail-only interface. One participant was unsure. While the difference is not significant, $X^2(1, N = 23) = 0.391, p < 0.532$, it nevertheless contradicts our hypothesis. Analyzing the users statements, we were able to identify two main reasons for this result:

- Most of the participants who were in favor of the detail-only interface stated that they preferred the larger size of the detail window. They found the system easier to use and preferred not having to decide which way to solve a task (8 participants).

- Furthermore, some users stated that they had problems with zooming and panning on the overview. Due to the small size of the window, they found these functions rather imprecise and difficult to use (5 participants). Our observations underlined these statements, especially regarding the scale functionality. Despite the fact that the users had been previously advised about the fixed aspect ratio of the bounding box, most participants still tried to draw boxes with a custom ratio and, since this did not work, became confused. Some users also became irritated by being unsure of when or how to use these additional navigation features.

Interestingly, five of the users who preferred the detail-only interface stated that they liked the overview window as an orientation help but either did not find the interaction possibilities useful or encountered problems using them. They therefore voted for the detail-only interface. This could indicate that a longer training phase might increase the acceptance of an overview window, because users would then become more certain which overview function is useful at a given time, and how to use it.

4.2.5.2   H2: Task-Completion Time

In our second hypothesis we assumed that participants would be able to solve tasks significantly faster using the detail-only interface. It took our participants on average 379.34 seconds to complete all 12 tasks with the detail-only interface but 452.65 seconds with the overview interface (Figure 4.9). This difference is highly significant, $F(1, 23) = 16.5, p < 0.001$, and therefore supports our hypothesis. A detailed analysis of the three different task types reveals that, for all of them, participants were significantly faster using the detail-only interface (task type 1: $F(1, 23) = 7.587, p < 0.05$; task type 2: $F(1, 23) = 7.569, p < 0.05$; task type 3 $F(1, 23) = 5.797, p < 0.05$).

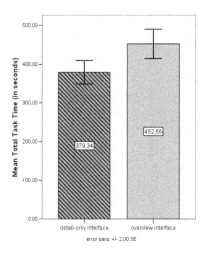

Figure 4.9: Comparing mean total task time between interface types

We also analyzed which of the interaction possibilities had the greatest influence on task-completion times. A stepwise regression analysis revealed that, for the detail-only interface, zooming attempts and panning attempts were the best predictors for task-completion time. Together they explained about 56 percent of the variance (ANOVA results: $F(2, 21) = 13.488, p < 0.001$). Panning distance was also nearly as good a predictor as panning attempts (also 56 percent explained variance). Regarding the overview interface, here again zooming attempts within the detail window and, in this case, panning distance in the detail window were the best predictors, explaining about 64 percent of the variance (ANOVA results: $F(2, 21) = 18.525, p < 0.001$). So regarding both interfaces, we can summarize by stating that distance panned and zooming attempts (both within the detail window) are mostly responsible for the differences in task-completion times between users. Moreover, we compared the zoom and pan actions within the detail window between both interface types. Analysis revealed that users panned and zoomed more often (Figure 4.10a, b) and over greater distances (Figure 4.10c, d) using the detail-only interface. For panning and zooming distance, this difference is significant (panning distance: $Mean = 4149$ pixels and $SD = 3392$ pixels compared to $Mean = 2670.5$ pixels and $SD = 3212$ pixels; $F(1, 23) = 4.837, p < 0.05$; zooming distance: $Mean = 2462$ level changes and $SD = 316$ level changes compared to $Mean = 1844$ level changes and $SD = 514$ level changes; $F(1, 23) = 26.684, p < 0.001$). This indicates that the overview window may have reduced the need for long-distance panning and zooming and, as shown by regression analysis, the panning distance is strongly correlated with task-completion time. However, since task-completion time for the overview interface was significantly higher, it seems as if the time needed for users to switch between views and to make up their minds about exactly how to use the overview outweighed this advantage, as predicted in our hypothesis.

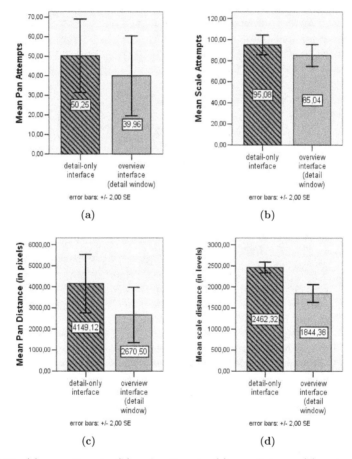

Figure 4.10: (a) pan attempts, (b) scale attempts, (c) pan distance, (d) scale distance - all within the detail window

4.2.5.3   H3: Low-Spatial Participants vs. High-Spatial Participants

Our third hypothesis suggested that low-spatial participants would need significantly more time to complete tasks than high-spatial participants, regardless of which interface type was used. To test this hypothesis, we first used the C-values of our spatial-ability test and tried a regression analysis with total task-completion time as the dependent variable. The analysis revealed that the spatial ability only explained 1.6 percent of the variance (ANOVA result: $F(1, 22) = 0.358$, p=n.s.). For further analysis, we dichotomized our spatial-ability variable into low-spatial users and high-spatial users. In the process, we excluded four participants around the median, leaving ten per group. We then compared these groups with a One-Way ANOVA using spatial group as the independent variable and total task time (sum for both interfaces) as the dependent variable. Our high-spatial users needed on average 809.6 seconds to complete all 24 tasks while it took our low-spatial users 822.6 seconds. The difference is not significant and therefore confirms the regression analysis. Given previous research, this result was rather unexpected. We analyzed our results from the spatial-ability test and discovered that, with regard to spatial ability, our users formed a rather homogeneous group (mean $C\text{-}Value = 7.46, SD = 0.977$). Moreover, the mean C-score of 7.46 was significantly above the population mean of 5 ($T(1, 23) = 12.326, p < 0.01$) and the mean C-Score of our low-spatial group was also significantly above the population mean (6.5 compared to 5, $T(1, 9) = 6.78, p < 0.01$). Thus our participants can all be considered as *high spatial* users, which might explain why we did not find a significant difference between our high and low-spatial participants.

4.2.5.4   H4: Overview Accommodates Spatial Differences

Our fourth and final hypothesis follows on from the third hypothesis. We predicted that the overview interface would reduce potential differences between low and high-spatial users. One-Way ANOVAs revealed that there was no significant difference between low and high-spatial users for both the detail-only interface and the overview interface (detail-only: 397 seconds for low-spatial users compared to 355 seconds, $F(1, 18) = 1.481, p = n.s.$; overview: 425 seconds for low-spatial users compared to 454 seconds, $F(1, 18) = 0.626, p = n.s.$). Nevertheless, it is interesting that high-spatial users were faster than low-spatial users while working with the detail-only interface but slower while working with the overview interface. To analyze this in more detail, we conducted a RM-ANOVA with interface type as the within-participants factor and spatial group as the between-participants factor. As expected, it again revealed no significant difference between the low and high-spatial users (Figure 4.11). Between interface type and spatial group, however, we found an interesting interaction effect that corresponds to the above finding, although just beneath the 0.05 significance level ($F(1, 18) = 3.759, p = 0.068$ n.s.). While task-completion times for low-spatial users were about equal for both interfaces (on average 397 seconds using the detail-only interface compared to 425 seconds, $F(1, 9) = 1.217, p = n.s.$), high-spatial users needed more time for the overview interface (on average 356 seconds using the detail only interface compared to 454 seconds). Furthermore, this difference within the high-spatial group is statistically significant ($F(1, 9) = 14.332, p < 0.05$). It therefore seems that the overview interface hindered high-spatial users while low-spatial users were relatively unaffected. However, there is no correlation between system preference and spatial group - four of the high-spatial users preferred the overview interface, and six the detail-only interface, meaning that the system preference of our high-spatial participants was not negatively affected by the significantly higher task-completion times for the overview interface.

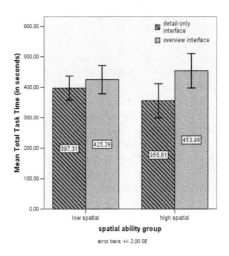

Figure 4.11: Comparing mean total task times between interface types separated by high and low spatial users

4.2.6 Additional Analysis

The analysis of the *Attrakdiff* scores revealed no significant difference between the two interfaces. Since they were very similar from a user perspective, this was a rather predictable result $(F(1, 22) = 2.157, p = n.s.)$. Regarding our pre-test data, there was no significant difference between users who had previously used a PDA and those who had not. In fact, participants who were already familiar with PDAs were slightly slower (868 seconds for users who previously had used a PDA compared to 813 seconds, $F(1, 22) = 0.792, p = n.s.$). Similar results were found for users who had previously used Google Earth. There was also no significant correlation between gender and spatial ability. The participant with the highest spatial ability was female.

After excluding a participant who never once used the pan function, the spatial ability C-Score correlated significantly with the panning distance for the detail-only interface $(r = 0.427, p < 0.05)$ and with distance panned per attempt $(r = 0.487, p < 0.05)$. This could indicate that low-spatial users pan in a more careful way and only small distances at a time. Regarding the error rate, we could not find a significant difference between the two interfaces. In both cases there was less than one incorrectly answered task on average. Because of the tasks selected, this result was expected - more complicated tasks would have been rather in the nature of memory tests for the users and would probably have covered other effects.

4.2.7   Interpretation

The performance advantage we measured for the detail-only ZUI indicates that, on small screens, a larger detail window can outweigh the benefits gained from an overview. For high-spatial users, we assume that the performance difference is also partly due to the rich navigation cues provided by scatterplot labels. Since the overview may not offer much of an orientation benefit for those users, it thus became more of a hindrance. Low-spatial participants, on the other hand, were less affected by the overview. Their task-completion times for the overview interface turned out to be nearly equal to those for the detail-only application. In this case, the overview may have actually supported the participants by preventing them from relying on their potentially incorrect mental model of the information space. However, the performance differences measured between the two user groups were not significant. We conjecture that this is mainly due to the rather small group size and cognitive homogeneity of our participants. For further research, we would recommend a broader testing approach as carried out, for example, by [215]. In that study, 74 individuals took the spatial-ability test initially. For the computer experiment, the researchers then selected 24 of the participants who fell into the extremes of the range.

Unlike a similar study for desktop applications that had identified a strong user preference for o+d interfaces [120], our experiment did not show a significant difference in preference between the two ZUIs. User statements suggest that not only the smaller detail view but also the difficulties experienced by the participants with zooming and panning in the overview led to a lower rating for the overview-supported interface. As was also found by various other studies, our results show once again that interface efficiency does not necessarily correlate with user satisfaction or preference.

Based on our findings, we recommend that overviews on small devices would be best used for information spaces without strong orientation cues. Moreover, designers must carefully consider the real estate trade-off as well as the increased level of visual and interaction complexity that an o+d interface means.

4.3   Design Iteration III: Focus+Context

While the o+d interface could not improve task-completion times or user satisfaction for a mobile starfield display, the previous experiment nevertheless showed that overview information can reduce the need for unnecessary navigation. A way to exploit this benefit without forcing users to switch between multiple views is to integrate both focus and context in a single view. Hence in our third starfield project (see [43]) we implemented a fisheye interface and compared it in a user study to an enhanced version of the smooth zooming detail-only application.

4.3.1   Interfaces

Apart from investigating orientation issues for improving the navigation performance, another main objective of the focus+context project was to highlight the scalability of the zoomable starfield approach by visualizing thousands of data records. The two experimental applications discussed in the following sections provide access to a book database.

4.3.1.1 Detail-only Starfield

Due to the experiences gained with the previous prototypes, we defined the following objectives for the second re-design of the detail-only ZUI:

- *Resolve overlappings*
  In the previous projects the geometric zoom was used to magnify scatterplot items so they would be easier to select by the users. However, given a large information space (i.e. scatterplot dimensions with a high granularity) and a high density of scatterplot data, there may be items that are completely overlapped by surrounding items. In the first prototype we had tried to reduce this problem by implementing a *shuffle* algorithm: each time the users tap an item, the previous item selected is moved to the head of the drawing queue, i.e. it is moved to background. While this workaround allowed users to *shuffle* through small clusters of items, for larger clusters a more efficient and precise solution is needed.

- *Improve orientation cues*
  Scatterplot labels are the most important orientation cues in zoomable starfield displays. These cues must be always visible to the users and adjust to the granularity of the current scale level.

- *Improve panning performance*
  When zooming in on a large information space, the distances between items can become very large. Due to its frequent need for clutching, the conventional drag&drop mechanism is not suitable for covering such distances in an acceptable time. A more effective panning solution must be provided.

- *Fluent content presentation.*
  Though the previous prototypes already provided a fluent transition from overview to detail in the sense that textual content and images were presented inside the scatterplot, the detail presentation itself had remained discrete (e.g. text was displayed on-demand or when reaching a certain scale level). The second re-design should feature a continuous content presentation to better exploit the potential of semantic zooming.

With regard to these objectives, we developed the detail-only application shown in Figure 4.12. As with the previous prototype, the users can start the scatterplot exploration by tapping a region of interest and holding the pen down on the display. The system responds by highlighting the item that is closest to the pen position. It becomes the focus item. After an initial delay of 150 milliseconds a fluent zoom animation is triggered, which consists of two steps: first, only the scatterplot pane is magnified (Figure 4.12b, the circles have been added to the screenshot to denote the position of the focus item). Book representations that are far away from the focus item drift out of sight while the focus item itself moves smoothly into the center of the view. This reflects the assumption that books with similar attribute values are of more interest to the users than those whose year of publication and sale price differ widely from those of the focus item. While zooming in, the space gained through clipping is allocated to the remaining items and causes data clusters to scatter. As soon as the decomposition has reached a level at which all overlappings have been resolved, the second zoom step based on semantic zooming takes effect. Gray pixels grow to small rectangles (Figure 4.12c) and then to record cards, which are used to display information about the books they represent (Figure 4.12d-f). As postulated by the re-design objectives, the presentation of detail information is fluent. During semantic zooming, the amount of content displayed on the record cards continuously changes according to the available display space. Hence the more the users zoom in, the fewer items are shown, but more details are presented. Overall, the two-step zoom algorithm ensures that each item can be displayed without occlusion, and that the users can control the ratio of overview and content information by the degree of scaling they perform.

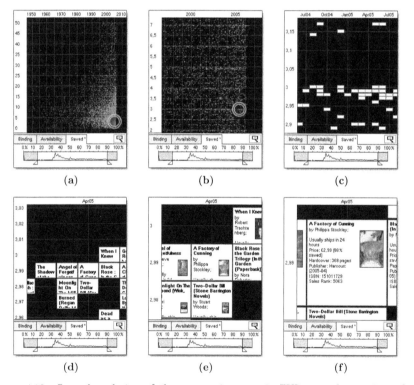

Figure 4.12: Second re-design of the geometric-semantic ZUI: smooth transition from overview to detail by tapping and holding the pen on the display.

Zooming in from the default scale to the maximum zoom level takes 1.8 seconds. Users can, at any time, interrupt the operation by lifting the pen. This would be necessary to examine the data distribution of a zoomed region, for instance, or to choose another focus item. If not interrupted, the animation continues until the record cards have reached a size of 50% of the view size. In this state, the focus item is always centered in the view window. Users can access book details while surrounding items remain partly visible (Figure 4.12f). To zoom out, users press the button showing the magnifying glass with the minus sign in it. It is located below the diagram. Scaling down, the diagram pane shrinks and the items change their appearance back to a single pixel representation before being aggregated to the initial distribution and density. Again, users can stop the operation by lifting the pen, otherwise the animation continues until the default scale of the diagram has been reached. Zooming out from the highest magnification level to the default scale takes 1.3 seconds.

To improve the orientation inside the diagram, the scatterplot labels are rapidly and continuously updated. In the default scale the X-axis is subdivided into decades and the Y-axis into units of EUR 5. While zooming in, labels and grid lines drift apart and new grid lines are drawn between them. For the X-axis the granularity levels are: 10 years, 5 years, year, and quarter (e.g. Jan01 means the first quarter in 2001) and for the Y-axis: 5 euro, 1 euro, 10 cent, 5 cent, and 1 cent.

Panning has been implemented as rate-based scrolling [240] via a pen gesture. Users tap the display and drag the pen in the direction they want to move the viewport. The speed of the animation that is triggered after the pen has moved at least 5 pixels away from its original position is defined by the overall distance it moves. Thus, during panning, users can control the direction and speed through the pen position in real time. If the pen is dragged back to its original position, the movement slows down. Using this kind of sliding, it is possible to travel long distances quickly. Users can bring the panning to a halt by lifting the pen. Another option for moving from one item in the view to another is *tap-to-center*, i.e. the users can tap an item to automatically move it to the center of the view. As in the previous application, the item tapped also becomes the focus item. Tap-to-center is particularly convenient for quickly navigating clusters of adjacent record cards.

4.3.1.2 Fisheye Starfield

As discussed in Chapter 2.4, the fisheye interface is a focus+context technique that integrates both overview and detail information into a single view. Our implementation shown in Figure 4.13 stems from the concept of a two-dimensional bifocal lens [213] and uses the navigation metaphor of stretching a rubber sheet [200] [201]. The rectangular nature of the distortion has the advantage that scatterplot items can always be mapped in straight lines to the diagram labels. Other types of fisheyes such as radial distortion may significantly deteriorate the readability of the interface.

To zoom into a part of the scatterplot, users first hit the box-icon button below the diagram. They can now draw a bounding-box denoting the region of interest (Figure 4.13a). As soon as the pen is lifted from the display, the application centers the focus region and magnifies it in a smooth animation (600 milliseconds) to about 50% of the diagram size

(Figure 4.13b). The surrounding regions contract. Objects that are not in focus are still visible but are allocated less space. In contrast, items in the focus region drift apart. A special characteristic of the distortion is that it only affects the underlying diagram pane. The one-pixel items in the information space behave as pins stuck in a rubber sheet. When the sheet is stretched by selecting a focus region, the pins in focus scatter, but their appearance remains undistorted. This way clusters of item representations can be easily resolved. However, depending on the given information density, users may have to apply the distortion recursively to completely isolate items (Figure 4.13c).

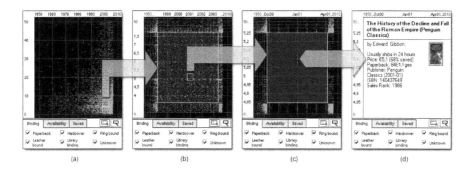

Figure 4.13: Fisheye interface: (a) and (b) recursive distortion to remove visual clutter, (c) the user taps an item to access its details (d) the record card representation.

Compared to the ZUI, the fisheye provides a better orientation by contracting and not clipping regions that are currently not of interest. That way, users can make informed decisions about where to navigate. By looking at the context, they may for instance prevent themselves from panning into regions where no items are located. Moreover, it is possible to move the focus directly into a context region without having first to zoom out. Users just need to draw a new bounding-box at the desired position. A drawback of the distortion technique is that the corner context regions are allocated less space than context areas orthogonal to the focus region and thus are likely to become more cluttered. Similar problems can also be observed in other rectangular fisheye applications such as the image browser presented in [187] (Chapter 2.4.3.1), or the PDA calendar DateLens [24] (Chapter 2.4.3.4), e.g. in Figure 2.34b: the next Monday after the focus day is assigned significantly less space than the Wednesday 7 weeks ago, for instance. This design decision is obviously not based on the degree of interest the user is likely to have in the next Monday, but is owed to the characteristics of the distortion.

The starfield can be undistorted by tapping and holding the button with the magnifying glass and the minus sign. If the button is only tapped but not held, the distortion settings of the previous step, if any, are restored. Since the compression of the information space eliminates the need for long-distance panning, the latter is implemented as conventional drag&drop. The users can move items in and out of the focus by dragging the diagram pane with the stylus. As with the detail-only application, the scatterplot labels are continuously updated during zooming operations, The same granularity levels are used. However, to avoid confusing overlapping of labels, the context regions are only labeled with the start or end unit of the axis.

The fisheye distortion allows the navigation in the abstract representation provided by the scatterplot. To access the actual details of book items, users tap in its vicinity. The item closest to the pen position zooms to full screen in 250 milliseconds and presents the book information on the familiar record card representation (Figure 4.13d). The zoom animation is further illustrated in Figure 4.14. Note that, unlike in the detail-only interface, only the single item is magnified, not the entire diagram. On tapping the magnified record card, the item zooms back to its original 1-pixel size and position. This mechanism is different to a conventional pop-up in that the animation leads the user's eye back to the previously focused point in the diagram. Thus reorientation is supported. Moreover, users can tap anywhere on the record card to remove it and do not need to hit an X-button in a fixed position. Overall, the zoomable pop-up allows the users to access the details of any non-overlapped item, regardless of whether the interface is distorted or not, and regardless of whether the item of interest is located in a focus or context region.

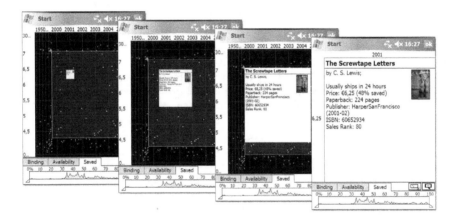

Figure 4.14: Item zooms to full screen in the fisheye interface.

4.3.1.3 Dynamic Queries

Both the fisheye view and the detail-only interface are enhanced with a set of dynamic query modules [6] (see Figure 4.12, 4.13 below the diagram window). By ticking checkboxes, users can filter out books based on binding type or availability. Next to that, they can also control the relative amount of money they wish to save compared to the current list price of each book. For this continuous attribute, we added a range slider that is also used to visualize the distribution of books against savings. When ticking the checkboxes or moving the slider, the diagram is rapidly updated, hiding those items that do not satisfy the filter requirements.

4.3.2   Implementation

The detail-only interface and the fisheye view consist of about 5,500 lines of C# code each and have been deployed for the .NET framework and the CF 2.0. Both applications are based on the interfaces developed for the overview+detail project. The following sections highlight some of the enhancements and modifications applied to the code.

Algorithm 8 shows an update of the zoom in procedure for the detail-only application that has been altered to resolve overlappings of scatterplot items. The constant zoom factor has been replaced by the number of steps (frames) a zoom animation should take to scale the view from the minimum to the maximum magnification factor, and vice versa. On loading the GUI, for each dimension the application checks the ratio of pixels available for each potential item in the scatterplot. In a dimension with overlapping item representations, this value is below one. Based on the current ratio, a target ratio (the size of an item at the highest magnification level) and the number of scale steps to perform, the application calculates individual zoom factors for both scatterplot dimensions X and Y, and for both zoom directions *in* and *out*.

During zooming, the ratio of pixels available per item increases continuously for both dimensions. While the value is below one, the item size in the corresponding dimension is set to the size of one pixel (line 14). This phase denotes the first part of the animation, in which the data points remain at a constant size, but scatter due to the growing size of the information space. The semantic zoom in phase two starts when more than one pixel becomes available. At this point the size of the items is linked to the increasing ratio (line 12) and thus grows steadily until the target size has been reached with the last zoom step.

The modified zoom algorithm ensures a chessboard-like pattern of adjacent record cards as shown in Figure 4.12c-f. This strategy minimizes the empty space between objects, and thus users need to perform fewer navigational actions to move the viewport from one item to another. A drawback may be that, for scatterplot dimensions in which the granularities of axis units differ by a large amount, the different scale factors temporarily lead to unevenly stretched rectangles as indicated in Figure 4.12d, for instance.

The layout algorithm for displaying item content during zooming is based on three information elements: book title, cover, and textual details (i.e. author, shipping etc.). As described by Algorithm 9, the allocation of screen space follows a priority rating. The objective is that users need to perform less zooming for high priority information such as book titles and more for low priority elements such as, say, the ISBN code. However, a possible improvement would be to replace the predefined layout by an intelligent solution that adjusts the priority rating of elements according to the user's specific information need. That way it would for instance be easier to compare book attributes across items.

To enable the continuously adjusting granularity of the scatterplot axes during zooming,

---

Algorithm 8 Altered zoom in

1: set the focus point for the zoom operation to be the center of the focus item
2: **if** the previous action was a zoom-out operation **then**
3:    set the zoom-in step counter to correspond to the current scale of the information space
4: **end if**
5: start the zoom animation
6: **while** zoom animation is running **do**
7:    **if** the maximum number of zoom-in steps has not been reached **then**
8:       increment the step counter by one
9:       **for** each scatterplot dimension **do**
10:          update the size of the information space with the zoom factor for the dimension

11:          **if** the current ratio of pixels available for each possible item in the scatterplot is greater than one **then**
12:             set the item size to be the ratio
13:          **else**
14:             set the item size to be one pixel
15:          **end if**
16:       **end for**
17:       translate the viewport rectangle to move in the direction of the focus point
18:       **if** the viewport rectangle is out of the boundaries of the information space **then**
19:          set the position of the viewport rectangle to the closest position within the information space
20:       **end if**
21:       screen update
22:    **else**
23:       stop the zoom animation
24:    **end if**
25:    process pen events
26: **end while**

Algorithm 9 display item information

1: **for** each item visible **do**
2:    display as many characters of the title as will fit into the enclosing item rectangle
3:    **if** there is vertical space left **then**
4:       scale and position the image cover to fit on the right hand side beneath the title
5:    **end if**
6:    **if** there is horizontal space left next to the cover **then**
7:       fill the remaining space with textual details
8:    **end if**
9: **end for**

---

all gridlines and labels are pre-calculated and stored in an array when loading the application. While the units for the lowest granularity levels (10 years for the X-axis and 5 euro for the Y-axis) are always visible, the other axes measures are displayed depending on the amount of screen space available. Hence while zooming, and for each of the higher granularity levels of each scatterplot dimension, the application repeatedly checks the ratio of available pixels per axis unit. For instance, for the Y-axis the higher granularity levels are: 1 euro, 10 cent, 5 cent, and 1 cent. A level is omitted if fewer than 10 pixels are available for each unit of the level. If there are more than 9 pixels but fewer than 16 pixels available, each visible unit is marked by a grid line. If more than 15 pixels are available, the gridline is also equipped with a scatterplot label. The labels are drawn using a 7-point sans-serif font.

Another modification of the original detail-only code concerns the event handlers for pen input. As discussed, these have been extended to support rate-based scrolling. When the users initiate a pan operation by dragging the pen, the program starts an animation loop that takes the current pen displacement and maps it linearly to a view translation. Lifting the pen interrupts the loop. Tap-to-center navigation is implemented as an animation of 4 frames, which moves the item in focus to the center of the view.

The algorithm implemented for the fisheye interface is similar to orthogonal stretching as described in [201]. The users define a focus region, which is stretched and centered to fill 70 % of the scatterplot width and height. A typical distortion splits the scatterplot in 9 segments, where the center segment is the focus region. For each item (and for each grid line) the drawing routine checks in which segment in the undistorted interface the object is located and then maps the relative position of that item to the corresponding distorted segment. To support the users' comprehension of the mapping, the initial scatterplot is transformed in several animated steps to the distorted fisheye view. The tweening between the two states of the interface is further manipulated by an easing function, which underlines the rubber-sheet metaphor.

Easing has also been used for the animation of the zoomable pop-up mechanism shown in Figure 4.14. When an item (i.e. a record card representation) zooms to full-screen, the motion is slow in the beginning to highlight where the item comes from. At the end of the movement the speed increases to reduce the overall duration of the animation. When the item zooms back to its one-pixel representation, the opposite motion is used: fast in the beginning to save time and slow in the end to emphasize the location of the item inside the scatterplot. For each frame of the animation, the easing function calculates the current position and size of the record card based on a non-linear motion. To improve the zoom performance the record card is initially drawn to an off-screen bitmap. In each frame the image is scaled and copied to the overall off-screen bitmap holding the scatterplot background.

4.3.3 User Evaluation

To compare the usability of the two interface solutions we conducted a user study in which the participants had to complete various search tasks on a collection of 7,500 books. While the information space may correspond to a realistic mobile retrieval scenario (e.g. searching the book collection of a retail store), the current generation of handheld devices is not yet powerful enough to cope with a highly animated starfield display of that size.

Thus we simulated a PDA interface using a pen-operated Tablet PC. The following sections describe our hypotheses and experimental settings.

4.3.3.1 Participants

For the study we selected 24 participants, 11 male and 13 female. 23 of them were students at the University of Konstanz. Their ages ranged from 19 to 33 years. The other participant was an engineer and aged 50. The fields of study varied, with psychology students (7 participants) being the largest group. Only one participant was a Ph.D. student in computer science. According to the data of a pre-test questionnaire, two of our participants owned a PDA and a further ten had at least tried one and were therefore familiar with the general pen interaction concept. All of our users were regular PC and Internet users. In order to test familiarity with zoomable user interfaces, we asked for Google Earth knowledge. Seventeen participants were aware of Google Earth but only one had used it.

4.3.3.2 Hypotheses

The hypotheses were:
1. *Task-completion time would be better for the fisheye interface.* In Chapter 2.4.1 we have discussed a number of studies that investigated the usability of fisheye views in comparison to other interfaces such as ZUIs and o+d interfaces. The results suggest that fisheye views can be more effective for monitoring [203] and navigation tasks [165] [104]. One explanation for this is that the fisheye view helps participants to concentrate directly on the task itself, resulting in quicker navigation and less unnecessary exploration [203]. For the scatterplot interface, we expected to obtain similar results. Users would need to perform less unnecessary navigation, which would compensate for the more time-consuming distortion technique of the fisheye view. On the other hand, tasks that require direct access to the information of a single item would be completed significantly faster when using the detail-only ZUI.

2. *Users would prefer the detail-only ZUI to the fisheye interface.* At first glance this statement may seem to contradict the first hypothesis, but it is based on the experience that interface efficiency does not necessarily correlate with user preference. Studies that compared ZUIs or overview+detail interfaces to a fisheye view found that, although the fisheye improved user performance for many task types, participants were still clearly in favor of the alternative interface [104] [121] [13]. It appears that the rather artificial distortion may discourage users and thus decrease user satisfaction. Moreover, we assumed that the detail-only ZUI would be preferred for its hedonic qualities. Due to the fly-through and slide metaphors, it reminds one in some ways of a computer game.

4.3.3.3 Evaluation Design

We used a counterbalanced within-subjects design, balancing the two interface types and task-sets. This resulted in four different groups mirroring all possible variations of interface and task-set order. We randomly assigned six participants to each group. For analysis, we mainly used repeated measures ANOVAs (RM-ANOVAs). Our independent variable was interface type (detail-only ZUI and fisheye interface). The dependent variables were task-completion time (in seconds), system preference (detail-only ZUI or fisheye interface), user-satisfaction (Attrakdiff PQ Scores), error-rate (number of incorrectly answered tasks), and navigation actions (panning and zooming attempts). Because of the different interaction techniques, we included navigation actions mainly for the sake of completeness but did not expect to be able to compare the two interfaces on the basis of this variable.

4.3.3.4   Tasks

During the experiment, and for each of the two interfaces, users had to solve a different set of 10 tasks after four training tasks (see Appendix C). A task set comprised three different types of questions:

1. *Visual Scan* (2)
   For example: how many books have been published since the year 2000 at a price of EUR 30?

2. *Information Access* (4)
   Who is the author of the most expensive book published in the year 2005?

3. *Comparison of Information objects* (4)
   Between August and November 2001 four books were published which are available at a price of EUR 8.53. Which is the one with the most pages?

4.3.3.5   Materials

For the test both applications were run as simulated PDA interfaces using a Wacom pen display connected to a 3 GHz Pentium 4 PC with 1 GB RAM. This allowed us to use pen-interaction while also being provided with sufficient processing power. As shown in Figure 4.15, the application interface took up a portion of 240 x 320 pixels of the Wacom display, mimicking the standard PDA resolution.

Next to using the screen-recording software Morae, which also recorded the audio stream, we logged task-completion times, and zooming and panning attempts directly within the application. To measure user satisfaction with regard to functionality, we used the pragmatic quality (PQ) dimension of the Attrakdiff questionnaire [109]. We supplemented the Attrakdiff with two questions regarding the quality of navigation and orientation features of the two interfaces, both of them measured on a 7-point scale. System preference was also measured with additional questions, directly asking the participants which of the two interfaces they preferred and furthermore if they thought that the less preferred interface was nevertheless superior for certain tasks. We also asked which interface they thought was more efficient in terms of task-completion times and which of the two panning techniques (sliding versus the conventional drag&drop) they preferred. A pre-test questionnaire was used to collect demographic data.

4.3.3.6   Procedure

The session started with a short written introduction and filling out the pre-test questionnaire. Users were then introduced to the pen handling on the Wacom display, during

Figure 4.15: Simulated PDA interface on a Wacom pen display.

which the pen was recalibrated by the participants themselves. Next, a tutorial video was shown, introducing the interaction of the first interface. After that, users had time to try the application on their own and ask questions. The test administrator asked participants to try the interaction techniques as shown in the video. When participants showed that they had understood the interface, each of the fourteen task questions was presented to them successively as a printout. The first four questions were labeled as training tasks and participants were still allowed to ask questions while working on them. Participants read all questions aloud and then pressed a *start task* button on the upper left of the screen. When they felt they could answer the question, users tapped a *say answer* button below the *start task* button. When the training tasks had been completed, no further support was given. After answering the questions in the first task-set, participants completed the Attrakdiff questionnaire. Subsequently, the same procedure was repeated for the second interface and the second task-set. At the end, participants also completed a preference questionnaire and were then given a movie theatre voucher worth EUR 10. Experiment sessions lasted about 60-75 minutes.

4.3.4   Results

The following sections describe the results of the study, with the focus on our two hypotheses. One thing to note is that during the analysis we discovered a significant interaction effect between system order, task-set order, and interface type. Further analysis traced this effect back to a single task in one of the two task sets, which unintentionally resulted in a bias towards one of the interface types. We therefore excluded this task from further analysis. Moreover, we also excluded one participant from our task-time analysis since their total task-completion time was identified as an outlier ($> 3 * St.Deviation$).

4.3.4.1 H1: Task-Completion Time

In our first hypothesis, we assumed that participants would be able to solve tasks significantly faster when using the fisheye interface. However, analysis revealed that it took users about the same time to complete the 10 tasks with both interfaces (623.8 seconds for the detail-only ZUI compared to 612.4 seconds for the fisheye interface, see Figure 4.16a). The small difference is not significant, $F(1,22) = 0,002$, p=n.s., and therefore contradicts our hypothesis. We then analyzed whether the interfaces differed for the three task types. We suggested that the detail-only interface might be faster for Information Access tasks but slower for the two other task types. Figures 4.16b to 4.16d show that this is indeed the case, however the rather small differences are also not significant.

Regarding navigation, the log data shows that the fisheye interface required far fewer actions but, since task times are similar, it seems that they required more time to execute. Hence we assume that drawing a bounding box is cognitively more demanding than the more direct zooming of the detail-only ZUI.

We also analyzed whether other variables such as gender had an influence on task-completion time. It took our male participants significantly less time to complete the tasks, regardless of the interface used (detail-only ZUI: 529 seconds compared to 646 seconds, $F(1,22) = 7.5, p = 0.012$; fisheye interface: 521 seconds compared to 650 seconds, $F(1,22) = 6.9, p = 0.016$). PDA experience, on the other hand, showed no effect on task-completion time. Our post-test questionnaire included one question where participants were asked to choose the interface with which they thought it had taken them less time to complete the tasks. About 30% guessed incorrectly. This is not surprising, however, bearing in mind the small differences in the overall task times (in most cases between one and two minutes per task-set). The interfaces did not differ in terms of task accuracy - in both cases, more than 90% of correct answers were given on average.

4.3.4.2 H2: Preference + Questionnaire Results

Our second hypothesis suggested that users would prefer the detail-only ZUI to the fisheye interface. The results obtained strongly contradict this assumption: 20 participants preferred the fisheye interface and only three the ZUI ($X^2(1, N = 23) = 12.565, p < 0.001$). In the search for reasons we first analyzed our Attrakdiff results. As can be seen in Figure 4.17, users rated the fisheye interface significantly better; 5.11 compared to 4.11, $F(1,23) = 20.84, p < 0.001$. Furthermore our two additional questions regarding navigation and orientation features were clearly rated in favor of the fisheye interface (navigation: 5.79 compared to 4.83, $F(1,23) = 9.6, p < 0.01$; orientation: 5.7 compared to 4.7 $F(1,23) = 9.9, p < 0.01$). Users gave as the reasons for their preference that the fisheye interface offered a better orientation (9 participants), that drawing bounding boxes was the easier way to get to a certain area (8 participants) and that it allowed a faster task completion (6 participants). Seven participants also mentioned that they had problems with the sliding technique of the detail-only interface. We assume that this was mainly caused by the users' unfamiliarity with this kind of panning, e.g. some participants were observed to accidentally trigger a zoom operation when trying to slide slowly. Nevertheless,

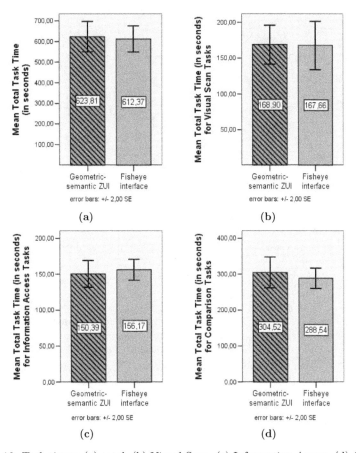

Figure 4.16: Task times: (a) total, (b) Visual Scan, (c) Information Access, (d) Comparison.

18 participants could think of a task where the non-preferred interface would be better. In the group that preferred the fisheye interface, seven participants stated that in the detail-only ZUI it was easier to compare books that were spatially close. Other statements were that, due to the zooming, it was easier to access a single book (3 participants), and one participant mentioned that the semantic zoom offered the possibility of discovering other books of potential interest while navigating to a certain area. Regarding the group that in general preferred the detail-only ZUI, two participants preferred the fisheye interface for tasks where they had to precisely access a given area of interest. Comparing the panning techniques, our participants preferred the more conventional drag&drop mechanism over the sliding technique (16:7, $X^2(1, N = 23) = 3.522, p = 0.061$, n.s.).

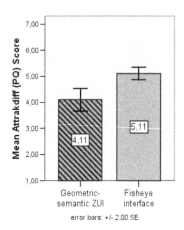

Figure 4.17: Comparing Attrakdiff PQ Scores between interface types

4.3.4.3   Interpretation

Unlike evaluations in previous research, in which the participants often favored other interfaces over fisheye views, we found a strong preference for our focus+context solution when compared to the detail-only ZUI. One reason for this contradiction could be that our rectangular distortion integrates particularly well with the abstract nature of the scatterplot diagram. This hypothesis also corresponds to [175] who suggest that the usability of fisheye views may decrease for domains such as maps, in which a higher degree of fidelity to the standard layout is essential. For these domains, the detail-only ZUI could provide the more efficient solution. We also believe that another strength of the ZUIs lies in exploration tasks. Unlike the fisheye view, in which detail access can only be performed sequentially, the semantic zoom allows the users to capture the content of several items during the course of navigation.

The preference results in favor of the fisheye view may also indicate that, when using a small screen, users place higher value on the ability to preserve navigational context. The user statements indicate that our participants particularly appreciated the better orientation cues of the fisheye. Given the PDA screen, this feature may have outweighed the common disadvantages of the distortion that usually have a negative effect on the user experience. However, it must be noted that our participants also emphasized the utility of the bounding box zoom of the fisheye. The test design does not allow us to resolve how much of the preference effect is accounted for by the orientation and zoom features individually.

In contrast to our expectations, we did not find a significant difference in task-completion time between the interfaces. Due to the context view, the fisheye interface required less navigation, but this advantage could not compensate for the slower interaction mechanism compared to the direct-zoom feature of the detail-only ZUI.

Apart from comparing the interfaces, the study showed that starfield displays, enhanced by an appropriate presentation technique, can scale to large information spaces on small screens.

4.3.5   Issues for Future Research

With regard to our work on mobile starfield displays, we want to propose a number of areas for further improvement and research:

- *3D APIs for 2.5D interfaces*
  The implementation of the experimental interfaces using the limited 2D drawing features of the .NET CF often proved to be difficult. In particular, much effort had to be invested in tweaking the performance of the zoom animations on PDAs. As suggested by [17], a more natural environment for developing ZUIs is provided by 3D graphics APIs. In that way, the application can also take advantage of hardware acceleration when available. With the release of CF 2.0, .NET developers can program managed Direct3D[2] applications to run on Windows Mobile 5.0 devices. Alternative 3D APIs are OpenGL ES[3] and Klimt[4]. The use of such libraries can simplify the development of mobile starfield displays, and significantly improve the graphics power. We actually used the desktop variant of Direct3D to implement a zoomable map application for a Tablet PC (see Chapter 5). We found the handling and the performance to be very convincing.

- *Scatterplot visualization*
  The starfield displays we developed focused almost exclusively on providing efficient scatterplot navigation. To be useful for complex data analysis tasks, the applications must be enhanced with well-known techniques from Information Visualization to allow the dynamic encoding of high-dimensionality data, e.g. one simple method already used in the original FilmFinder was to map categorical attributes to item color. Another sensible feature could allow the users to select a small subset of items to be displayed in a table for easy comparison. Moreover, the clutter of items at the default scale should be reduced by using clustering or point displacement algorithms as discussed in Chapter 2.2.5.3. This would give the users a more precise impression of the distribution and density of data in the scatterplot.

- *Automatic overviews*
  Automatic overviews have been presented in Chapter 2.3.3.2. Unlike the static layout used in the overview+detail project, this kind of presentation technique provides overview information without (permanently) cropping the size of the detail view. More research must be conducted to investigate the general usability of these widgets, including the effect of transparent windows. Another point is the development of

---

[2]The mobile DirectX and Direct3D namespaces implement a subset of the classes available in DirectX 9. According to Microsoft, the supported functionality is comparable to the one provided by DirectX 8: http://msdn2.microsoft.com/en-us/library/ms172504(VS.80).aspx

[3]http://www.khronos.org/

[4]http://studierstube.icg.tu-graz.ac.at/klimt/

intelligent display mechanisms that better detect the time spans in which the users need overview information.

- *Fisheye preference*
  In the interpretation of the focus+context project, we hypothesized that a fisheye view may have a less negative effect on the user experience when used for an abstract information space, as opposed to distortions applied to a more natural domain such as maps. Further research should clarify that point.

- *Halos*
  As shown in Chapters 2.4.2 and 2.4.3.3, halos are a focus+context technique to visualize clipped objects, and have already been successfully applied to mobile devices. In the context of the detail-only starfield, highlighting items in the off-screen space could improve the navigation when zoomed in. However, a drawback of halos is the approach's limited scalability, i.e. thousands of rings would lead to extensive clutter in the interface. Hence intuitive means must be found to limit the spatial scope of halos, or to provide expressive clustering methods. Another issue for research, as proposed by [125], is that of interaction techniques to quickly iterate over halo-enhanced off-screen objects.

- *Advanced Dynamic Queries*
  So far our prototypes are only equipped with basic dynamic query widgets including filter check boxes and a range slider. To support powerful text filtering, more sophisticated filter techniques such as an alphaslider must be implemented. Alphasliders, as has been briefly discussed in Chapter 3.2, allow users to rapidly search and explore lists with thousands of alphanumeric items when only limited screen space is available for the graphical user interface. However, a drawback of the approach is that using such a slider can be exhaustive and even error-prone. In a separate project ([44]) we therefore proposed to enhance the conventional alphaslider design with a novel text filter to dynamically limit the slider range. In this way, users are supported in locating target items and in identifying records that are missing. The results of a comparative user evaluation run on a Personal Digital Assistant showed that 8 out of 12 participants preferred the filter widget to the classic interface. Moreover, we suggested an improved visual design to speed up user interaction. Incorporating such a widget would greatly enhance the search capabilities of the mobile starfield interface.

- *Continuous and concurrent interaction*
  The interaction design featured by the experimental applications was optimized for ZUIs. However, the nature of pen input still limits the users' ability to fluently navigate the 2.5D space. The reasons for this problem, and how it may be overcome, form the research topic discussed in the following chapter.

- *Zooming with multiple devices*
  We also experimented with using PDAs for interacting with large screens. Together with Joachim Böttger and Vladimir Bondarenko from the University of Konstanz we developed a client-server application: a high resolution image was shown on a wall-size display (5.20m x 2.15m, 9 megapixels), and users could zoom and pan

the image information space via a PDA. The viewport of each handheld client was denoted by a colored rectangle on the wall-size display (see Figure 4.18). That way it was possible to observe the movements of all users inside the information space. We found the look and feel of the interaction promising and plan to enhance the application's functionality.

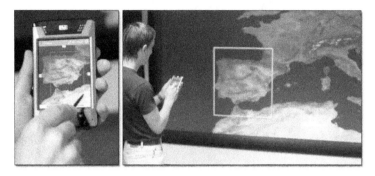

Figure 4.18: Zooming an information space using a PDA and a wall-size display.

4.4 Summary

Chapter 4 presented several interface strategies that we have implemented and evaluated for improving the usability of starfield displays on mobile devices. In the first project we introduced smooth geometric and semantic zooming to provide a consistent transition from overview to detail information within a multiscale starfield display. While users found this technique appealing and easy-to-use, they still showed difficulties in preserving their orientation while navigating. To investigate and reduce this problem, the second project compared an improved detail-only interface with an overview+detail approach. The results of a quantitative usability evaluation with 24 participants showed that the separate overview window was not able to improve user satisfaction and moreover, due to the small size of the control and the cognitive costs of visual switching, it worsened task-completion times. Hence in the third project we proposed a fisheye view for starfield displays. Due to distortion, this interface can preserve overview information without requiring visual switching between separate views. Another usability evaluation with 24 participants was conducted to compare the focus+context solution to a second design-iteration of the detail-only ZUI. While task-completion times remained similar to the ZUI, users significantly preferred the fisheye view. This is an important result that may encourage designers to employ distortion strategies when displaying abstract information spaces on small screens. However, for less abstract data such as maps, the detail-only interface featuring the geometric semantic zoom may still provide the better solution, especially when enhanced by techniques such as halos. Overall, we found our starfield displays to be an elegant and efficient solution for visualizing and exploring retrieval data on mobile devices.

Chapter 5

Interaction Design for Pen-Operated Mobile ZUIs

Contents

5.1 Research Objectives

As discussed in the previous chapters, ZUIs can provide an effective solution for displaying large data sets on small screens. In this part of the dissertation we want to investigate how the usability of ZUIs on pen-operated devices may be further improved by advanced interaction techniques such as speed-dependent automatic zooming (SDAZ) [123]. SDAZ combines zooming and panning into a single operation where the displacement of a pointing device is mapped to the direction and velocity of a continuous pan movement (rate-based scrolling [240]). At the same time, the faster the users pan the view, the more the system zooms out, and vice versa. SDAZ has been found to improve the performance for basic navigation tasks [66] [202], and unlike many other interaction techniques developed for desktop computers, SDAZ may be well suited for application on pen-operated mobile devices. Pen input is good for freeform note-taking and sketching, but due to its limited states and events it does not cover the full set of interface primitives (click, track, drag, double-click, and right-click) that most desktop software is built on [48] [47] [114]. In contrast, SDAZ only requires a dragging state with two linear input dimensions and thus can be conveniently controlled with a regular stylus. However, there may also be two potential drawbacks related to automatic zooming:

- While SDAZ has been proposed for accelerating map browsing, the tasks tested across studies consisted mostly of rather abstract speed tasks. For more real-life navigation tasks, which require users to constantly read and analyze map information, the binding of zooming and panning may turn out to be rather counter-productive.

- Most studies on SDAZ have been conducted in a desktop environment with a large screen. For smaller screens such as featured by PDAs, a recent work by Jones et al. [132] indicates that the effectiveness of SDAZ may be decreased. While the experiment did not include a control group, the authors assumed that the unexpected performance results were due to the lower number of contextual cues provided by the smaller display.

Considering map-based ZUI navigation, there are two alternatives to the binding of zooming and panning as featured by SDAZ: the first one is to allow for sequential navigation only, i.e. the users can either zoom or pan, but cannot perform both operations at the same time. This type of interface is very common on pen-operated devices, and its performance strongly depends on the time it takes the users to switch between the navigation styles. For instance, a comparably slow technique is to provide a tool palette, e.g. the hand and magnifying tools in Adobe Acrobat (see Figure 2.8). Such a widget forces the users to frequently move the pen back and forth between the palette and the focus area, which adds up to a significant amount of travel time [150] [147]. However, more advanced techniques such as tracking menus [84] can reduce switching costs to a minimum.

The second option is to support concurrent, but separate, control of zooming and panning. While this type of interface provides the most flexible navigation, it also assumes the most complex input device. Apart from the 2D position tracking of the pen, which we want to use for controlling rate-based panning, an additional input mechanism is needed to manipulate the scale. A straightforward strategy would be to enhance the device with buttons. These can be placed on the pen, on the bezel of the device display, or as virtual buttons on a touchscreen as in [161] [236], for instance. However, providing a button always means making an assumption about how the users will hold the device and push the button [10]. In consequence, there are many situations in which buttons are awkward to press [237] [97] or may even result in an unstable grip of the device [137]. So instead, we want to focus on two interaction techniques that we believe can integrate more seamlessly with the ergonomics of pen-operated mobile devices, namely pen pressure and inertial sensors. With a pressure-sensitive pen, the users can manipulate all three navigation parameters simultaneously with one hand. Inertial sensors such as accelerometers and gyroscopes may be attached to, or incorporated into, the device. Assuming that panning is controlled by the pen, the users can simultaneously zoom by moving or rotating the handheld. Hence, in contrast to pen pressure, this interface would require bimanual interaction.

Based on the different interface options discussed above we implemented a map viewer application and carried out a research project with the following objectives:

1. Evaluate and compare the usability of (i) automatic zooming, (ii) sequential zooming and panning, and (iii) concurrent but separate zooming and panning for navigating a map on a pen-operated device. For concurrent but separate navigation, the

experiment tests one unimanual approach employing pen pressure and a bimanual approach based on both pen and sensor input.

2. Analyze the effect that different task types of varying navigation complexity would have on the usability results for each interface.

3. Analyze the effect that different screen sizes (600x600 pixels versus 300x300 pixels) would have on the usability results for each interface.

In the following sections we will first review related work, and then explain the settings and hypotheses of our experiment. Later, we present the results and interpret the findings. Issues for further research are also highlighted.

5.2 Related Work

This section summarizes previous research in the fields of SDAZ, pressure interfaces, and inertial sensors. It also highlights some design guidelines that we found helpful for implementing the experimental application.

5.2.1 Speed-Dependent Automatic Zooming

As discussed, SDAZ couples rate-based scrolling with scaling and was developed to avoid visual blur when navigating large information spaces at high speed [123]. The users control the velocity of a continuous panning operation by dragging the pointing device. To keep the visual flow constant, the system automatically zooms out when the scrolling speed increases and zooms back in when the scrolling speed decreases. This behavior also maps the design intuition that the users desire a high level of detail when moving slowly, while for covering large distances quickly, overview information becomes more important.

Previous research reports a number of experiments investigating the usability of SDAZ on desktop computers. A preliminary informal study with 7 participants focused on basic 1D and 2D navigation [123]. The first task required the users to locate target images in a long web document using SDAZ and vertical scrolling. For SDAZ, the custom web browser was enhanced with semantic zooming, i.e. with an increasing scrolling speed (and thus a decreasing magnification) the headings of the document became salient to guide navigation (see Figure 5.1). The results showed that the user performance was approximately equal for both navigation techniques. Nevertheless, six out of the seven participants preferred to use the automatic zooming technique. The second task was to navigate to a target point in a flat map view. The latter consisted of an abstract image showing non-representational shapes. The location of the target point was indicated by a small radar window in a corner of the map view. To reach the target, the participants used SDAZ and a conventional zoom and pan interface, where both interaction techniques were controlled via a joystick. Again, the difference in task-completion times between the two interfaces was found to be non-significant. Four participants preferred SDAZ, and three the scrolling interface [123].

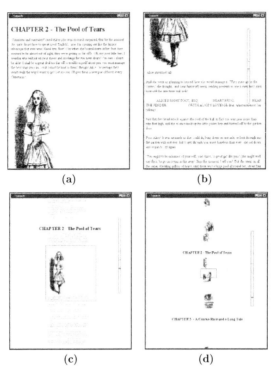

Figure 5.1: Speed-dependent automatic zooming in a web browser; the scale of the document decreases with an increasing scroll speed and the section headings and images become salient: (a) default view, (b) scrolling slowly, (c) scrolling fast, (d) scrolling very fast [123].

In contrast to the moderate results discussed above, some follow-up studies indicate that SDAZ can dramatically improve user performance. In [66] the authors presented an OpenGL implementation of SDAZ that employed hardware acceleration to provide a smooth animation performance at a high frame-rate. A usability study with 12 participants was conducted to evaluate SDAZ when compared to a variety of manual zooming, panning and scrolling facilities as provided by standard commercial applications (Acrobat Reader and Paint Shop Pro). The test tasks required the users to find images and headings in a PDF document, and to navigate to named locations on a road map. The target locations were cued by compass direction or route descriptions such as highways or rivers to follow. For both document and map navigation, the participants solved the tasks significantly faster using SDAZ. Subjective preferences and workload measures also strongly favored the automatic zooming technique. Similar results were obtained in another study [67], which compared SDAZ for 1D document navigation to scrolling, rate-based scrolling and a variant of automatic zooming that implemented optimal pan-zoom trajectories based on the work of van Wijk and Nuij [221]. SDAZ was found to significantly improve the user performance and preference values.

In some cases, the powerful coupling of navigation in SDAZ can also be considered a potential drawback. For instance, the users are not able to zoom out without increasing the pan speed, or to maintain a constant scale without moving. With regard to this limitation, Savage et al. [202] conducted an experiment in which SDAZ was compared to an interface that allowed concurrent but separate navigation control: the users could drag the mouse to pan the view via rate-based scrolling, and press two keyboard keys for stepwise zooming in and out with 5 discrete scale levels. Apart from browsing documents and maps, a globe ZUI was also tested. During the evaluation, 35 participants were asked to navigate to a target object continuously cued by an arrow positioned in the window center. It was found that automatic zooming significantly reduced task-completion times, that it was preferred by the users, and that it caused less subjective workload. However, this finding does not correspond to the results of a study by Appert & Fekete [8], in which the authors proposed a 1D multiscale navigation technique called OrthoZoom Scroll. With OrthoZoom the users can control rate-based scrolling by moving the mouse cursor along the Y dimension, while the granularity of the information space is manipulated by dragging the cursor orthogonally. Hence this approach allows concurrent but separate view navigation. A controlled experiment with 12 participants was conducted to compare OrthoZoom to SDAZ for pointing tasks with indices of difficulty up to 30 bits (see Fitts' law [83]). During navigation, the target was continuously cued by arrows and concentric circles. The researchers found that OrthoZoom performed twice as fast as SDAZ and that all participants preferred to use the OrthoZoom technique.

In previous research there have also been attempts to examine the effectiveness of automatic zooming on small screens. In [171] a variant of SDAZ was applied to vertically navigate a photo collection in a small window on a desktop PC. Unlike the original design, the reference point for scale and velocity was not the initial mouse-down position but the center of the screen. In an evaluation with 72 participants, the technique was compared to two alternative solutions: a scrollable thumbnail view and an interface called GestureZoom, which is similar to OrthoZoom scrolling, i.e. vertical dragging of the mouse is mapped to rate-based scrolling while horizontal dragging controls the zoom level of the view. All experimental applications were controlled by a computer mouse. Across different search tasks the performance of SDAZ and GestureZoom for searching images turned out to be at least equal to, or better than, that for the scrolling interface [171]. Less promising results were found in a study by Jones et al. [132], in which 12 participants used SDAZ on a simulated PDA screen to search documents and city maps. Again, all test applications were operated by a mouse. Surprisingly, even though the control interface was limited to sequential mode-based navigation, SDAZ produced longer task-completion times. In the case of the 1D document navigation, the difference was significant. The authors assumed that the discrepancy of the results compared to the success of SDAZ in desktop-based studies was due to the smaller view size. However, the study did not comprise a control group for screen size and thus more research must be conducted to clarify this point.

5.2.2   Pressure Sensing

When talking about pen-operated devices, we mean devices that are controlled by a touch-screen or an electromagnetic digitizer located behind a LCD.[1] Touchscreens are usually found in PDAs and an increasing number of smartphones; they can sense any object (stylus or finger) touching the surface. The electromagnetic digitizer is commonly used in Tablet PCs and graphics tablets such as a Wacom display (see Figure 4.15). While they can only be operated with a special pen, many digitizers provide advanced sensing features including measuring the pressure of the pen tip applied to the display.

One of the earliest works on controlling user interfaces with pressure was published almost thirty years ago [111]. The device setup consisted of a glass pane with piezoelectric transducers, with the pane being mounted on a display tube with strain gauges (see Figure 5.2). The researchers conducted an informal experiment to investigate the users' ability to perform basic interface interaction by applying pressure to the screen. The tasks were to manipulate a cursor's position and speed, as well as to push, pull, disperse and rotate virtual objects. The authors found that pressure sensing provided a rich channel for direct manipulation and multidimensional interaction.

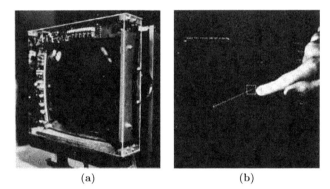

(a)   (b)

Figure 5.2: An early pressure interface: (a) apparatus consisting of a touch sensitive digitizer mounted on a display with strain gauges to sense pressure normal and parallel to the surface, (b) a force cursor; the arrow's origin is located at the touch position, its angle maps to the direction of the force, and its length is proportional to the force [111].

Pressure input can be used to control a continuous parameter or to produce discrete signals. A discrete design may be used, for instance, to trigger click events while pointing. Buxton [48] found that just two levels of pressure already provide a stylus with a set of states comparable to a one-button mouse, and that the input can thus be used to control direct manipulation interfaces. Another example of a discrete pressure interface is the pen-operated 2.5D virtual desktop that was presented in [1]. The users applied maximum pen pressure to switch from a dragging mode to manipulating desktop objects (e.g. a pile

---

[1]Another pen technology is the light pen, but since it only works with CRT monitors it is hardly used any longer.

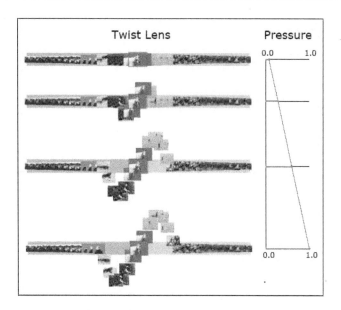

Figure 5.3: Navigating the frames of a video using a TwistLens slider widget. The amplitude of the twist lens changes with the pen pressure [180].

of files).

The most common application for mapping pressure to a continuous parameter is to control the width or color opacity of a brush tool in a drawing program. This functionality, which was originally suggested in [48], is supported by Adobe Photoshop and Illustrator, for instance. A more advanced scenario for employing continuous pressure is the TwistLens slider widget shown in Figure 5.3. In the example, the slider is used to navigate the frames of a video sequence. Frames in focus are enlarged via a fisheye zoom, while the users can morph the linear layout via pressure to an s-shape to avoid occlusions among thumbnails. The amplitude of the lens grows with an increasing force [180].

Surprisingly, to date there have been only a few evaluations of pressure input. In [164], an interface is presented, in which pen pressure was used to define a throwing distance for a virtual object in a multi-display reaching task. In an experiment with 18 participants, the authors found that the technique was inferior in both performance and user preference to several non-pressure techniques (e.g. pick-and-drop [189] and push-and-throw [108]). They concluded that one potential reason for the result was the poor control of pressure with the pen. They also acknowledged the need to study pressure-based input devices more carefully to make them easier to control.

Another study [150] investigated pressure input for rapid mode switching between ink and command gestures on a Tablet PC. The pressure space was divided into two levels, where

pen strokes with light to medium pressure were interpreted as ink, and strokes with strong
pressure were treated as commands. In a usability evaluation with 15 participants, the
pressure technique was compared to 4 other mode switching techniques: dwelling, pressing
a button with the non-preferred hand, pressing the barrel button of the pen, and using
the eraser of the pen. The pressure-based interface was found to have a moderate performance among the techniques. A significant problem detected was that some participants
showed difficulties in adapting to the uniform pressure threshold. The threshold had been
selected based on a preliminary evaluation, but could not compensate for the high variance
of individual differences in applying pressure.

An experimental application whose design requirements were quite similar to the ones for
the present work has been introduced in [181]. A pressure-sensitive stylus was used as an
integrated device for zooming a parameter's scale space while concurrently manipulating
the parameter's value within that scale space. The authors conducted a usability study,
in which 12 participants were asked to vertically scroll and zoom an abstract document to
reach targets of different widths and located at varying distances from the viewport. The
pressure-based widget was compared to two bimanual interaction techniques, where the
position sensing of the pen input was used in conjunction with either an isometric button
or two discrete keyboard keys controlled by the non-dominant hand. The results showed
no significant difference in task-completion times between the techniques. Preference ratings were also mixed, but participants commented that 'it felt right' and 'natural' to zoom
using a pressure-sensitive pen as an integrated device. In contrast, the participants who
favored one of the bimanual techniques liked the fact that zooming and scrolling were
decoupled by using two hands. However, other users found it demanding to coordinate
the two-handed navigation.

Overall, previous research seems to indicate that pressure interfaces, though promising,
are difficult to implement in such a way that they can be controlled accurately and with
ease. The following list summarizes some common implementation and usability issues:

- *Lifting the pen*
  Depending on the speed with which the pen is lifted from the display, the pressure
  decreases gradually, which may trigger unwanted operations [179]. In the case of
  multidimensional input, the lifting movement can also cause an unintentional fluctuation of the pen's spatial position just before it loses contact with the device [48]
  [181]. Appropriate filtering of the signals should eliminate or at least reduce both
  problems.

- *Number of pressure levels*
  The human ability to reliably discriminate discrete levels within the pressure space
  is rather limited. The proposed maximum numbers of levels are 6 [182], between 5
  and 7 [163], and between 3 and 7 [48].

- *Friction*
  For finger input, an increasing pressure force also increases the friction between the
  finger and the display, which can hamper smooth, sweeping gestures [111] [48] [179].
  To a less significant degree this problem also applies to pen input.

- *Maintaining a pressure level*
  Moving a pen decreases the users' ability to maintain a constant pressure level, which in the case of multidimensional input can hamper precise parameter manipulation. In such cases a filter mechanism for signal stabilization is recommended [181].

- *Low-pressure spectrum*
  Users have less pressure control at low levels of pressure [182]. The transfer function in a continuous mapping, or the pressure thresholds in a discrete mapping should outweigh this effect.

- *Individual differences*
  Users have been reported to vary a lot in the range and values of their pressure spaces [150], i.e. some people use a lower or greater overall pressure for drawing with a pen. Calibration was suggested to adjust the pressure sensitivity of the interface to the individual pressure space.

Another important factor for easing the control of pressure input is the provision of continuous visual feedback [48]. In a study [182] about target selection via discrete pressure levels, after one hour of practice with a continuous feedback feature the participants were asked to switch to a more limited feedback variant, which required them to rely primarily on their haptic memory. The user performance decreased significantly as a result. On the one hand, the authors assumed that the one hour of practice with continuous feedback might not have been sufficient to train the users. On the other hand, they also considered the possibility that the performance difference may persist, regardless of the amount of practice.

The design of appropriate feedback is strongly dependent on the task to be performed and the type of pressure mapping used. If applicable, however, the feedback should not only indicate the current amount of pressure applied, but also indicate the consequences of varying the pressure level [180] [162]. An example of such an approach is shown in Figure 5.4. The widget provides continuous visual feedback with preview icons for the previously discussed TwistLens slider (see Figure 5.3). Apart from visual feedback, auditory feedback may also be beneficial in some scenarios, e.g. [181].

5.2.3   Sensor-Augmented Mobile Devices

Sensor-based interaction has become a continually growing area of research during the last ten years. An example of the rich input potential provided by this approach is the video console Wii[2]. The users play games using a wireless controller that, as well as serving as an infrared pointing device, also detects motion and rotation in three dimensions. Since its release in late 2006 the console has been a great success, with millions of units sold worldwide. Other devices that provide tilt-control are recent mobile phones such as the Nokia 5500 Sport[3] and the Samsung SCH-S310[4].

---

[2]http://wii.nintendo.de/
[3]http://www.nokia.com
[4]http://www.samsung.com

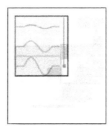

Figure 5.4: A pressure widget providing visual feedback for the TwistLens slider. A series of icons reflect the consequences of varying the pen pressure with respect to the s-shape of the video sequence [180] (also see Figure 5.3).

An early research prototype investigating sensor-based interaction was the Chameleon system [86] [85]. The main idea was that a small palmtop should act as a viewport to a large virtual workspace. By moving the display in 3D, the users could navigate the workspace accordingly. Chameleon consisted of a 4-inch color monitor simulating a future palmtop device, and a back-end workstation for doing all the processing and graphics rendering. The monitor was equipped with a 6-degree-of-freedom input device, whose signals were used by the workstation to detect user gestures in terms of position and tilt. The visual output produced by the workstation was fed back to the palmtop via a video camera. Ten years later a more advanced prototype of a spatially aware display was presented by Yee [235]. Based on a peephole metaphor, the system allowed users to navigate lists and maps, draw images larger than the screen, or, as shown in Figure 5.5, navigate a calendar application. Unlike Chameleon, the peephole display was intended for bimanual usage combining the position-tracking of the device with pen input.

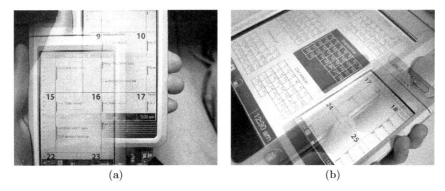
(a)   (b)

Figure 5.5: Navigating a calendar using a spatially aware peephole display (photos were blended together): (a) panning by vertical and horizontal movement, (b) semantic zooming by holding the PDA closer or further away from the body [235].

Though not implemented, the developers of Chameleon had also discussed how their interaction model could benefit from tilting gestures. Apart from triggering automatic view shifts in 3D navigation, they saw a great potential for this type of interaction in controlling 2D rate-based scrolling [86]. Since then many experimental systems have investigated tilt-control, with scrolling probably being the most common application domain. For instance, Harrison et al. [107] employed tilting for browsing sequential lists on a handheld device. Different scrolling rates could be achieved by altering the device angle. The same mechanism has been proposed in [211] to navigate an electronic newspaper device. In addition, the prototype was supposed to feature position-tracking similar to that of Chameleon or the peephole display. Pushing the device away from the body would result in a smooth zoom out, giving the reader an overview of several news stories. By pulling the display closer to the body, the users could zoom back into a particular story. A way to control both zooming and panning by tilting alone was examined in [81]. To navigate a text document on a PDA, the authors coupled tilt input around the X axis with speed-dependent automatic zooming. The results of an informal usability study suggested that the handling of tilt-based SDAZ was comparable to that of a pen-based SDAZ implementation.

Rekimoto [188] presented a palmtop display that employed tilting around the vertical and horizontal axes as continuous input to navigate cylindrical and pie menus, and to browse a 3D map. In the case of the map, when dipping the device edge to one side, the view was panned, rotated, and zoomed to provide a perspective overview of the current location (see Figure 5.6). As another example application, the author had implemented a 3D object viewer, in which the orientation of the view was coupled to the orientation of the display. Thus users could inspect the virtual object from different directions by rotating the device.

Figure 5.6: Using tilt-control to browse a 3D road map [188].

An advanced prototype of a small-sized appliance with built-in sensors was presented by Bartlett [10]. Users could control the device by performing tilting and fanning gestures in different directions and around the two axes of the device. In Figure 5.7 such a gesture is used to select a thumbnail image in a photo album application. Based on the handheld prototype the author conducted an informal study with 15 participants, in which tilt-control was used to scroll through text and images, to navigate an interactive floor plan, and to play a simple chase game. On the one hand, it was found that the majority of participants rapidly learned to master the interaction. On the other hand, when comparing the technique to a four-way rocker switch button, the preferences of the users were mixed. The participants who favored tilt-control found this technique more natural and intuitive to use. The other group preferred the button because of the greater precision it provided.

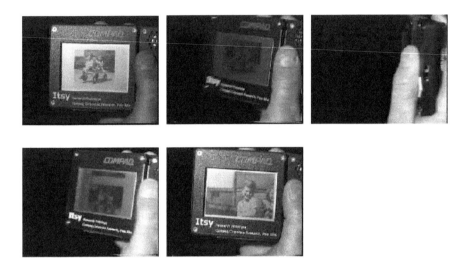

Figure 5.7: Using a fanning gesture around the Y axis of the device to select an image from a thumbnail view to be displayed at full size (sequence runs from top left to bottom right) [10].

Using tilt-control for navigating a spreadsheet was proposed in [117] [116]. The researchers experimented with different transfer functions for controlling 2D rate-based scrolling via tilt angles, and found single axis control to be the most promising, i.e. scrolling was limited to either vertical or horizontal scrolling at a time. Though this approach hampers diagonal movements, it allows for rapid scrolling across a long distance without drifting off-axis. Another result was that the 5 participants in an informal usability test seemed to like tilt-to-scroll better than using a rocker switch button. In particular, they preferred tilting for its intuitiveness, and because it was easier to control with one hand. Negative user statements were that it was easy to overshoot a target with tilting, and that it took time to get used to it. Similar results were gained in another handheld study [62] that compared tilt-to-scroll with using navigation buttons and an iPod wheel for searching images in a photo collection. Most effective with regard to overshooting, travel distance, and performance time was the button-based input. Nevertheless, the 7 participants slightly preferred tilting to the other techniques, though they also rated it more difficult to control.

The previous literature indicates that sensor-based interaction, and especially tilting, may provide an intuitive input dimension for controlling handheld devices. Unlike position-tracking in 3D, tilting requires less physical activity and less space, which makes gesturing more comfortable. As with pen pressure, there have been only very few quantitative studies on tilting, but problems have been reported with regard to input precision. Furthermore, the following issues should be considered when implementing tilt-control:

- *Physical limitations of tilting input*
  The users' physical ability to tilt around the two device axes may not be equal for each direction. For instance, the results of an evaluation [70] examining PDA tilt-control in a target-acquisition task indicated a lower performance and accuracy for upward pitch motions. Mantyjarvi et al. [159], who used discrete tilt events to navigate a virtual museum guide on a PDA, reported that the majority of the participants in an informal user test found tilting around the X axis of the device more difficult than tilting around the vertical axis.

- *Toggle tilt-control*
  Tilt-sensitive devices must provide a functionality to disable and engage sensor input, otherwise accidental gestures can be difficult to avoid. One solution is to provide a simple toggle mechanism such as pressing a button [159], squeezing the device [107], or performing a tilting gesture [10]. Even then, the users may simply forget to turn the sensitivity off. Hence other designs propose a clutch button that must be kept depressed during navigation (e.g. [86] [188] [211]). Obviously, this method may become tedious if the navigation continues over a longer time span. An alternative technique that does not require muscle tension is to use a touch sensor on the bezel of the display [117]. The tilt-sensitivity is enabled until the users release contact. However, as acknowledged by the authors, inadvertent contact can be a problem.

- *Neutral angle*
  A touch sensor [117] or a gesture [10] may also provide a flexible way to set a device's neutral orientation, relative to which tilt interaction takes place. In contrast, a pre-defined angle as in [107], though derived from in-laboratory testing, may not be appropriate for different user postures.

- *Display visibility*
  Several researchers have experienced difficulties with display visibility due to reflections and extreme viewing angles, e.g. [107] [81] [70] [10]. Hinckley et al. [117] proposed to compensate for the loss of apparent contrast during tilting by continuously adjusting the contrast settings of the device. However, as noted by Cho et al. [62], the introduction of wide viewing angle LCD and OLED technology may significantly reduce the problem in the near future.

5.3   User Evaluation

Based on SDAZ, pen pressure, and tilt-control, we implemented three interaction interfaces for controlling a ZUI on pen-operated mobile devices. A standard interface relying on sequential interaction was also developed. We conducted a formal usability study, in which we compared the approaches in terms of task-completion times, user preference, and workload. The study required the participants to solve navigation and search tasks by zooming and panning a Munich city map. The map consisted of three semantic layers and was displayed in a viewport of either 600x600 pixels or 300x300 pixels. The following sections discuss the experimental settings and our hypotheses.

5.3.1 Experimental Interfaces

In a first attempt we implemented our experimental map viewer application using C# and the .NET framework. However, for the large map bitmaps used, the graphics performance was unsatisfactory. Thus, we reimplemented the application using managed DirectX 9.0, which allowed us to take advantage of hardware acceleration. Since the map viewer is essentially a 2.5D interface, we simply wrapped the map bitmap in a sprite object, which is translated and scaled during navigation according to the user input. This approach provided us with smooth zooming and panning at 50 frames per second. We were also able to reuse some of the code from the previous prototype.

In order to simplify the administration and evaluation of the experiment, the map viewer reads in the test parameters (e.g. number of tasks to perform, task types, task set, view size etc.) from an Excel file, which is also used to store logged data. From Excel the log can then be easily copied to a statistics software package such as SPSS.

Each of the different interaction techniques is implemented as custom event handlers. Apart from zooming and panning, all interfaces also support a click mechanism by quickly tapping the screen with the stylus. Except for the standard interface, panning is implemented as rate-control, i.e. the speed of an animated and continuous pan movement increases with the distance the pen is dragged on the display. For rate-control, we defined a maximum pan speed along with a maximum drag distance at which the maximum speed would be reached. The drag range was set to be a fraction of the smaller dimension of the view size because the users quickly reach the end of the display when dragging a pen on a PDA or a smartphone screen. Being stuck at the bezel, the pen is significantly impaired in the way it can be moved. By setting the maximum drag distance to a fraction of the view size, the users can reach the maximum speed and, without decreasing the speed of the movement, still have sufficient space left before reaching the bezel to freely change the pan direction.

Figure 5.8 shows the general layout of the map-viewer application based on the example of the pressure interface. The GUI consists of controls for the test administrator, a compass rose, and the viewport to the map information space. A cross-hair is drawn in the center of the map view. Visual feedback, apart from the implicit map transformation, is provided by each event handler individually. Furthermore, the rate-controlled interfaces provide the users with a visual reference point of the pen displacement. Dragging the pen over the display causes the system to draw an arrow with its origin in the center of the view. The direction of the arrow is equal to the direction of the pen movement and the length mirrors the current drag distance. While interacting, the arrow is continuously updated. For measuring the effect of display size, the map view could be set to either 600x600 pixels or 300x300 pixels. The smaller view corresponds roughly to the display size of a PDA-like device.

The parameters used for the interaction techniques (e.g. maximum pan speed, zoom rate, etc.) were determined in a preliminary test with 6 participants. For this purpose, the variables were mapped to interface controls so they could be dynamically adjusted during testing. Such a control panel is shown in Figure 5.8a on the right hand side of the screenshot. This panel was only visible in the preliminary test.

5.3.1.1 SDAZ Interface

The SDAZ interface maps both rate-based 2D scrolling and zooming to the pen position. For the relationship between pan speed and scale, the prototype implements the original design as proposed by Igarashi & Hinckley [123], i.e. we set the scale exponential to the pan movement to achieve a perceptually constant scale change for a growing displacement of the pointing device. In a second step, we calculated the pan speed based on the current scale. In the preliminary user test, however, the smooth decrease in scale proved to be a problem for more complex navigation tasks. For instance, given that the view was set to an area of interest, the users wanted to gain an overview of the region at a low magnification level, but when zooming out the implicit panning caused the initial location to quickly move into the offscreen space. Thus the users frequently had to backtrack to the start position, which they found rather annoying and confusing. To minimize this problem, we manipulated the rate of change of the scale to be more significant at first, leading to a lower magnification level when panning slowly.

As recommended by Igarashi & Hinckley, we defined a maximum falling rate to ease the transition between zoomed-out and zoomed-in views. Otherwise, when lifting the pen or reversing the drag direction, the map would abruptly zoom in to full size because the pan rate defined by the pen displacement drops to zero or crosses zero. This has a very disorienting effect, in particular when dealing with semantic zooming.

To provide the users with a notion of the zoom level, a scale bar is drawn within an outlined box in the upper-left corner of the view. The size of the white bar reflects the current zoom level proportional to the scale range and is continuously updated during navigation (see Figure 5.9). When the box is all white, the map is shown at the highest magnification level.

5.3.1.2 Pressure Interface

With the pressure interface, the users pan via rate-control and manipulate the scale by adjusting the pressure of the pen on the display. The test device used in the evaluation provides a pressure space from 0 to 255. Considering that the users were expected to zoom and pan in parallel, the application required a robust mapping that would resist significant but unintentional fluctuations of the pen pressure. Hence, we avoided a continuous mapping and defined two thresholds that would tile the pressure space into three discrete intervals. Each interval corresponds to a zoom command: when the input value lies within one of the outer intervals, the scale is continuously increased or decreased by a constant

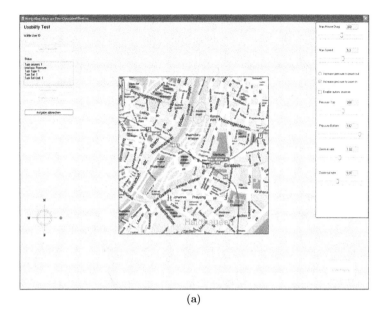

(a)

(b)

Figure 5.8: Layout of the experimental map viewer application: (a) the 600x600 pixels view (with the manipulation panel used in the preliminary test), (b) the 300x300 pixels view.

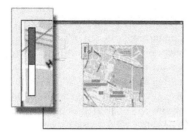

Figure 5.9: Scale bar feedback for SDAZ. The white bar grows with an increasing magnification level.

factor; when within the range of the middle interval, the current scale is maintained. Such an all-or-none response for parallel zooming and panning has already been found beneficial in [37]. Moreover, the design of only three command intervals is a good match for the limited human ability to discriminate a larger number of pressure levels.

Which outer interval to map to which zoom direction proved to be a difficult decision. When developing the interface, the first design intuition was that the map should zoom out when applying strong pressure (the input value enters the top interval). This corresponds to pushing a physical map away from the body. Accordingly, applying only little pressure would cause the map to rise, i.e. to zoom in. We found, however, that the users in the preliminary test expected the opposite mapping, and when trying out this opposite mapping they also found it more natural to control. They associated the high pressure with diving deeper into the information space and thus with magnifying the map. We also experimented with different pressure thresholds and eventually settled on the following values:

- *Zoom in with constant speed:* [205,255]

- *Maintain the current scale:* [142,204]

- *Zoom out with constant speed:* [0,141]

These thresholds agree with the previous literature reviewed in Chapter 5.2.2 in that our users showed more difficulties in controlling the low-pressure spectrum. This resulted in a zoom-out interval that is almost three times the size of the zoom-in interval in the high-pressure spectrum.

It is important to note that, compared to SDAZ, the pressure interface does not force the users to zoom and pan in parallel. If desired, they can control each navigation parameter independently. Another feature is that when the users lift the pen from the display the current view freezes. This allows examination of a portion of the map in a more relaxed state. With SDAZ, the users must permanently circle over an area of interest to avoid losing the current scale and position of the view.

An implementation issue we experienced with freezing the view was that, when lifting the pen, the pressure input inevitable crosses the lowest pressure spectrum. When the users had previously zoomed in or maintained the scale, this then caused a slight but annoying drop in scale. A similar problem occurred when initially pressing the pen on the display to either pan at the current scale or to zoom in. The input value would gradually rise from 0 to above 141 and thus temporarily decrease the scale. To overcome these effects we introduced a timer that is set each time the pressure input enters the lowest pressure interval. The corresponding zoom-out operation is not triggered until the timer executes after 100 milliseconds. If the pressure value exceeds the low-pressure interval within that timeframe, the operation is cancelled. The delay of 100 milliseconds is too short to be noticed by the users, but sufficient to reliably filter out the pressure fluctuation when lifting or setting the pen.

The visual feedback of the pressure interface as shown in Figure 5.10 enhances the scale feedback of SDAZ by an additional box in which the horizontal lines mirror the two pressure thresholds proportional to the pressure space. Within the box outline, the current pressure value is denoted as a red dot that rises with a growing pressure. The interval that currently contains the pressure dot is further highlighted by a blue background color.

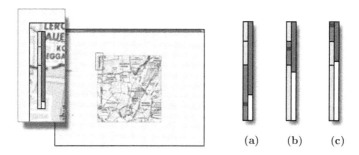

(a)   (b)   (c)

Figure 5.10: Visual feedback for the pressure interface, consisting of a pressure bar and a scale bar. The tiles of the pressure bar mirror the three pressure intervals, and the dark dot represents the current pressure input: (a) low pressure interval, the interface zooms out, (b) middle pressure interval, the current scale is maintained, (c) high pressure interval, the interface zooms in. The white scale bar indicates the current zoom level.

5.3.1.3 Tilt Interface

The tilting interface offers the same functionality as the pressure interface but it is controlled by two-handed interaction based on Guiard's model of the Kinematic Chain [98]. According to the model, in real-life human action the non-dominant hand sets a frame of reference in which the dominant hand operates. Moreover, the action of the non-dominant hand precedes that of the dominant hand and the level of detail at which the dominant hand works is finer than that of the non-dominant hand. We applied this design to the map viewer application by assigning the comparably coarse task of controlling the scale (the frame of reference) to the non-dominant hand via device tilting. Accordingly, the fine granular task of rate-based panning (view pointing) is left to the dominant hand via pen input.

For controlling the zoom, only a single tilt dimension is needed. We limited the interaction to rotation around the X axis of the device, because tilting the device around the Y axis with the display pointing away from the dominant hand makes it ergonomically difficult to operate the device using the pen. In contrast, tilting around the X axis ensures a relatively constant level of ease-of-access for pen input.

The tilt-control is based on the data from the accelerometer of the test device. For mapping the input to the scale of the view, we used the same threshold strategy as for the pressure interface. However, an important difference is that the thresholds are not defined as absolute values, but as angular distances relative to a neutral orientation of the device. The neutral orientation is set to the current tilt input value each time the users put the pen on the display. Hence the neutral orientation is frequently and automatically initialized without requiring any extra action by the users.

Based on the preliminary study, we set the relative thresholds to be 6 degrees from the neutral orientation when tilting the device upwards (rotating the upper edge of the device away from the body) and 2 degrees from the neutral orientation when tilting it downwards. The difference in the angular distances is due to the special settings of the test device, in which downward tilting decreases the visibility of the display more significantly than upward tilting. Given the two thresholds, the users have an angular range of 8 degrees in which the current scale is maintained. When the tilt angle exceeds the range, the zoom operation corresponding to the respective tilt direction is triggered. Apart from being easy to control, the threshold design with all-or-none response also helps to avoid extreme device angles.

When assigning the zoom commands to the two tilt directions, we again faced the problem that there seems to be no definite natural mapping. However, most participants of the preliminary test preferred to zoom in when tilting upwards, and to reduce the magnification when tilting the device downwards. Zooming is at constant speed.

As with the pressure interface, the display freezes when the pen is lifted from the display. While this functionality forces the users to place the pen on the display even when they only want to zoom without panning, it has the benefit of providing an effective clutch mechanism for toggling tilt-control.

The same visual feedback as shown in Figure 5.10 is provided, but in this case the left box visualizes the angular thresholds along with the current tilt input.

5.3.1.4   Standard Interface

In the standard interface the users can control the scale by dragging a slider thumb or by tapping plus and minus buttons (see Figure 5.11). 11 discrete zoom levels are provided.

While the slider design is visually similar to the one used in Google Maps, for instance, one difference is that it provides direct feedback, i.e. the view is updated while dragging the thumb and not just when it is released. Panning is implemented as conventional drag&drop, i.e. the users drag the information space with the pen. Compared to the other interaction techniques, the standard interface is limited to discrete and, in particular, sequential interactions. Advantages may be the more precise navigation control, and the fact that the users can perform larger changes in scale more quickly. Since the slider widget already indicates the current scale level, no further visual feedback is provided for the standard interface. To reduce occlusion by the user's hand when operating the slider, we placed the control on the right side of the map view (the study included right-handed participants only).

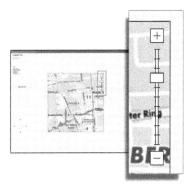

Figure 5.11: Zoom slider of the standard interface with 11 discrete levels. The users can also increase or decrease the current level stepwise by tapping the plus and the minus buttons.

5.3.2   Map Information Space

Most geographic ZUIs make use of semantic zooming, in which the granularity of the map information changes with the scale. For the evaluation, we therefore created a simple semantic information space consisting of three bitmaps that show the same city map of Munich at different scales[5]. The first map layer has a size of 6000x6000 pixels and shows the city at a high level of detail (scale: 1:10,000). The layer includes a complete labeling of main roads, small streets, public transport lines, tourist landmarks, official buildings, parks, etc. The second layer shows the map at a scale of 1:20,000. The granularity is reduced in that small streets and buildings are omitted. The public transport lines are still visible, but without labels. In contrast, the labels of the city districts are highlighted. The third layer has a scale of 1:40,000 and accordingly the amount of detail information is further reduced. Only some of the main roads are labeled, and the landmarks and

---

[5]For the maps see http://www.stadtplandienst.de.

transport lines have been completely removed.

For the standard interface, the semantic layers are swapped according to the scale values of the distinct zoom level, i.e. when zooming out from the highest magnification of the map, the first layer will be scaled down with each zoom level until it is replaced by the second layer, which in turn is scaled down until the third layer is eventually displayed.

For the three alternative interfaces that support continuous zooming, we were not satisfied with the abrupt swapping effect, given the otherwise fluent zoom. Thus we enhanced the transitions between the layers with fluent alpha blending. For instance, the transition between the first layer and the second layer starts at a scale of 0.8 and ends at scale 0.6. During this scale range the second layer is blended onto the first layer with a continuously decreasing transparency that is proportional to the value of the current scale within the transition range. Hence when the scale has reached a value of 0.6, the second layer is shown at full opacity while the first layer is no longer visible.

The alpha blending effect resulted in a smooth semantic zoom, which was found to be very appealing and natural by all of the participants in the preliminary test. In fact, the users did not perceive the map as three distinct bitmaps, but as a single, dynamically changing information space. Initially, we were also concerned that if the users were, by chance, to stop zooming exactly midway between a transition of two layers, the blending effect might disturb them. However, as it turned out, this transition-situation happened too seldom to cause a serious problem.

5.3.3 Tasks

When developing the following four task types, our objective was to cover a variety of use cases ranging from simple speed tasks to complex search and map navigation tasks. Each task starts with the view being set to the maximum magnification level of the map. For a complete list of the tasks used see Appendix D.

1. *Halo-navigation*
   The users were asked to navigate to an offscreen target as quickly as possible. The target consisted of a circle (radius 20 pixels at maximum scale), which was continuously cued by a red halo (see Chapter 2.4.3.3). Targets were only tappable at the highest magnification level, which was further indicated by the circle changing its color from gray to red. Upon a successful hit, the system produced a beep of 150 milliseconds, the circle was removed from the display, and a new halo-enhanced offscreen target was generated. In total the users had to reach ten targets in succession. The targets were located at a distance of 2500 pixels from each other and the directions were set at random but within the bounds of the map. Unlike in the original design by Baudisch [14], the halos in our application did not disappear once the target objects entered the viewport. Instead they became an outer concentric circle (radius 25 pixels) of the onscreen target. We found that this approach improved the

identification of the target, and particularly so when the circle was drawn in a highly cluttered map region.

The main purpose of halo-navigation was to measure speed. It may correspond to the rather rare scenario in which the users are highly familiar with a given map and know in which direction and distance a point-of-interest is located. The most effective strategy to reach the target is to zoom out, pan, and, once the target object appears on the screen, to zoom in on it. While the halos are rendered without any relation to the underlying information space, the map was nevertheless displayed to provide additional visual feedback to the users.

2. *Follow-route*

   The users had to find and tap a named station by following an underground line. When starting the task, the view was automatically positioned such that the relevant underground line crossed the view. The label of the target station was highlighted with a red rectangle, which was only visible (and tappable) at the highest magnification level. Due to the fact that the underground lines in Munich are of similar length, we were able to keep the distance between the initial view position and the target station rather equal for all tasks. To support the users in case they became lost (e.g. accidentally switched to another line at an intersection), the start location was marked by a red halo. Moreover, we enhanced the 1:10,000 map with additional labeling to better distinguish between the individual transport lines.

   With the follow-route tasks, our main interest lay in evaluating the panning functionality. Zooming did not provide a performance benefit, as the station labels were hardly readable or simply not visible at scales other than the highest magnification level. Adjacent stations were also positioned very close to each other on the map, which would have required users to constantly zoom in and out to check the name for every station.

   Example task: follow the underground line number 5 from Odeonsplatz (start) to Laimer Platz (destination). The destination is located west of the start position.

3. *Find-route*

   This task type asked the users to find a route between two given landmarks (e.g. a slip road, a park, etc.) that, due to their distance apart, could not be displayed in a single view. The route had to be submitted orally as driving directions based on street names. The start and destination landmarks were marked by differently colored halos. The participants were instructed to choose the shortest route based on the main streets (colored yellow on the map). The task ended when the participants tapped a red target circle positioned at the destination.

   Routing is probably the most common real-life task when reading maps. In the experiment it was also the most complex task type to solve. It usually required the participants to frequently zoom out to maintain the overview of the route, and then to zoom to a higher magnification level to be able to read the street names more easily.

Example task: find a route from Theodor-Heuss-Platz to the Ostbahnhof.

4. *Find-landmark*
   The users were given a printout showing a map clipping of 225x225 pixels. On this clipping a target position (e.g. a street crossing) was marked by a red dot. The users had to locate and tap the target position, which on the digital map was highlighted by a red circle. The target was only visible at the highest magnification level.

   For each interface the users had to solve three find-landmark tasks in succession, with each task being based on a clipping of another semantic layer of the map interface. All clippings contained an item of symbolic or alphanumeric information that was represented on all three map layers. This task type may correlate to a typical map exploration, in which the users browse an information space in search of certain visual information.

5.3.4 Apparatus

For the evaluation we used a Toshiba Portégé Tablet PC running Windows XP Tablet PC Edition. The device is equipped with a Pentium M 1.6 GHz processor, 1GB of RAM, a 12.1 inch LCD display, a built-in dual axis accelerometer and a digitizer with 255 levels of pressure. The experiment was conducted at a resolution of 1400x1050 pixels. For pen input the participants used a standard Tablet PC pen.

While the Tablet PC allowed us to simulate two different display sizes, it is too heavy (2 kilo) to be held for a longer period with one hand, and thus would have rendered tilt-control unusable. To overcome this problem, we used a metal rack equipped with springs that held the Tablet PC in an upright position and counterbalanced its weight (see Figure 5.12a, b). In this way, the users could rest their non-dominant arm on a table and tilt the device with a minimum of force and arm movement. We believe that the apparatus provided us with a reasonable approximation of tilting a smaller, lightweight device such as a PDA. Nevertheless, the differences in ergonomics have to be taken into account when interpreting the results.

The rack enables a total tilting range of 41 degrees. In the default position (Figure 5.12a), the Tablet PC is fixed at an orientation of 24 degrees (measured from a vertical axis). Since this is not the most convenient angle for reading the display, we hoped that it would motivate the users to tilt the device to an individual orientation right from the start (image c). This was especially important for the tilt interface, since for zooming in and out the users needed to pitch the device in two directions from the current orientation when setting the pen on the display. Tilting the device all the way upwards resulted in a maximum angle of 65 degrees (image d). The metal rack was used for all interaction techniques. To simulate a display bezel we used two differently sized passepartouts cut out of cardboard and attached to the Tablet PC screen (images e, f).

5.3.5   Hypotheses

We defined the following hypotheses to test with our experiment:

1. *The task-completion times for halo-navigation would be equal for the 600x600 pixels and the 300x300 pixels interfaces.*
   Halo-navigation tasks as defined in Chapter 5.3.3 are identical to what has been termed multiscale pointing tasks: the participants have to reach and tap a continuously cued target object located in a ZUI. No semantic information needs to be processed; the users mechanically follow the cues as quickly as possible. The implication of view size on such tasks has been investigated in [100] [99]. The authors found that display miniaturization has a cost in terms of navigation time, but the study also indicated a ceiling effect at a rather low level, i.e. for displays smaller than about 80x60 pixels. This constraint may therefore be more applicable to wrist-watch interfaces, for instance, than to PDAs and smartphones. With regard to the larger view settings tested in our evaluation, we expected that display size would not have an effect on task-completion time for halo-navigation tasks.

2. *The total task-completion time for semantic tasks (task types 2 to 4) would be better for the 600x600 pixels interface compared to the 300x300 pixels interface.*
   In typical multiscale pointing tasks, little space is needed to effectively cue the target object, for instance by using a halo [14] or concentric circles [100]. Given a certain minimum size of the display, the users therefore do not benefit from a larger view. This is different for semantic tasks in which the content of the information space is essential for solving the task. The larger the view, the more context information is displayed, which may reduce unnecessary navigation [203] [43]. Hence we expected that for the semantically more demanding task types the smaller display size would decrease the task-completion time.

3. *The users would be faster using the tilt interface compared to the pen pressure interface.*
   The tilt and pressure interfaces provide equal functionality to the users in the sense that they both allow for concurrent, but independent, zooming and panning. While we are not aware of any previous research comparing the usability of these two input techniques, there has been extensive work on investigating unimanual versus bimanual interface control. Two-handed input has been found beneficial in various scenarios (e.g. positioning and scaling [46], document scrolling [239], and image alignment [148]), but its performance appears to be strongly dependent on the type of task to be performed [135]. Owen et al. [170] recommended that bimanual input should be used for tasks that are visually and conceptually integrated, which is the case for ZUI navigation (see also [127] for zooming and panning as an integral task). In fact, many studies on ZUI interaction have successfully employed bimanual input. For instance, in [101] [100] [99] users controlled zooming by a joystick with their non-dominant hand and panning via a mouse or a stylus on a tablet with their dominant

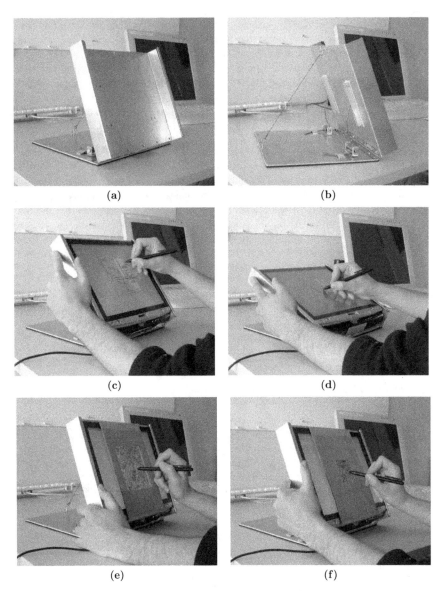

Figure 5.12: Experimental apparatus: (a) the metal rack, (b) two springs are fixed to the back of the rack to counterbalance the weight of the Tablet PC; the string is used to hold the device in an upright position, (c) the rack with the Tablet PC inserted, (d) the user tilts the device upward to the maximum angle, (e) the apparatus with a 600x600 pixels cardboard passepartout attached to the display, (f) the 300x300 pixels passepartout.

hand. Two studies [38] [37] specifically examined the effect that bimanual and parallel input may have on user performance in a ZUI. The results showed that multiscale pointing performance strongly depends on the degree of pan-zoom parallelism, and that a higher degree of parallelism is better supported by two-handed input. Hence we expected the bimanual tilt interface to outperform the unimanual pressure-based interface. Another reason for this hypothesis was our impression that, due to the separate input devices (device tilting and pen position), the tilt interface required less fine-motor skills compared to the integrated pen input.

4. *Both the tilt and pressure interfaces would be faster than the standard interface.*
This hypothesis was again based on the two studies by Bourgeois & Guiard [38] [37], which indicate that users are able to perform zooming and panning in parallel, and that such parallelism improves task-completion times in multiscale pointing tasks. While parallel actions are supported by the tilt and the pressure interface, the standard interface is limited to sequential navigation. However, we were also aware that the users' unfamiliarity with the non-standard interfaces may reduce the performance benefit; for instance, when the users failed to take advantage of a parallel strategy as described in [46].

5. *SDAZ would be faster for halo-navigation compared to the other interfaces.*
As found in previous literature and discussed in Chapter 5.2.1, the binding of zooming and panning can provide an effective solution for basic navigation and browsing tasks [66] [171] [67] [202]. We expected to observe the same effect for our halo-navigation tasks, in which the underlying map information can be ignored by the users.

6. *SDAZ would be slower for semantic tasks (task types 2 to 4) compared to the other interfaces.*
We believed that there is a mismatch between the demands of supporting real-life map-navigation tasks and the interaction provided by SDAZ. Reading cluttered semantic information such as map symbols or small-sized street names in different orientations requires the users to temporarily reduce the pan speed or to bring the movement to a complete halt. However, doing so will cause the SDAZ interface to increase the zoom level, which changes the view and thus requires the users to reorient. Moreover, with semantic zoom [172], some data may only be present at a certain scale level. To read such information, the users must pan back and forth, but with each change in direction the current zoom factor is lost and the users need time to readjust it. Another serious drawback of SDAZ is that when releasing the pointing device the current view state is not locked; instead, the interface falls back to the highest magnification level. This is particularly troublesome when using pen-operated mobile devices since (a) in a mobile context the users may frequently have to interrupt the navigation (e.g. when being spoken to), and (b) having located an area of interest at a lower magnification level, the users may want to view the map clipping without the physical effort and occlusion of constantly pressing the pen on the display. To sum up, SDAZ is a highly unsteady interface for focusing on detail information within a limited navigation radius at a lower magnification level. The enforced need for continuous panning to maintain a constant scale level can

easily lead to time-consuming disorientation [132]. Hence, the feature of independent zooming and panning provided by the other interfaces may be more effective for solving the semantic tasks.

7. *If constrained to use the smaller view of 300x300 pixels, the performance decrease for semantic tasks (task types 2 to 4) would be most distinct for SDAZ compared to the other interfaces.*
In hypothesis 2 we assumed that a smaller screen increases task-completion times for semantic tasks due to insufficient context. Since the lack of context is likely to lead to otherwise unnecessary navigation, we expected that the decrease in performance would be most notable for SDAZ, where each change in pan direction brings the further disadvantage of losing the current zoom level. This would also partly conform to the results of Jones et al. [132] (see Chapter 5.2.1).

8. *The participants would prefer the standard interface and reject the SDAZ interface.*
The standard interface benefits from the users' familiarity with sliders and drag&drop, which we believed would increase user confidence and thus result in a comparatively positive user rating. While SDAZ has also been found easy to learn (e.g. [66] [171]), its potential inadequacy for semantic tasks (see hypothesis 6) would cause a high amount of user frustration, leading to the lowest rating. The tilt and pressure interfaces offer the most flexible navigation features, but require the users to control an additional input dimension by a fairly unusual interaction mechanism. Moreover, in previous research novice users have been repeatedly reported to have difficulties with accurately controlling pen pressure and device tilting. We assume that these results are at least partially due to insufficient training, which, given the limited time frame of an evaluation, can hardly be avoided. In summary, we expected our tilt and pressure interfaces to result in a rather moderate rating.

9. *Across the different task types, the subjective workload would be lower for the standard interface compared to SDAZ.*
In previous research SDAZ has been found to produce less subjective workload than conventional scroll and zoom-pan approaches [66] [202] [67]. However, with respect to the semantic task types tested, we expected that the participants would find the decoupled interaction of the standard interface less demanding than SDAZ. This assumption corresponds to hypothesis 6.

5.3.6 Participants

For the study we selected 32 subjects, 14 male and 18 female. All of them were students or Ph.D. students at the University of Konstanz. Their ages ranged from 20 to 33 years, with 24.47 years as the mean value and a standard deviation of 3.25 years. Their fields of study varied greatly. No participant was a computer science student and they had been students for a mean time of 6.52 semesters. The pre-test questionnaire showed that two of our subjects actually owned a PDA, and 13 more had at least tried one and were therefore familiar with the general pen-interaction concept. All of our users were regular PC and internet users. In order to test familiarity with zoomable user interfaces for maps, we asked for Google earth knowledge. 31 participants were aware of Google earth and

19 had actually tried it once. We also asked participants if they used paper street maps for navigation, which 30 of them affirmed. They also had to rate their competence in dealing with such paper maps on a 5-point scale where 5 was perfect performance and 1 poor performance. The result was a mean of 3.8 and a standard deviation of 0.9. Since we used a map of Munich for our experiment, we also asked our participants about their knowledge of Munich. None of them actually came from Munich and on a 5-point scale (1 = no familiarity at all, 5 perfect familiarity) they rated their familiarity with a mean of 1.59 and a standard deviation of 0.76. Furthermore, no participant rated his familiarity higher than 3. Out of the 32 participants, three had already participated in one of the experiments discussed in Chapter 4. These experiments dealt with zooming a starfield display on a pen-based device.

5.3.7 Experimental Design

We used a 2x4x4 split-plot design, the first being a between-subjects factor and the latter two being within-subjects factors. The between-subjects factor was *view size* (300x300 pixels and 600x600 pixels) resulting in two different groups, each of 16 participants. The within-subjects factors were *interface type* (four different levels) and *task type* (four different levels). For each interface, a different task set was developed to reduce learning effects. We used a latin square design to counterbalance the interface types and the task sets, resulting in four groups (with four subjects each) per interface order and four groups per task-set order. We randomly assigned each participant to one of the resulting 16 groups. The dependent variables were task-completion time (in seconds), interface preference, and subjective workload. The workload was measured with the NASA Task Load Index questionnaire (NASA TLX).

5.3.8 Procedure

The session started with a short written introduction and the pre-test questionnaire. After that, the users were introduced to the pen handling on the TabletPC. During this process, the pen was recalibrated by the participants themselves. Next, the test administrator explained the general procedure and handed out the first interface explanation. The explanation was a written description of the interface functionality. Participants were allowed and encouraged to ask questions. Subsequently, they were given time to try the application with a London Underground map. Each participant had to complete two halo-navigation tasks before advancing to the test interface. When participants showed that they had understood the interface, the Munich map was loaded and each of the eleven tasks was presented to them successively as a printout. The first two tasks were halo-navigation tasks, followed by three follow-route tasks, then three find-route tasks, and finally three find-landmark tasks. Since every task type required a different strategy for each interface type, we excluded the first task of each type from the analysis and marked them as training tasks, without the knowledge of the participants. Participants read all questions aloud and then pressed a start-task button on the lower right of the screen. To complete a task, a marked target had to be tapped (see the task descriptions listed in Chapter 5.3.3). The participants could also cancel a task by pressing a button on the left hand side. Moreover, a time-out routine was defined, which interrupted the task automatically after 5 minutes. Upon completion of a task the screen immediately turned black. After finishing all tasks for the first interface type, the participants had to fill out a paper version of the NASA TLX translated into German, the participants' native language. The questionnaire measured the average workload on six scales, each weighted through a pairwise comparison procedure. Subsequently, the same procedure was repeated in succession for the remaining three interfaces and the corresponding task sets. As the last step, the participants completed a preference questionnaire and were then handed a movie theatre voucher worth EUR 10,-. Experiment sessions lasted about 90 to 120 minutes, and were recorded and video taped for documentation purposes.

5.4 Results

For the analysis of the task-completion times we used mainly RM-ANOVA, a priori contrast analysis, and post-hoc pairwise comparisons, the latter two with Bonferroni adjusted significance levels when needed. For our main 2x4x4 design including two levels for the between-subjects factor view size and four levels each for the within-subjects factors interface type and task type, we could assume sphericity for our within-subjects factor interface type but not for task type, which is why we used the Greenhouse-Geisser degree of freedom adjustment in this case. Throughout the analysis we used a significance level of 5 percent. For four participants we logged a cancellation (3) or a timeout (1) of a task, but each time only a single task within a task type for an interface was affected. Hence, in those cases the generated mean was equal to the task-completion time of the corresponding second task, which was properly completed.

5.4.1 H1: Influence of different view sizes for halo-navigation tasks

Based on prior research, our first hypothesis suggested that display size would not affect the performance for halo-navigation tasks. Our results show that it took our participants about 92.6 seconds on average to complete the halo-navigation tasks on the large display, but only 84.25 seconds on average on the small display (standard error: 3.14 seconds). However, an RM-ANOVA analyzing the main effect of the between-subjects factor view size shows that this difference is not significant on the 5 percent significance level ($F(1, 30) = 3.532, p = 0.07$). While this result seems at first glance to agree with previous research [100] [99], it must be noted that, due to the relatively low observed power of 0.444 (resulting in a type 2 error of 56.6 %), the test cannot provide clear empirical evidence that halo-navigation is not affected by view size.

5.4.2 H2: Influence of different view sizes for semantic tasks

In the second hypothesis we assumed that for semantic tasks (task types 2 to 4), task-completion times would be faster for the 600x600 pixels view in comparison to the 300x300 pixels view. To analyze the main effect for our between-subjects factor, we used a 2x4x3 design, excluding the halo-navigation tasks. The results show that there is indeed a difference between the large and small view sizes, resulting in an average task-completion time of 34.25 seconds for the 600x600 pixels view compared to 42.35 seconds for the 300x300 pixels view (standard error: 2.07). Furthermore, this difference is significant, the significance being backed up by a relatively large effect size ($F(1,30) = 7.662, p = 0.01, hp^2 = 0.203$). Hence, we can accept the experimental hypothesis and reject the null hypothesis. An in-depth analysis of the pairwise comparisons reveals that task-completion times for task types 2 and 3 differ significantly, but not for task type 4 (one-sided, Bonferroni adjusted t-tests, see Table 5.1 and Figure 5.13).

	600x600 pixels	300x300 pixels	std. error	sig
task type 2	25.49 sec	33.05 sec	2.09 sec	0.008
task type 3	40.71 sec	49.26 sec	2.96 sec	0.025
task type 4	36.54 sec	44.73 sec	3.73 sec	0.0655

Table 5.1: Influence of the two view sizes for semantic tasks.

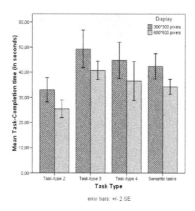

Figure 5.13: The difference in task-completion time between the two view sizes is significant for the task types 2 and 3 for semantic tasks.

5.4.3 H3: Comparing the performance of the tilt interface and the pressure interface

Our third hypothesis stated that users would be faster using the tilt interface compared to the pressure interface. However, the times logged do not support this assumption. It took the participants about 46.33 seconds on average to complete the tasks with the pressure interface (standard error: 2.42 seconds) and 45.90 seconds on average with the tilt interface (standard error: 1.73 seconds). This difference is non-significant (analyzing simple contrasts: $F(1,30) = 0.019, p = 0.891$). Also, further in-depth pairwise comparisons do not show any significant effect for one of our four task types. Therefore we have to reject the hypothesis and confirm the null hypothesis for the time being.

With regard to navigation behavior, we logged the time the users spent for panning and zooming in parallel while using these two interfaces. The analysis reveals that the participants spent more time panning and zooming in parallel while using the pressure interface

(3.58 seconds on average per task, standard error: 0.232 seconds) than while using the tilt interface (2.92 seconds on average per task, standard error: 0.26 seconds). This difference is significantly in favor of the pressure interface ($F(1, 30) = 8.587, p = 0.006, hp^2 = 0.223$) and indicates that, in contrast to our expectations, the integrated pen input seems to have encouraged parallel zooming and panning more than the bimanual approach of the tilt interface. However, considering the mean task-completion times of about 46 seconds, our participants relied strongly on separate zooming and panning regardless of which of the two interfaces they used.

5.4.4 H4: Comparing the performance of tilt and pressure with the standard interface

The fourth hypothesis was built upon the assumption that performing zooming and panning in parallel would improve task-completion time [38] [37]. Therefore the users should have been faster with the tilt and the pressure interfaces compared to the standard interface, which does not offer parallel movement. Since the previous analysis already indicated that our participants made only very limited use of concurrent zooming and panning, it is not surprising that this hypothesis does not hold. Moreover, our analysis shows that both the pressure and the tilt interfaces are slower than the standard interface (46.33 seconds for pressure and 45.90 seconds for the tilt interface compared to 43.15 seconds and a standard error of 1.72 seconds for the standard interface). A contrast analysis (simple contrasts) shows that this difference is not significant (standard vs. pressure: $F(1, 30) = 1.714, p = 0.4$, standard vs. tilt: $F(1, 30) = 1.22, p = 0.556$, Bonferroni adjusted). Investigating a possible influence of the view size, it seems that the difference in task-completion time results from the small view size (see Table 5.2 and Figure 5.14).

	standard	pressure	tilt
600x600 pixels	43.16 sec	41.67 sec	42.93 sec
300x300 pixels	43.15 sec	50.99 sec	48.87 sec

Table 5.2: The mean task-completion times for the tilt, pressure, and standard interfaces with respect to view size.

However, a contrast analysis does not show a significant main interaction effect for interface x view size (standard vs. pressure: $F(1, 30) = 3.68, p = 0.128$; standard vs. tilt: $F(1, 30) = 1.43, p = 0.484$, Bonferroni adjusted). Nevertheless, we performed single sided pairwise comparisons comparing the standard interface with the pressure and the tilt interfaces for the small view size. The results are significant only for the standard interface compared to the pressure interface (standard vs. pen-pressure: $p = 0.03$; standard vs. tilt: $p = 0.114$; Bonferroni adjusted). Furthermore, the results show that the standard interface does not benefit at all from the larger view size and even performs slightly worse than the other two interfaces for the 600x600 pixels view, though this difference is not significant.

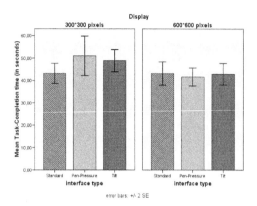

Figure 5.14: Unlike the pressure and the tilt interfaces, the standard interface does not benefit from the larger view size of 600x600 pixels.

5.4.5 H5: Comparing the SDAZ interface to the three other interfaces for halo-navigation

In hypothesis 5 we assumed that the SDAZ interface would perform significantly better than the other three interfaces for halo-navigation tasks. The mean task-completion times for this task type are listed in Table 5.3 and displayed in Figure 5.15. An RM-ANOVA reveals that the four interface types differ significantly ($(F3, 90) = 12.764, p = 0.000, hp^2 = 0.198$). Further in-depth single-sided pairwise comparisons for the SDAZ interface show that the observed difference is significant compared to the pressure and the tilt interfaces (in each case $p = 0.000$), but not to the standard interface, although it is close to being significant ($p = 0.55$, Bonferroni adjusted alpha level).

	mean time	std. error
SDAZ	76.34 sec	3.12 sec
standard	83.9 sec	2.45 sec
pressure	94.8 sec	3.31 sec
tilt	98.66 sec	4.18 sec

Table 5.3: The mean task-completion times for halo-navigation tasks.

5.4.6 H6: Comparing the SDAZ interface to the three other interfaces for semantic tasks

We predicted that the SDAZ interface would produce longer task-completion times for semantic tasks compared to the other three interfaces. However, our results indicate that, despite the SDAZ interface being the slowest, this hypothesis does not hold. The task-completion times using the different interfaces for the task types 2 to 4 are listed in Table 5.4 and displayed in Figure 5.16. A contrast analysis comparing the SDAZ

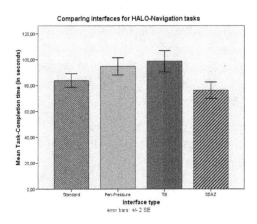

Figure 5.15: SDAZ is significantly faster for halo-navigation compared to the pressure and the tilt interfaces.

mean task-completion time with the three other interfaces shows that the difference is not significant (SDAZ vs. standard: $F(1, 30) = 3.26, p = 0.83$; SDAZ vs. pressure: $F(1, 30) = 1.58, p = 0.218$; SDAZ vs. tilt: $F(1, 30) = 1.84, p = 0.185$)).

	mean time	std. error
SDAZ	41.47 sec	2.84 sec
standard	36.36 sec	1.84 sec
tilt	37.11 sec	1.78 sec
pressure	38.26 sec	2.53 sec

Table 5.4: The mean task-completion times for the task types 2 to 4.

5.4.7 H7: Influence of view size on solving the semantic tasks with the SDAZ interface in comparison to the other interfaces

Hypothesis 7 stated that the SDAZ interface performance would decrease significantly more than that of the other three interfaces when using the small 300x300 pixels view size for tasks types 2 to 4. To analyze this hypothesis, we first had to create a new variable reflecting the difference between the mean task-completion time and the mean for the corresponding view size. We then performed an RM-ANOVA with this variable as the within-subjects factor (and no between-subjects factor, since the view size was already represented in this variable). An RM-ANOVA shows that there is no significant main effect for the four different interfaces ($F(3, 93) = 1.255, p = 0.294$). Contrast analysis furthermore reveals that the SDAZ interface is not influenced more than any of the other interfaces (SDAZ vs. standard: $F(1, 31) = 2.272, p = 0.142$; SDAZ vs. pressure: $F(1, 31) = 0.125, p = 0.726$; SDAZ vs. tilt: $F(1, 31) = 0.193, p = 0.663$). Table 5.5

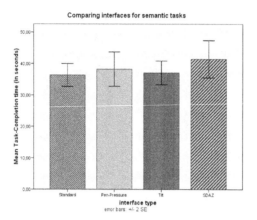

Figure 5.16: The difference in performance between the SDAZ interface and the other experimental interfaces for semantic tasks is non-significant.

and Figure 5.17 display the differences from the mean of the two view sizes. The high error values give further support for the contrast analysis being non-significant. We must therefore reject the hypothesis.

	diff. from the mean	std. error
SDAZ	5.24 sec	2.79 sec
standard	0.98 sec	1.85 sec
pressure	6.13 sec	2.49 sec
tilt	3.85 sec	1.76 sec

Table 5.5: The differences from the mean of the two view sizes for semantic tasks (higher values indicate that the interface was more influenced by the different view sizes).

5.4.8   H8: Interface Preferences

Regarding the users' preferences, we assumed that users would prefer the standard interface because of their familiarity with it and reject the SDAZ interface because of its potential limitations for semantic tasks. Our participants ranked the four interfaces after using them from 1 (best) to 4 (worst). Across the two view sizes, the frequencies for being voted into first place by the 32 participants were: standard: 13, pressure: 9, tilt: 9, and SDAZ: 1. Standard, pressure, and tilt received about the same number of second- and third-place votes, but the latter two were ranked more often in the last place than the standard interface (four times for the pressure interface and five times for the tilt interface). Analyzing the results for the two view sizes separately gives the distribution of first-place votes as listed in Table 5.6. These votes give the impression that, while for the 600x600 pixels view the participants slightly preferred the novel pressure and tilt techniques even

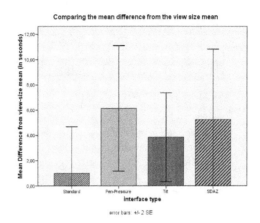

Figure 5.17: For semantic tasks the SDAZ interface is not influenced more than the other experimental interfaces by the different view sizes.

more than the highly familiar standard interface, the latter interface proved to be more resilient to the constraints of a smaller view size. As assumed, the SDAZ interface was strongly rejected.

	standard	pressure	tilt	SDAZ
600x600 pixels	4 votes	5 votes	6 votes	1 votes
300x300 pixels	9 votes	4 votes	3 votes	0 vote

Table 5.6: First-place votes out of 16 votes for each view regarding interface preference.

We also analyzed these results using an RM-ANOVA, which shows a significant main effect for the mean ranks for the four interfaces ($F(3, 90) = 14.154, p = 0.000, hp^2 = 0.269$). The mean ranks are listed in Table 5.7. A contrast analysis indicates that SDAZ was ranked significantly lower compared to the other three interfaces (SDAZ vs. standard: $F(1, 30) = 44.190, p = 0.000, hp^2 = 0.596$; SDAZ vs. pressure: $F(1, 30) = 18.868, p = 0.000, hp^2 = 0.386$; SDAZ vs. tilt: $F(1, 30) = 13.652, p = 0.003, hp^2 = 0.313$; Bonferroni adjusted). Pairwise comparisons did not reveal any further significant differences between the three other interfaces. Regarding the influence of the view size on preference, we did not find a significant difference between the pressure, the tilt, and the standard interface for either the 300x300 view or the 600x600 view.

5.4.9 H9: Subjective Workload

The last hypothesis was that, in contrast to previous research, the standard interface would lead to less subjective workload than SDAZ. The total mean scores for the four interfaces as measured by the TLX questionnaire are shown in Table 5.8. An RM-ANOVA shows a significant main effect for interface type ($F(3, 90) = 7.456, p = 0.000, hp^2 = 0.199$)

	mean rank	std. error
SDAZ	3.469	0.16
standard	1.938	0.158
pressure	2.281	0.183
tilt	2.344	0.191

Table 5.7: Mean ranks for interface preference votes.

and a significant interaction effect for interface type x view size $(F(3, 90) = 3.897, p = 0.011, hp^2 = 0.115)$. We therefore analyzed the simple effects through pairwise comparisons. The results indicate that the standard interface caused significantly lower workload than each of the other three interfaces (pressure: $p = 0.009$, tilt: $p = 0.008$, and SDAZ: $p = 0.001$). The differences between the other interfaces are not significant. Moreover, analyzing the simple interaction effects, we found that the differences only occur for the 300x300 pixels view size (standard: 31.40, pressure: 48.96, tilt: 45.69, SDAZ: 60.90). Again, only the differences compared to the standard interface are significant. In contrast, the 600x600 pixels view resulted in more or less equal workloads for all four interfaces (standard: 40.19 points, pressure: 44.10 points, tilt: 44.67 points, SDAZ: 44.96 points).

	workload score	std. error
SDAZ	52.93	3.79
standard	35.79	2.20
pressure	46.53	3.67
tilt	45.18	2.93

Table 5.8: Subjective workload scores.

While the TLX results seem to support the experimental hypothesis, an unexpected result was that the workload for the standard interface increased when using the larger view. In contrast, the other three interfaces seem to have benefited from the large display size in terms of a reduced workload. In our opinion, this effect borders on the inexplicable, since one must assume that a larger view size would be more convenient to work with, regardless of the interaction technique used. We are therefore rather sceptical of the validity of the TLX results. One aspect that further supports this doubt is the observation that many participants felt bothered by the frequent questionnaires and particularly so by the weighting procedure. In some cases this may have resulted in more or less random scoring.

5.4.10   Further Analysis

We also analyzed the influence of additional variables such as gender or PDA experience. Our 14 male participants needed on average 41.05 seconds (standard error: 1.85 seconds) while our female participants needed 47.57 seconds (standard error 1.74 seconds) to complete a task. This difference is significant $(F(1, 25) = 10.581, p = 0.017, hp^2 = 0.208)$. The same result can be observed when analyzing the effect of PDA experience. 15 participants who had used a PDA at least once needed 41.53 seconds (standard error 1.87

seconds) compared to 49.11 seconds (standard error 1.63 seconds) for those participants who had never used a PDA before. This difference is significant ($F(1,25) = 9.358, p = 0.005, hp^2 = 0.272$). However, 10 out of the 15 participants who were familiar with a PDA were male, which results in a significant correlation (Pearson's $r = 0.434, p = 0.013$) So one might suggest that only one aspect - either gender, or PDA experience - influences the task-completion time.

The frequency of Google Earth usage also had a significant impact on task-completion time. 13 participants had never used it and 19 had used it at least once. Comparing the latter two groups, an RM-ANOVA indicated that it took the group who had never used it 50.4 seconds (standard error 2.17 seconds) compared to only 42.01 seconds (standard error 1.73 seconds) for the other group. This difference is significant ($F(1,30) = 9.792, p = 0.004, hp^2 = 0.246$). We again analyzed the results for possible correlations. Pearson's r did not turn out to be significant for sex and Google usage ($r = 0.322, p = 0.077$), but it did so for PDA usage and Google usage ($r = 0.504, p = 0.004$). It seems, therefore, that these three variables are not independent of each other, although our analysis cannot reveal the exact dependencies.

Finally, the differences in Munich knowledge and subjective streetmap skills (both measured on a 5-point scale in the pre-test questionnaire) did not seem to have any effect.

5.5 Interpretation

The experiment conducted led to a variety of interesting results. First, we found that the performance for tasks that require the users to read semantic map information was significantly decreased by a smaller view size of a 300x300 pixels view compared to a 600x600 pixels view. The task types responsible for this effect were follow-route and find-route, for which context information seems to be most important. The find-location tasks, which focused on exploration, were less affected by the change of the view size. Previous research indicates that display miniaturization also increases navigation time for multiscale pointing tasks (similar to halo-navigation), but with the performance loss taking effect at a much lower view size, i.e. for displays smaller than about 80x60 pixels [100] [99].

The results for the SDAZ interface were mixed. As expected, for simple halo-navigation tasks, automatic zooming provided a better performance than the other interfaces, with significant differences to the pressure and the tilt interfaces. This result partly corresponds to previous research. In terms of task-completion times, SDAZ also provided a reasonable solution for solving more realistic map navigation tasks, which required the users to constantly read and process semantic information. Though SDAZ was slower than the other interfaces, the differences were non-significant. However, the predicted inappropriateness of SDAZ for such tasks was nevertheless indicated by the preference ratings and user comments. The participants clearly rejected automatic zooming compared to the other interfaces. Frequent comments were that it was difficult to solve tasks using SDAZ because of the coupled zooming and panning, which for the semantic task types was found tedious, imprecise and hard to control. Positive comments were that SDAZ was found to be particularly effective for halo-navigation, which corresponds to the performance results regarding that task type.

We did not find evidence that SDAZ may be less effective than other interfaces for a smaller view size. The moderate results of SDAZ on a simulated PDA screen as reported by Jones et al. [132] may be due more to implementation issues. As has already been suggested by Cockburn & Savage [66], the usability of SDAZ depends strongly on the smoothness of zooming and panning, which may not have been supported by the Java prototype used in [132].

Regarding the overall handling of SDAZ for map navigation, we believe the interaction may be improved by introducing a mechanism that allows the users to view a scaled sub-set of the map without movement. For instance, the view could freeze when the users lift the pen from the display, with the last position of the pen being marked by an icon. If the users want to automatically zoom back in they just tap anywhere on the display (this could also be implemented as point-directed zooming). If they want to continue the previous zoom and pan movement, they tap and drag the icon. While this strategy means a more complex interaction, it may result in a more stable interface.

Both the pressure and the tilt interfaces provided the users with concurrent but separate control of zooming and panning. During the experiment, however, the users hardly ever took advantage of parallel movement, which corresponds to a similar observation in [46]. It seems that, in the test scenario, the users felt more comfortable solving the tasks with the easier-to-control discrete zoom and pan operations. We assume that more extensive training would change the navigation behavior, as was also the case, for instance, with our expert users, i.e. the colleagues who accompanied the development of the interaction techniques over weeks and tested them frequently. With the navigation strategy used by the participants, both interfaces resulted in comparable task-completion times across task types. When compared to the standard interface, the performance was significantly decreased when using the small view, but on the larger view the mean task-completion times were fairly equal for the three interfaces.

The preference ratings indicate that the participants liked the pressure and tilt control almost as much as the standard interface. For the larger view of 600x600 pixels, the tilt interface was actually the most preferred technique. The user comments suggest that tilting was fun, as well as fast and easy to use, while the pressure interface was mostly appreciated for its intuitiveness and the low effort it required.

Considering the users' high familiarity with the standard interface, both the preference and the performance results for the novel pressure and tilt techniques are highly encouraging. Moreover, there seems to be room to further improve the usability of these approaches. The more critical user comments that were collected indicate strong individual differences in how well participants coped with each of the two interfaces. While some users explicitly stated that the pressure-based zoom was difficult to control, many users were observed to frequently trigger zoom-in or zoom-out operations by accident. In a real-life application, this problem may be reduced by individual calibration of the pressure threshold settings.

As expected, the tilt-controlled interface seemed to require less fine-motor skills, but the mapping of the tilt movement to the zoom direction was found less intuitive compared to the pressure interface. Some participants were observed to frequently tilt the device in the wrong direction. One solution for this issue may be to extend the visual feedback to emphasize more clearly the effect a certain tilt movement will have. Overall, we think that the results of the tilt interface also provide a positive feedback for the apparatus setup. In the future we would like to verify the findings for the tilt interface with a PDA device.

An issue we observed for both the pressure and the tilt interfaces was that some participants initially became confused by the fact that the pen did not serve as a device for point-directed zooming. For instance, in a situation in which the target object is already visible in the view, the users seemed to assume that by tapping the target, they would automatically zoom in on it. However, as previously described pen strokes are interpreted as relative navigation commands for steering the view. This mismatch of navigation style and user expectation may be worth investigating in further research.

The standard interface proved to give a reliably high performance across the different task types compared to the other three interfaces. This is despite the accumulated travel time enforced by the need to frequently move the pen back and forth between the zoom slider and the focus area. Moreover, the separation of zooming and panning was not perceived as a limitation by many participants, but as a feature to enable more accurate view movement. Another interesting property of the standard interface is that the preference and performance values turned out to be particularly good for the small view size of 300x300 pixels. This may indicate that, on a smaller screen such as featured by mobile devices, precise control becomes an increasingly important usability factor. Hence, another issue for further research may be the equipping of the pressure and the tilt interfaces with more concise navigation elements that better match the users' needs on PDA-like screens. One method, for instance, may be to employ drag&drop panning instead of the quicker, but harder to control, rate-based approach.

Chapter 6

Conclusion

This work investigated the potential of zoomable user interfaces to ease access to large information spaces on mobile devices. Based on a review of presentation techniques and the scientific field of Information Visualization, we provided an extensive overview of state-of-the-art experimental and commercial user interfaces targeting PDAs and smartphones. The review also served as the basis for our research projects, in which we implemented various prototype applications. The prototypes were tested in four usability evaluations with a total of 86 participants. As test devices, we used PDAs, a Wacom display, and a Tablet PC enhanced by a custom metal rack.

The first part of our research focused on mobile starfield displays, which are search interfaces encoding abstract information as a zoomable scatterplot visualization. We enhanced the concept with smooth semantic zooming to provide a fluent and intuitive transition from overview to detail information in a movie database. Other features proposed were the presentation of multiple-data-points as nested information objects, and the use of the same scatterplot for visualizing user-generated information spaces such as a query history and a bookmark selection. The positive feedback we gained in an informal user study motivated us to pursue the interface strategy. However, the results also indicated the need for improvement with regard to interaction design and orientation support.

To investigate and reduce orientation drawbacks in mobile ZUIs, we developed a starfield display featuring an additional overview window. Inside the window a field-of-view box continuously highlighted the position and scale of the detail view. When evaluating the usability of the interface in a comparative user study, we found that, while the overview reduced the need for navigation, the participants nevertheless solved search tasks significantly faster using a detail-only starfield. We concluded that this result was due to the increased interface complexity and the extra time needed for visual switching between the two views. In contrast to similar studies for desktop applications, there was no significant difference in user preference between the interfaces. Individual differences in spatial ability as measured by a psychometric test did not have a significant effect on task-completion times, although results suggest that participants with higher spatial ability were slowed down by the overview more than low spatial-ability users were.

In another attempt to support user orientation, we developed a starfield display with a rectangular fisheye view. The latter integrated both detail and context information into a single view by employing distortion. Thus the users were not required to switch between separate views to preserve their orientation. We conducted another user study, in which the participants had to solve search tasks on a book database using the fisheye and an improved version of the smooth zooming starfield. While the results showed no significant difference in task-completion times, a clear majority of the users preferred the fisheye view to the zoom interaction. In addition, other dependent variables such as user satisfaction and subjective rating of orientation and navigation support revealed a preference for the fisheye distortion. These findings partly contradict previous research, in which fisheyes have often been found to decrease user satisfaction compared to undistorted interfaces. We assumed that this discrepancy is due to rectangular distortion integrating well with the abstract nature of the scatterplot visualization. The user perception of the fisheye may be different for domains such as maps, in which a higher degree of fidelity to the standard layout is essential

Overall, we found that scatterplot displays enhanced with semantic zooming and distortion capabilities reduced the detail-context tension when displaying information spaces larger than the screen. This concept may be particularly interesting for data-retrieval interfaces on next-generation PDAs and smartphones, which will have matured from disconnected personal organizers to powerful mobile information systems.

The second part of this work presented research on advanced interaction techniques for navigating map-based ZUIs on pen-operated devices. We investigated the performance of four interfaces for navigation control:

- Standard approach: the users are limited to sequential interaction.

- Speed-dependent automatic zooming (SDAZ): zooming and rate-based panning are controlled concurrently via pen displacement.

- Pressure: rate-based panning is mapped to the pen position, while zooming is controlled by the pen pressure.

- Tilt: rate-based panning is mapped to the pen position, while the users can zoom in and out by tilting the device with their non-dominant hand.

Due to the additional input dimensions, the two latter approaches allow for concurrent, but separate, control of both zooming and panning. An important difference, however, is that the pressure interface is based on unimanual interaction, while the tilt interface is controlled bimanually.

We compared the four techniques in a usability study with 32 participants. Apart from analyzing the performance for solving tasks of varying complexity, we were also interested in how two different view sizes (600x600 pixels and 300x300 pixels) would affect the usability of each interface. In contrast to our expectations, we found that SDAZ not only performed well for simple speed tasks, but - given more realistic navigation tasks - also led to completion times that were not significantly slower than the ones measured for the other interfaces. This is a surprising result, since the coupled interaction of SDAZ suffers from severe navigation limitations (e.g. the users cannot zoom out without panning the view). However, the shortcomings of this approach were still indicated by the interface preference votes and the user comments we collected. SDAZ was clearly rejected by the participants and the majority found the coupled zooming and panning difficult and irksome to control.

The novel pressure and tilting techniques were much liked by the participants, especially when considering their unfamiliarity with these interaction approaches. As it turned out, however, the participants took hardly any advantage of the ability to control zooming and panning in parallel. Instead, they performed discrete navigation; for the larger view, this resulted in task-completion times comparable to those for the standard interface. For the smaller 300x300 pixels view, the standard interface was actually significantly faster than the two novel techniques. This ratio is also reflected in the preference votes. While for the larger 600x600 pixels view the tilt interface was the most popular, the standard interface was rated highest for the 300x300 pixels view. We concluded that precise control may become an increasingly important usability factor for progressively smaller displays. Accordingly, designers should take this finding into account when developing interfaces for small-sized mobile devices.

Appendix A

Experiment 1

The test started with a think-aloud session, in which the users were asked to try out the interface on their own and then to perform a search for the term "apoc" (query retrieved the movie "Apocalypse Now"). The tasks have been translated from German, the participants' native language.

Tasks

1. Start a new query for the keyword "Maria". How many movies are retrieved? What is the title of the oldest movie from the result set and what is the year of the movie's production? Which movie has the highest popularity rating?

2. Start a new query for the keyword "almo". Which movie from 2000 is listed in the section Theatre? What does the poster of the movie Kika show?

3. Start a new query for the keyword "John". How many movies are retrieved? Which section contains more movies, Theatre or American Studies?

4. Which of the movies you bookmarked has the highest lending frequency? What is the movie's lending rate?

5. Which of the queries stored in the query history returned the largest result set?

Appendix B

Tasks Experiment 2

The notation for the different task types is: *(a)* visual scan, *(b)* information access, *(c)* comparison of information objects. The tasks have been translated from German, the participants' native language.

Task Set 1

1. Which movie has the worst popularity rating? *(a)*

2. Which movie from 1997 has a popularity rating of 3.6? *(b)*

3. Which movie, produced in 1985 or 1984 and with a popularity rating of 6.2, has several writers? *(c)*

4. Who is the director of the movie having a popularity rating of 4.4? *(b)*

5. How many movies produced in 1990 have a popularity rating smaller or equal to 7? *(a)*

6. Compare the oldest and most recent movie having a popularity rating of 5.2. Which of these movies is longer? *(c)*

7. How many movies from 2003 featured the actress Drew Barrymore? *(c)*

8. Compare the amount of movies which have a popularity rating smaller or equal to 4 with the amount of movies having a popularity rating greater or equal to 7. Which movies are more? *(a)*

9. Who is the director of the only movie produced in 1986? *(b)*

10. How many movies from 1997 featured the actress Uma Thurman? *(b)*

11. What is the title of the movie whose poster shows a black hand? The movie was produced after 1990 and has a rating between 5 and 7. *(c)*

12. How many posters of movies having a popularity rating of smaller or equal to 4 show persons? *(a)*

Task Set 2

1. What is the title of the oldest movie? *(a)*

2. Which movie from 1984 has a popularity rating of 7.2? *(b)*

3. Which of the two movies from 1990 having a rating of 6.3 and 6 is longer? *(c)*

4. How long is the movie having a popularity rating of 8.1? *(b)*

5. How many movies produced after 1985 have a popularity rating equal to 5? *(a)*

6. Compare the movies with the greatest and smallest rating from the year 2000. Which of these movies has more writers? *(c)*

7. Which movie has a rating of greater or equal to 8 and featured the actor Kenneth Branagh. *(c)*

8. Does the collection hold more movies from the sixties or the nineties? *(a)*

9. What is the language of the only movie having a popularity rating of 5.4? *(b)*

10. Which actor played the main character in two movies from 1990? *(b)*

11. Which movie has a poster showing a drawing? The movie was produced after 1994 and has a popularity rating greater to 6,8. *(c)*

12. Which movie with a popularity rating of smaller than 5 has a poster showing a moon? *(a)*

Appendix C

Tasks Experiment 3

The notation for the different task types is: *(a)* visual scan, *(b)* information access, *(c)* comparison of information objects. The questions have been translated from German, the participants' native language. The first four questions were used as training questions.

Task Set 1

1. Does the collection contain more paperbacks or hardcover books? *(a)*

2. Which book from the fifties has an unusually high price? *(b)*

3. In October 2002 three books were published at a price of about 4 EUR. Which of these books is currently out of stock? *(c)*

4. How many books with a leather-binding does the collection contain? Please name the authors of these books. *(a)*

5. How many books have been published since the year 2000 at a price of 30 EUR ? *(a)*

6. Name the author of the most expensive book from 2005. *(b)*

7. From August 2001 until November 2001 four books were published subsequently at a price of 8.52 EUR. Which of these books has the most pages? *(c)*

8. In January 2005 a book by John Grisham was published, which costs between 3 and 4 EUR. Name the book's title - is it in stock (ships in 24 hours)? *(b)*

9. You are looking for books costing 10 EUR, which were published in 2005. Which of the books has the best sales rank? *(c)*

10. How many books from October 2001 cost between 4 and 5 EUR? *(a)*

11. You are now looking for books which offer a discount of at least 60%. From these books choose the one which costs more than 10 EUR and has the most recent date of publication. Name the title of this book. *(b)*

12. In the first quarter of 1998 two books were published at a price of 6 EUR each. Name the author of the book with the most pages. *(c)*

13. Who wrote the book which was published in October 2005 at a price of 6.92 EUR? *(b)*

14. Look for books which have been published in April 1987 and cost between 3 and 4 EUR. Who wrote the book published by Fawcett? *(c)*

Task Set 2

1. Does the collection contain more books which are currently out of stock, or "special orders"? *(a)*

2. Have a look at the books, which are marked as "not released / not published" and cost less than 10 EUR. Which of these books stands out for what reason? *(b)*

3. Have a look at the books from the nineties which cost exactly one Cent. Which book by Shakespeare is included in this subset? *(c)*

4. How many books have been published since the year 2000 at a price of 20 EUR? *(a)*

5. Count the books which have been published in October 2002 and cost between 9 and 10 EUR. *(a)*

6. Which book has been published in April 2003 and costs 4.90 EUR? *(b)*

7. Which of the books from 1999 costing 3.99 EUR offers the most discount? *(c)*

8. Who published the book "Smillas Sense of Snow" in 1995? The book costs 6 EUR. *(b)*

9. Have a look at the books from 1999, which cost 7 EUR. Please name the author of the book offering the smallest discount. *(c)*

10. How many books have been published after 1995 at a price between 8 and 9 EUR? *(a)*

11. Define a filter such that paperbacks which are out of stock are removed from the scatterplot display. Which of the remaining books is the most expensive one and how much does it cost? *(b)*

12. Who wrote the book from 2004, which cost 7 EUR and has the most pages? *(c)*

13. Have a look at the books from the fifties, which offer a discount of at least 40%. Which of these books has the earliest year of production and who wrote it? *(b)*

14. Who wrote the book from 2003 which costs between 9 and 10 EUR and was published by Bantam? *(c)*

Appendix D

Tasks Experiment 4

Please note that due to copyright constraints we are not able to reproduce the map clippings used for the Find-landmark tasks. The questions have been translated from German, the participants' native language.

Task Set 1

Follow-Route Tasks

1. Follow the U1 from the main station (start position) to the Olympia Einkaufszentrum (target position). The Einkaufszentrum is situated north-west.

2. Follow the U1 from the main station (start position) to the Mangfallplatz (target position). The Mangfallplatz is situated southward.

3. Follow the U2 from the main station (start position) to Feldmoching (target position). Feldmoching is situated northward.

Find-Route Tasks

1. Find a route from the A8 to the A96.

2. Find a route from the A8 to the A9.

3. Find a route from the main station to the Olympiaturm.

Task Set 2

Follow-Route Tasks

1. Follow the U2 from the Sendlinger Tor (start position) to Moosfeld (target position). Sendlinger Tor is situated eastward.

2. Follow the U3 from Odeonsplatz (start position) to Olympiazentrum (target position). Olympiazentrum is situated northward.

3. Follow the U3 from Odeonsplatz (start position) to Baxler Strasse (target position). Baxler Strasse is situated south-west.

Find-Route Tasks

1. Find a route from the A94 to A96.

2. Find a route from the A94 to A9.

3. Find a route from Zamilapark to Ostpark.

Task Set 3

Follow-Route Tasks

1. Follow the U4 from Karlsplatz (start position) to Westendstrasse (target position). Westendstrasse is situated westward.

2. Follow the U4 from Karlsplatz (start position) to Arabella Park (target position). Arabella Park is situated northward.

3. Follow the U6 from Sendlinger Tor (start position) to Fröttmaning (target position). Fröttmaning is situated northward.

Find-Route Tasks

1. Find a route from the A9 to A96.

2. Find a route from the A94 to A995.

3. Find a route from Cosimapark to Ostfriedhof.

Task Set 4

Follow-Route Tasks

1. Follow the U5 from Odeonsplatz (start position) to Laimer Platz (target position). Laimer Platz is situated westward

2. Follow the U5 from Odeonsplatz (start position) to Neuperlach-Süd (target position). Neuperlach-Süd is situated south-east.

3. Follow the U6 from Sendlinger Tor (start position) to Holzapfelkreutz (target position). Holzapfelkreutz is situated south-westward.

Find-Route Tasks

1. Follow the route from the A995 to the A9.

2. Follow the route from the A95 to the A94.

3. Follow the route from Theodor-Heuss-Platz to Ostbahnhof.

Bibliography

[1] Anand Agarawala and Ravin Balakrishnan. Keepin' it real: pushing the desktop metaphor with physics, piles and the pen. In *CHI '06: Proceedings of the SIGCHI conference on Human Factors in computing systems*, pages 1283–1292, New York, NY, USA, 2006. ACM Press.

[2] Christopher Ahlberg. Spotfire: an information exploration environment. *SIGMOD Rec.*, 25(4):25–29, 1996.

[3] Christopher Ahlberg and Ben Shneiderman. The alphaslider: a compact and rapid selector. In *CHI '94: Proceedings of the SIGCHI conference on Human factors in computing systems*, pages 365–371, New York, NY, USA, 1994. ACM Press.

[4] Christopher Ahlberg and Ben Shneiderman. Visual information seeking: tight coupling of dynamic query filters with starfield displays. In *CHI '94: Proceedings of the SIGCHI conference on Human factors in computing systems*, pages 313–317, New York, NY, USA, 1994. ACM Press.

[5] Christopher Ahlberg and Ben Shneiderman. Visual information seeking using the filmfinder. In *CHI '94: Conference companion on Human factors in computing systems*, pages 433–434, New York, NY, USA, 1994. ACM Press.

[6] Christopher Ahlberg, Christopher Williamson, and Ben Shneiderman. Dynamic queries for information exploration: an implementation and evaluation. In *CHI '92: Proceedings of the SIGCHI conference on Human factors in computing systems*, pages 619–626, New York, NY, USA, 1992. ACM Press.

[7] Bryce Allen. Information space representation in interactive systems: relationship to spatial abilities. In *DL '98: Proceedings of the third ACM conference on Digital libraries*, pages 1–10, New York, NY, USA, 1998. ACM Press.

[8] Caroline Appert and Jean-Daniel Fekete. Orthozoom scroller: 1d multi-scale navigation. In *CHI '06: Proceedings of the SIGCHI conference on Human Factors in computing systems*, pages 21–30, New York, NY, USA, 2006. ACM Press.

[9] Michelle Q. Wang Baldonado, Allison Woodruff, and Allan Kuchinsky. Guidelines for using multiple views in information visualization. In *AVI '00: Proceedings of the working conference on Advanced visual interfaces*, pages 110–119, New York, NY, USA, 2000. ACM Press.

[10] Joel F. Bartlett. Rock 'n' scroll is here to stay. *IEEE Comput. Graph. Appl.*, 20(3):40–45, 2000.

[11] Patrick Baudisch, Nathaniel Good, and Paul Stewart. Focus plus context screens: combining display technology with visualization techniques. In *UIST '01: Proceedings of the 14th annual ACM symposium on User interface software and technology*, pages 31–40, New York, NY, USA, 2001. ACM Press.

[12] Patrick Baudisch and Carl Gutwin. Multiblending: displaying overlapping windows simultaneously without the drawbacks of alpha blending. In *CHI '04: Proceedings of the SIGCHI conference on Human factors in computing systems*, pages 367–374, New York, NY, USA, 2004. ACM Press.

[13] Patrick Baudisch, Bongshin Lee, and Libby Hanna. Fishnet, a fisheye web browser with search term popouts: a comparative evaluation with overview and linear view. In *AVI '04: Proceedings of the working conference on Advanced visual interfaces*, pages 133–140, New York, NY, USA, 2004. ACM Press.

[14] Patrick Baudisch and Ruth Rosenholtz. Halo: a technique for visualizing off-screen objects. In *CHI '03: Proceedings of the SIGCHI conference on Human factors in computing systems*, pages 481–488, New York, NY, USA, 2003. ACM Press.

[15] Patrick Baudisch, Xing Xie, Chong Wang, and Wei-Ying Ma. Collapse-to-zoom: viewing web pages on small screen devices by interactively removing irrelevant content. In *UIST '04: Proceedings of the 17th annual ACM symposium on User interface software and technology*, pages 91–94, New York, NY, USA, 2004. ACM Press.

[16] David V. Beard and John Q. Walker. avigational techniques to improve the display of large two-dimensional spaces. *Behaviour and Information Technology*, 9(6):451–466, 1990.

[17] Ben Bederson and Jon Meyer. Implementing a zooming user interface: experience building pad++. *Softw. Pract. Exper.*, 28(10):1101–1135, 1998.

[18] Ben B. Bederson, Larry Stead, and James D. Hollan. Pad++: advances in multiscale interfaces. In *CHI '94: Conference companion on Human factors in computing systems*, pages 315–316, New York, NY, USA, 1994. ACM Press.

[19] Ben B. Bederson, Larry Stead, and James D. Hollan. Pad++: advances in multiscale interfaces. In *CHI '94: Conference companion on Human factors in computing systems*, pages 315–316, New York, NY, USA, 1994. ACM Press.

[20] Benjamin B. Bederson. Fisheye menus. In *UIST '00: Proceedings of the 13th annual ACM symposium on User interface software and technology*, pages 217–225, New York, NY, USA, 2000. ACM Press.

[21] Benjamin B. Bederson. Photomesa: a zoomable image browser using quantum treemaps and bubblemaps. In *UIST '01: Proceedings of the 14th annual ACM symposium on User interface software and technology*, pages 71–80, New York, NY, USA, 2001. ACM Press.

[22] Benjamin B. Bederson. Interfaces for staying in the flow. *Ubiquity*, 5(27):1–1, 2004.

[23] Benjamin B. Bederson and Angela Boltman. Does animation help users build mental maps of spatial information? In *INFOVIS '99: Proceedings of the 1999 IEEE Symposium on Information Visualization*, page 28, Washington, DC, USA, 1999. IEEE Computer Society.

[24] Benjamin B. Bederson, Aaron Clamage, Mary P. Czerwinski, and George G. Robertson. Datelens: A fisheye calendar interface for pdas. *ACM Trans. Comput.-Hum. Interact.*, 11(1):90–119, 2004.

[25] Benjamin B. Bederson and James D. Hollan. Pad++: a zooming graphical interface for exploring alternate interface physics. In *UIST '94: Proceedings of the 7th annual ACM symposium on User interface software and technology*, pages 17–26, New York, NY, USA, 1994. ACM Press.

[26] Benjamin B. Bederson and James D. Hollan. Pad++: a zoomable graphical interface system. In *CHI '95: Conference companion on Human factors in computing systems*, pages 23–24, New York, NY, USA, 1995. ACM Press.

[27] Benjamin B. Bederson, James D. Hollan, Jason Stewart, David Rogers, and David Vick. A zooming web browser. *Human Factors in Web Development*, 1998.

[28] Benjamin B. Bederson, Jon Meyer, and Lance Good. Jazz: an extensible zoomable user interface graphics toolkit in java. In *UIST '00: Proceedings of the 13th annual ACM symposium on User interface software and technology*, pages 171–180, New York, NY, USA, 2000. ACM Press.

[29] Eric Bergman. *Information Appliances and Beyond*. Morgan Kaufmann Publishers Inc., San Francisco, CA, USA, 2000.

[30] Enrico Bertini and Giuseppe Santucci. Improving 2d scatterplots effectiveness through sampling, displacement, and user perception. In *IV '05: Proceedings of the Ninth International Conference on Information Visualisation (IV'05)*, pages 826–834, Washington, DC, USA, 2005. IEEE Computer Society.

[31] Enrico Bertini and Giuseppe Santucci. Give chance a chance: modeling density to enhance scatter plot quality through random data sampling. *Information Visualization*, 5(2):95–110, 2006.

[32] Eric Bier, Kris Popat, Lance Good, and Alan Newberger. Zoomable user interface for in-depth reading. In *JCDL '04: Proceedings of the 4th ACM/IEEE-CS joint conference on Digital libraries*, pages 424–424, New York, NY, USA, 2004. ACM Press.

[33] Eric A. Bier, Maureen C. Stone, Ken Pier, William Buxton, and Tony D. DeRose. Toolglass and magic lenses: the see-through interface. In *SIGGRAPH '93: Proceedings of the 20th annual conference on Computer graphics and interactive techniques*, pages 73–80, New York, NY, USA, 1993. ACM Press.

[34] Staffan Björk, Lars Erik Holmquist, Peter Ljungstrand, and Johan Redström. Pow-erview: structured access to integrated information on small screens. In *CHI '00: CHI '00 extended abstracts on Human factors in computing systems*, pages 265–266, New York, NY, USA, 2000. ACM Press.

[35] Staffan Björk, Lars Erik Holmquist, Johan Redström, Ivan Bretan, Rolf Danielsson, Jussi Karlgren, and Kristofer Franzén. West: a web browser for small terminals. In *UIST '99: Proceedings of the 12th annual ACM symposium on User interface software and technology*, pages 187–196, New York, NY, USA, 1999. ACM Press.

[36] Staffan Björk, Johan Redström, Peter Ljungstrand, and Lars Erik Holmquist. Pow-erview: Using information links and information views to navigate and visualize information on small displays. In *HUC*, pages 46–62, 2000.

[37] Frédéric Bourgeois and Yves Guiard. Multiscale pointing: facilitating pan-zoom co-ordination. In *CHI '02: CHI '02 extended abstracts on Human factors in computing systems*, pages 758–759, New York, NY, USA, 2002. ACM Press.

[38] Frédéric Bourgeois, Yves Guiard, and Michel Beaudouin Lafon. Pan-zoom coordi-nation in multi-scale pointing. In *CHI '01: CHI '01 extended abstracts on Human factors in computing systems*, pages 157–158, New York, NY, USA, 2001. ACM Press.

[39] Stefano Burigat, Luca Chittaro, and Silvia Gabrielli. Visualizing locations of off-screen objects on mobile devices: a comparative evaluation of three approaches. In *MobileHCI '06: Proceedings of the 8th conference on Human-computer interaction with mobile devices and services*, pages 239–246, New York, NY, USA, 2006. ACM Press.

[40] Thorsten Büring. Interaktionsstrategien für punktdiagramm-visualisierungen auf kleinen bildschirmen. *i-com, Zeitschrift für interaktive und kooperative Medien*, 5(2):32–37, 2006.

[41] Thorsten Büring. *Handbook of Research on User Interface Design and Evaluation for Mobile Technology (in press)*, chapter Navigation Support for Exploring Starfield Displays on Personal Digital Assistants. Information Science Reference, 2007.

[42] Thorsten Büring, Jens Gerken, and Harald Reiterer. Usability of overview-supported zooming on small screens with regard to individual differences in spatial ability. In *AVI '06: Proceedings of the working conference on Advanced visual interfaces*, pages 233–240, New York, NY, USA, 2006. ACM Press.

[43] Thorsten Büring, Jens Gerken, and Harald Reiterer. User interaction with scat-terplots on small screens - a comparative evaluation of geometric-semantic zoom and fisheye distortion. *IEEE Transactions on Visualization and Computer Graph-ics (Proceedings Visualization / Information Visualization 2006)*, 12(5):829–836, September-October 2006.

[44] Thorsten Büring, Jens Gerken, and Harald Reiterer. Dynamic text filtering for improving the usability of alphasliders on small screens. In *IV '07: Proceedings of the Eleventh International Conference on Information Visualisation (IV'07) (in press)*, Zuerich, Switzerland, 2007. IEEE Computer Society.

[45] Thorsten Büring and Harald Reiterer. Zuiscat: querying and visualizing information spaces on personal digital assistants. In *MobileHCI '05: Proceedings of the 7th international conference on Human computer interaction with mobile devices & services*, pages 129–136, New York, NY, USA, 2005. ACM Press.

[46] W. Buxton and B. Myers. A study in two-handed input. In *CHI '86: Proceedings of the SIGCHI conference on Human factors in computing systems*, pages 321–326, New York, NY, USA, 1986. ACM Press.

[47] William Buxton. A three-state model of graphical input. In *INTERACT '90: Proceedings of the IFIP TC13 Third International Conference on Human-Computer Interaction*, pages 449–456, Amsterdam, The Netherlands, The Netherlands, 1990. North-Holland Publishing Co.

[48] William Buxton, Ralph Hill, and Peter Rowley. Issues and techniques in touch-sensitive tablet input. In *SIGGRAPH '85: Proceedings of the 12th annual conference on Computer graphics and interactive techniques*, pages 215–224, New York, NY, USA, 1985. ACM Press.

[49] Orkut Buyukkokten, Hector Garcia-Molina, Andreas Paepcke, and Terry Winograd. Power browser: efficient web browsing for pdas. In *CHI '00: Proceedings of the SIGCHI conference on Human factors in computing systems*, pages 430–437, New York, NY, USA, 2000. ACM Press.

[50] Donald Byrd. A scrollbar-based visualization for document navigation. In *DL '99: Proceedings of the fourth ACM conference on Digital libraries*, pages 122–129, New York, NY, USA, 1999. ACM Press.

[51] Xiang Cao and Ravin Balakrishnan. Interacting with dynamically defined information spaces using a handheld projector and a pen. In *UIST '06: Proceedings of the 19th annual ACM symposium on User interface software and technology*, pages 225–234, New York, NY, USA, 2006. ACM Press.

[52] Stuart K. Card, Jock D. Mackinlay, and Ben Shneiderman, editors. *Readings in information visualization: Using vision to think*. Morgan Kaufmann Publishers, San Francisco, 1999.

[53] Stuart K. Card, George G. Robertson, and Jock D. Mackinlay. The information visualizer, an information workspace. In *CHI '91: Proceedings of the SIGCHI conference on Human factors in computing systems*, pages 181–186, New York, NY, USA, 1991. ACM Press.

[54] M. Sheelagh T. Carpendale, David J. Cowperthwaite, and F. David Fracchia. Extending distortion viewing from 2d to 3d. *IEEE Comput. Graph. Appl.*, 17(4):42–51, 1997.

[55] Chaomei Chen. Individual differences in a spatial-semantic virtual environment. *Journal of the American Society of Information Science*, 51(6):529–542, 2000.

[56] Chaomei Chen. *Information Visualization - Beyond the Horizon*. Springer, 2 edition, 2004.

[57] Chaomei Chen. Top 10 unsolved information visualization problems. *IEEE Comput. Graph. Appl.*, 25(4):12–16, 2005.

[58] Chaomei Chen, Mary Czerwinski, and Robert Macredie. Individual differences in virtual environments-introduction and overview. *Journal of the American Society of Information Science*, 51(6):499–507, 2000.

[59] Chaomei Chen and Mary P. Czerwinski. Spatial ability and visual navigation: An empirical study. *The New Review for Hypertext and Multimedia*, 3:40–66, 1997.

[60] Chaomei Chen and Mary P. Czerwinski. Empirical evaluation of information visualizations: an introduction. *Int. J. Hum.-Comput. Stud.*, 53(5):631–635, 2000.

[61] Richard Chimera. Value bars: an information visualization and navigation tool for multi-attribute listings. In *CHI '92: Proceedings of the SIGCHI conference on Human factors in computing systems*, pages 293–294, New York, NY, USA, 1992. ACM Press.

[62] Sung-Jung Cho, Younghoon Sung, Roderick Murray-Smith, Kwanghyeon Lee, Changkyu Choi, and Yeun-Bae Kim. Dynamics of tilt-based browsing on mobile devices. In *CHI '07: Proceedings of the SIGCHI conference on Human factors in computing systems*, pages 815–820, New York, NY, USA, 2007. ACM Press.

[63] Andy Cockburn. Revisiting 2d vs 3d implications on spatial memory. In *AUIC '04: Proceedings of the fifth conference on Australasian user interface*, pages 25–31, Darlinghurst, Australia, Australia, 2004. Australian Computer Society, Inc.

[64] Andy Cockburn and Bruce McKenzie. 3d or not 3d?: evaluating the effect of the third dimension in a document management system. In *CHI '01: Proceedings of the SIGCHI conference on Human factors in computing systems*, pages 434–441, New York, NY, USA, 2001. ACM Press.

[65] Andy Cockburn and Bruce McKenzie. Evaluating the effectiveness of spatial memory in 2d and 3d physical and virtual environments. In *CHI '02: Proceedings of the SIGCHI conference on Human factors in computing systems*, pages 203–210, New York, NY, USA, 2002. ACM Press.

[66] Andy Cockburn and Joshua Savage. Comparing speed-dependent automatic zooming with traditional scroll, pan, and zoom methods. In *People and Computers XVII: British Computer Society Conference on Human Computer Interaction*, pages 87–102, 2003.

[67] Andy Cockburn, Joshua Savage, and Andrew Wallace. Tuning and testing scrolling interfaces that automatically zoom. In *CHI '05: Proceedings of the SIGCHI conference on Human factors in computing systems*, pages 71–80, New York, NY, USA, 2005. ACM Press.

[68] Tammara T. A. Combs and Benjamin B. Bederson. Does zooming improve image browsing? In *DL '99: Proceedings of the fourth ACM conference on Digital libraries*, pages 130–137, New York, NY, USA, 1999. ACM Press.

[69] Donald A. Cox, Jasdeep S. Chugh, Carl Gutwin, and Saul Greenberg. The usability of transparent overview layers. In *CHI '98: CHI 98 conference summary on Human factors in computing systems*, pages 301–302, New York, NY, USA, 1998. ACM Press.

[70] Andrew Crossan and Roderick Murray-Smith. Variability in wrist-tilt accelerometer based gesture interfaces. In *Mobile HCI*, pages 144–155, 2004.

[71] Mary P. Czerwinski and K. Larson. The new web browsers: They're cool but are they useful? In B. O'Conaill Thimbleby and P. Thomas, editors, *People and Computers XII: Proceedings of HCI'97*, Berlin, 1997. Springer Verlag.

[72] N. Dahlbäck, K. Höök, and M. Sjölinder. Spatial cognition in the mind and in the world: The case of hypermedia navigation. In *Proceedings of the 18th Annual Meeting of the Cognitive Science Society University of California, San Diego*, 1996.

[73] Alan Dix and Geoffrey Ellis. Starting simple: adding value to static visualisation through simple interaction. In *AVI '98: Proceedings of the working conference on Advanced visual interfaces*, pages 124–134, New York, NY, USA, 1998. ACM Press.

[74] William C. Donelson. Spatial management of information. In *SIGGRAPH '78: Proceedings of the 5th annual conference on Computer graphics and interactive techniques*, pages 203–209, New York, NY, USA, 1978. ACM Press.

[75] Misha Donskoy and Victor Kaptelinin. Window navigation with and without animation: a comparison of scroll bars, zoom, and fisheye view. In *CHI '97: CHI '97 extended abstracts on Human factors in computing systems*, pages 279–280, New York, NY, USA, 1997. ACM Press.

[76] M. D. Dunlop and N. Davidson. Visual information seeking on palmtop devices. In *Proceedings of HCI2000, volume 2*, pages 19–20, 2000.

[77] M. D. Dunlop, A. Morrison, S. McCallum, P. Ptaskinski, C. Risbey, and F. Stewart. Focussed palmtop information access through starfield displays and profile matching. In F. Crestani, M. Jones, and S. Mizzaro, editors, *Proceedings of workshop on Mobile and Ubiquitous Information Access, LNCS v2954*, pages 79–89. Springer, 2004.

[78] Daniel E. Egan. Individual differences in human-computer interaction. In M. Helander, editor, *Handbook of Human-Computer Interaction*. Elsevier Science Publishers B.V, 1988.

[79] Dennis E. Egan and Louis M. Gomez. Assaying, isolating and accomodating in-
     dividual differences in learning a complex skill. In Dillon R. F., editor, *Individual
     Differences In Cognition*, volume 2. Academic Press, New York, 1985.

[80] Geoffrey Ellis and Alan Dix. The plot, the clutter, the sampling and its lens: oc-
     clusion measures for automatic clutter reduction. In *AVI '06: Proceedings of the
     working conference on Advanced visual interfaces*, pages 266–269, New York, NY,
     USA, 2006. ACM Press.

[81] Parisa Eslambolchilar and Roderick Murray-Smith. Tilt-based automatic zooming
     and scaling in mobile devices - a state-space implementation. In *Mobile HCI*, pages
     120–131, 2004.

[82] Jean-Daniel Fekete and Catherine Plaisant. Interactive information visualization of a
     million items. In *INFOVIS '02: Proceedings of the IEEE Symposium on Information
     Visualization (InfoVis'02)*, page 117, Washington, DC, USA, 2002. IEEE Computer
     Society.

[83] Paul Morris Fitts. The information capacity of the human motor system in control-
     ling the amplitude of movement. *Journal of Experimental Psychology*, 47(6):381–391,
     1954.

[84] George Fitzmaurice, Azam Khan, Robert Pieké, Bill Buxton, and Gordon Kurten-
     bach. Tracking menus. In *UIST '03: Proceedings of the 16th annual ACM symposium
     on User interface software and technology*, pages 71–79, New York, NY, USA, 2003.
     ACM Press.

[85] George W. Fitzmaurice. Situated information spaces and spatially aware palmtop
     computers. *Commun. ACM*, 36(7):39–49, 1993.

[86] George W. Fitzmaurice, Shumin Zhai, and Mark H. Chignell. Virtual reality for
     palmtop computers. *ACM Trans. Inf. Syst.*, 11(3):197–218, 1993.

[87] David Fox. *Tabula Rasa: A Multi-scale User Interface System*. PhD thesis, New
     York University, 1998.

[88] Andrew U. Frank and Sabine Timpf. Multiple representations for cartographic ob-
     jects in a multi-scale tree - an intelligent graphical zoom. *Computers & Graphics*,
     18(6):823–829, 1994.

[89] G. W. Furnas. Generalized fisheye views. In *CHI '86: Proceedings of the SIGCHI
     conference on Human factors in computing systems*, pages 16–23, New York, NY,
     USA, 1986. ACM Press.

[90] G. W. Furnas. The fisheye view: a new look at structured files. pages 312–330, 1999.

[91] George W. Furnas. A fisheye follow-up: further reflections on focus + context. In
     *CHI '06: Proceedings of the SIGCHI conference on Human Factors in computing
     systems*, pages 999–1008, New York, NY, USA, 2006. ACM Press.

[92] George W. Furnas and Benjamin B. Bederson. Space-scale diagrams: understanding multiscale interfaces. In *CHI '95: Proceedings of the SIGCHI conference on Human factors in computing systems*, pages 234–241, New York, NY, USA, 1995. ACM Press/Addison-Wesley Publishing Co.

[93] Jade Goldstein and Steven F. Roth. Using aggregation and dynamic queries for exploring large data sets. In *CHI '94: Proceedings of the SIGCHI conference on Human factors in computing systems*, pages 23–29, New York, NY, USA, 1994. ACM Press.

[94] Lance Good and Benjamin B. Bederson. Zoomable user interfaces as a medium for slide show presentations. *Information Visualization*, 1(1):35–49, 2002.

[95] Lance Everett Good. *Zoomable User Interfaces for the Authoring and Delivery of Slide Presentations*. PhD thesis, University of Maryland, USA, 2003.

[96] Guido Grassel, Roland Geisler, Elina Vartiainen, Deepika Chauhan, and Andrei Popescu. The nokia open source browser. In *MobEA IV 2006 - Empowering the Mobile Web*, 2006.

[97] Tovi Grossman, Ken Hinckley, Patrick Baudisch, Maneesh Agrawala, and Ravin Balakrishnan. Hover widgets: using the tracking state to extend the capabilities of pen-operated devices. In *CHI '06: Proceedings of the SIGCHI conference on Human Factors in computing systems*, pages 861–870, New York, NY, USA, 2006. ACM Press.

[98] Yves Guiard. Asymmetric division of labor in human skilled bimanual action: The kinematic chain as a model. *Journal of Motor Behavior*, 19(4):486–517, 1987.

[99] Yves Guiard and Michel Beaudouin-Lafon. Target acquisition in multiscale electronic worlds. *Int. J. Hum.-Comput. Stud.*, 61(6):875–905, 2004.

[100] Yves Guiard, Michel Beaudouin-Lafon, Julien Bastin, Dennis Pasveer, and Shumin Zhai. View size and pointing difficulty in multi-scale navigation. In *AVI '04: Proceedings of the working conference on Advanced visual interfaces*, pages 117–124, New York, NY, USA, 2004. ACM Press.

[101] Yves Guiard, Michel Beaudouin-Lafon, and Denis Mottet. Beyond the 10-bit barrier: Fitts' law in multi-scale electronic worlds. In *People and Computers XV - Interaction without frontiers*, pages 573–587. Springer Verlag, 2001.

[102] Carl Gutwin. Improving focus targeting in interactive fisheye views. In *CHI '02: Proceedings of the SIGCHI conference on Human factors in computing systems*, pages 267–274, New York, NY, USA, 2002. ACM Press.

[103] Carl Gutwin and Chris Fedak. A comparison of fisheye lenses for interactive layout tasks. In *GI '04: Proceedings of the 2004 conference on Graphics interface*, pages 213–220, School of Computer Science, University of Waterloo, Waterloo, Ontario, Canada, 2004. Canadian Human-Computer Communications Society.

[104] Carl Gutwin and Chris Fedak. Interacting with big interfaces on small screens: a comparison of fisheye, zoom, and panning techniques. In *GI '04: Proceedings of the 2004 conference on Graphics interface*, pages 145–152, School of Computer Science, University of Waterloo, Waterloo, Ontario, Canada, 2004. Canadian Human-Computer Communications Society.

[105] Carl Gutwin, Mark Roseman, and Saul Greenberg. A usability study of awareness widgets in a shared workspace groupware system. In *CSCW '96: Proceedings of the 1996 ACM conference on Computer supported cooperative work*, pages 258–267, New York, NY, USA, 1996. ACM Press.

[106] Carl Gutwin and Amy Skopik. Fisheyes are good for large steering tasks. In *CHI '03: Proceedings of the SIGCHI conference on Human factors in computing systems*, pages 201–208, New York, NY, USA, 2003. ACM Press.

[107] Beverly L. Harrison, Kenneth P. Fishkin, Anuj Gujar, Carlos Mochon, and Roy Want. Squeeze me, hold me, tilt me! an exploration of manipulative user interfaces. In *CHI '98: Proceedings of the SIGCHI conference on Human factors in computing systems*, pages 17–24, New York, NY, USA, 1998. ACM Press/Addison-Wesley Publishing Co.

[108] Mountaz Hascoët. Throwing models for large displays. In *HCI'03: British HCI Group*, pages 73–77, 2003.

[109] Marc Hassenzahl, Axel Platz, Michael Burmester, and Katrin Lehner. Hedonic and ergonomic quality aspects determine a software's appeal. In *CHI '00: Proceedings of the SIGCHI conference on Human factors in computing systems*, pages 201–208, New York, NY, USA, 2000. ACM Press.

[110] Christopher G. Healey, Kellogg S. Booth, and James T. Enns. Visualizing real-time multivariate data using preattentive processing. *ACM Trans. Model. Comput. Simul.*, 5(3):190–221, 1995.

[111] Christopher F. Herot and Guy Weinzapfel. One-point touch input of vector information for computer displays. In *SIGGRAPH '78: Proceedings of the 5th annual conference on Computer graphics and interactive techniques*, pages 210–216, New York, NY, USA, 1978. ACM Press.

[112] Ron R. Hightower, Laura T. Ring, Jonathan I. Helfman, Benjamin B. Bederson, and James D. Hollan. Padprints: graphical multiscale web histories. In *UIST '98: Proceedings of the 11th annual ACM symposium on User interface software and technology*, pages 121–122, New York, NY, USA, 1998. ACM Press.

[113] William C. Hill, James D. Hollan, Dave Wroblewski, and Tim McCandless. Edit wear and read wear. In *CHI '92: Proceedings of the SIGCHI conference on Human factors in computing systems*, pages 3–9, New York, NY, USA, 1992. ACM Press.

[114] Ken Hinckley. Input technologies and techniques. pages 151–168, 2002.

[115] Ken Hinckley, Edward Cutrell, Steve Bathiche, and Tim Muss. Quantitative analysis of scrolling techniques. In *CHI '02: Proceedings of the SIGCHI conference on Human factors in computing systems*, pages 65–72, New York, NY, USA, 2002. ACM Press.

[116] Ken Hinckley, Jeff Pierce, Eric Horvitz, and Mike Sinclair. Foreground and background interaction with sensor-enhanced mobile devices. *ACM Trans. Comput.-Hum. Interact.*, 12(1):31–52, 2005.

[117] Ken Hinckley, Jeff Pierce, Mike Sinclair, and Eric Horvitz. Sensing techniques for mobile interaction. In *UIST '00: Proceedings of the 13th annual ACM symposium on User interface software and technology*, pages 91–100, New York, NY, USA, 2000. ACM Press.

[118] Lars Erik Holmquist. Focus+context visualization with flip zooming and the zoom browser. In *CHI '97: CHI '97 extended abstracts on Human factors in computing systems*, pages 263–264, New York, NY, USA, 1997. ACM Press.

[119] Wolfgang Horn. *Leistungspruefsystem*. Hogrefe Verlag fuer Psychologie, Goettingen, 1983.

[120] Kasper Hornbæk, Benjamin B. Bederson, and Catherine Plaisant. Navigation patterns and usability of zoomable user interfaces with and without an overview. *ACM Trans. Comput.-Hum. Interact.*, 9(4):362–389, 2002.

[121] Kasper Hornbæk and Erik Frøkjær. Reading of electronic documents: the usability of linear, fisheye, and overview+detail interfaces. In *CHI '01: Proceedings of the SIGCHI conference on Human factors in computing systems*, pages 293–300, New York, NY, USA, 2001. ACM Press.

[122] Kasper Hornbæk and Erik Frøkjær. Reading patterns and usability in visualizations of electronic documents. *interactions*, 11(1):11–12, 2004.

[123] Takeo Igarashi and Ken Hinckley. Speed-dependent automatic zooming for browsing large documents. In *UIST '00: Proceedings of the 13th annual ACM symposium on User interface software and technology*, pages 139–148, New York, NY, USA, 2000. ACM Press.

[124] Alfred Inselberg and Bernard Dimsdale. Parallel coordinates: a tool for visualizing multi-dimensional geometry. In *VIS '90: Proceedings of the 1st conference on Visualization '90*, pages 361–378, Los Alamitos, CA, USA, 1990. IEEE Computer Society Press.

[125] Pourang Irani, Carl Gutwin, and Xing Dong Yang. Improving selection of off-screen targets with hopping. In *CHI '06: Proceedings of the SIGCHI conference on Human Factors in computing systems*, pages 299–308, New York, NY, USA, 2006. ACM Press.

[126] Edward W. Ishak and Steven K. Feiner. Content-aware scrolling. In *UIST '06: Proceedings of the 19th annual ACM symposium on User interface software and technology*, pages 155–158, New York, NY, USA, 2006. ACM Press.

[127] Robert J. K. Jacob, Linda E. Sibert, Daniel C. McFarlane, and Jr. M. Preston Mullen. Integrality and separability of input devices. *ACM Trans. Comput.-Hum. Interact.*, 1(1):3–26, 1994.

[128] Mikkel R. Jakobsen and Kasper Hornbæk. Evaluating a fisheye view of source code. In *CHI '06: Proceedings of the SIGCHI conference on Human Factors in computing systems*, pages 377–386, New York, NY, USA, 2006. ACM Press.

[129] D. F. Jerding and J. T. Stasko. The information mural: a technique for displaying and navigating large information spaces. In *INFOVIS '95: Proceedings of the 1995 IEEE Symposium on Information Visualization*, page 43, Washington, DC, USA, 1995. IEEE Computer Society.

[130] N. K. Jog and B. Shneiderman. Starfield visualization with interactive smooth zooming. In *Proceedings of the third IFIP WG2.6 working conference on Visual database systems 3 (VDB-3)*, pages 3–14, London, UK, UK, 1995. Chapman & Hall, Ltd.

[131] Jeff A. Johnson. A comparison of user interfaces for panning on a touch-controlled display. In *CHI '95: Proceedings of the SIGCHI conference on Human factors in computing systems*, pages 218–225, New York, NY, USA, 1995. ACM Press/Addison-Wesley Publishing Co.

[132] Steve Jones, Matt Jones, Gary Marsden, Dynal Patel, and Andy Cockburn. An evaluation of integrated zooming and scrolling on small screens. *Int. J. Hum.-Comput. Stud.*, 63(3):271–303, 2005.

[133] Patrick W. Jordan. Pleasure with products: the new human factors. pages 303–328, 2001.

[134] Susanne Jul and George W. Furnas. Critical zones in desert fog: aids to multiscale navigation. In *UIST '98: Proceedings of the 11th annual ACM symposium on User interface software and technology*, pages 97–106, New York, NY, USA, 1998. ACM Press.

[135] Paul Kabbash, William Buxton, and Abigail Sellen. Two-handed input in a compound task. In *CHI '94: Proceedings of the SIGCHI conference on Human factors in computing systems*, pages 417–423, New York, NY, USA, 1994. ACM Press.

[136] Victor Kaptelinin. A comparison of four navigation techniques in a 2d browsing task. In *CHI '95: Conference companion on Human factors in computing systems*, pages 282–283, New York, NY, USA, 1995. ACM Press.

[137] Amy K. Karlson, Benjamin B. Bederson, and John SanGiovanni. Applens and launchtile: two designs for one-handed thumb use on small devices. In *CHI '05: Proceedings of the SIGCHI conference on Human factors in computing systems*, pages 201–210, New York, NY, USA, 2005. ACM Press.

[138] Bernd Karstens, Uwe Rauschenbach, and Heidrun Schumann. Information presentation on mobile handhelds. In *IRMA 2003 Proceedings 14th International Conference of the Information Resources Managment Association*, 2003.

[139] Daniel A. Keim and Annemarie Herrmann. The gridfit algorithm: an efficient and effective approach to visualizing large amounts of spatial data. In *IEEE Visualization*, pages 181–188, 1998.

[140] Daniel A. Keim, Christian Panse, Jörn Schneidewind, and Mike Sips. Geo-spatial data viewer: From familiar land-covering to arbitrary distorted geo-spatial quadtree maps. In *WSCG*, pages 213–220, 2004.

[141] Daniel A. Keim, Christian Panse, Mike Sips, and Stephen C. North. Visual data mining in large geospatial point sets. *IEEE Comput. Graph. Appl.*, 24(5):36–44, 2004.

[142] Amir Khella and Benjamin B. Bederson. Pocket photomesa: a zoomable image browser for pdas. In *MUM '04: Proceedings of the 3rd international conference on Mobile and ubiquitous multimedia*, pages 19–24, New York, NY, USA, 2004. ACM Press.

[143] Robert Kincaid and Heidi Lam. Line graph explorer: scalable display of line graphs using focus+context. In *AVI '06: Proceedings of the working conference on Advanced visual interfaces*, pages 404–411, New York, NY, USA, 2006. ACM Press.

[144] K. Koffka. *Principles of Gestalt Psychology*. Harcourt Brace, New York, 1935.

[145] Heidi Lam and Patrick Baudisch. Summary thumbnails: readable overviews for small screen web browsers. In *CHI '05: Proceedings of the SIGCHI conference on Human factors in computing systems*, pages 681–690, New York, NY, USA, 2005. ACM Press.

[146] Edward Lank and Son Phan. Focus+context sketching on a pocket pc. In *CHI '04: CHI '04 extended abstracts on Human factors in computing systems*, pages 1275–1278, New York, NY, USA, 2004. ACM Press.

[147] Edward Lank, Jaime Ruiz, and William Cowan. Concurrent bimanual stylus interaction: a study of non-preferred hand mode manipulation. In *GI '06: Proceedings of the 2006 conference on Graphics interface*, pages 17–24, Toronto, Ont., Canada, Canada, 2006. Canadian Information Processing Society.

[148] Celine Latulipe, Craig S. Kaplan, and Charles L. A. Clarke. Bimanual and unimanual image alignment: an evaluation of mouse-based techniques. In *UIST '05: Proceedings of the 18th annual ACM symposium on User interface software and technology*, pages 123–131, New York, NY, USA, 2005. ACM Press.

[149] Y. K. Leung and M. D. Apperley. A review and taxonomy of distortion-oriented presentation techniques. *ACM Trans. Comput.-Hum. Interact.*, 1(2):126–160, 1994.

[150] Yang Li, Ken Hinckley, Zhiwei Guan, and James A. Landay. Experimental analysis of mode switching techniques in pen-based user interfaces. In *CHI '05: Proceedings of the SIGCHI conference on Human factors in computing systems*, pages 461–470, New York, NY, USA, 2005. ACM Press.

[151] H. Lieberman. A multi-scale, multi-layer, translucent virtual space. In *IV '97: Proceedings of the IEEE Conference on Information Visualisation*, page 126, Washington, DC, USA, 1997. IEEE Computer Society.

[152] Henry Lieberman. Powers of ten thousand: navigating in large information spaces. In *UIST '94: Proceedings of the 7th annual ACM symposium on User interface software and technology*, pages 15–16, New York, NY, USA, 1994. ACM Press.

[153] Feng Liu and Michael Gleicher. Automatic image retargeting with fisheye-view warping. In *UIST '05: Proceedings of the 18th annual ACM symposium on User interface software and technology*, pages 153–162, New York, NY, USA, 2005. ACM Press.

[154] David F. Lohman. Spatial ability and g. *Human abilities: Their nature and assessment*, pages 97–116, 1996.

[155] Saturnino Luz and Masood Masoodian. A mobile system for non-linear access to time-based data. In *AVI '04: Proceedings of the working conference on Advanced visual interfaces*, pages 454–457, New York, NY, USA, 2004. ACM Press.

[156] Bonnie MacKay, David Dearman, Kori Inkpen, and Carolyn Watters. Walk 'n scroll: a comparison of software-based navigation techniques for different levels of mobility. In *MobileHCI '05: Proceedings of the 7th international conference on Human computer interaction with mobile devices & services*, pages 183–190, New York, NY, USA, 2005. ACM Press.

[157] Jock Mackinlay. Automating the design of graphical presentations of relational information. *ACM Trans. Graph.*, 5(2):110–141, 1986.

[158] Jock D. Mackinlay, George G. Robertson, and Stuart K. Card. The perspective wall: detail and context smoothly integrated. In *CHI '91: Proceedings of the SIGCHI conference on Human factors in computing systems*, pages 173–176, New York, NY, USA, 1991. ACM Press.

[159] Jani Mantyjarvi, Fabio Paternò, Zigor Salvador, and Carmen Santoro. Scan and tilt: towards natural interaction for mobile museum guides. In *Mobile HCI*, pages 191–194, 2006.

[160] Linn Marks, Jeremy A.T. Hussell, Tamara M. McMahon, and Richard E. Luce. Activegraph: A digital library visualization tool. *International Journal on Digital Libraries, Special Issue on Information Visualization Interfaces for Retrieval and Analysis*, 2005.

[161] Nobuyuki Matsushita, Yuji Ayatsuka, and Jun Rekimoto. Dual touch: a two-handed interface for pen-based pdas. In *UIST '00: Proceedings of the 13th annual ACM symposium on User interface software and technology*, pages 211–212, New York, NY, USA, 2000. ACM Press.

[162] Sachi Mizobuchi, Mark Chignell, and David Newton. Mobile text entry: relationship between walking speed and text input task difficulty. In *MobileHCI '05: Proceedings of the 7th international conference on Human computer interaction with mobile devices & services*, pages 122–128, New York, NY, USA, 2005. ACM Press.

[163] Sachi Mizobuchi, Shinya Terasaki, Turo Keski-Jaskari, Jari Nousiainen, Matti Ryynanen, and Miika Silfverberg. Making an impression: force-controlled pen input for handheld devices. In *CHI '05: CHI '05 extended abstracts on Human factors in computing systems*, pages 1661–1664, New York, NY, USA, 2005. ACM Press.

[164] Miguel A. Nacenta, Dzmitry Aliakseyeu, Sriram Subramanian, and Carl Gutwin. A comparison of techniques for multi-display reaching. In *CHI '05: Proceedings of the SIGCHI conference on Human factors in computing systems*, pages 371–380, New York, NY, USA, 2005. ACM Press.

[165] Dmitry Nekrasovski, Adam Bodnar, Joanna McGrenere, François Guimbretière, and Tamara Munzner. An evaluation of pan & zoom and rubber sheet navigation with and without an overview. In *CHI '06: Proceedings of the SIGCHI conference on Human Factors in computing systems*, pages 11–20, New York, NY, USA, 2006. ACM Press.

[166] Chris North and Ben Shneiderman. Snap-together visualization: a user interface for coordinating visualizations via relational schemata. In *AVI '00: Proceedings of the working conference on Advanced visual interfaces*, pages 128–135, New York, NY, USA, 2000. ACM Press.

[167] Kenton O'Hara and Abigail Sellen. A comparison of reading paper and on-line documents. In *CHI '97: Proceedings of the SIGCHI conference on Human factors in computing systems*, pages 335–342, New York, NY, USA, 1997. ACM Press.

[168] Kenton O'Hara, Abigail Sellen, and Richard Bentley. Supporting memory for spatial location while reading from small displays. In *CHI '99: CHI '99 extended abstracts on Human factors in computing systems*, pages 220–221, New York, NY, USA, 1999. ACM Press.

[169] Chris Olston, Allison Woodruff, Alexander Aiken, Michael Chu, Vuk Ercegovac, Mark Lin, Mybrid Spalding, and Michael Stonebraker. Datasplash. In *SIGMOD '98: Proceedings of the 1998 ACM SIGMOD international conference on Management of data*, pages 550–552, New York, NY, USA, 1998. ACM Press.

[170] Russell Owen, Gordon Kurtenbach, George Fitzmaurice, Thomas Baudel, and Bill Buxton. When it gets more difficult, use both hands: exploring bimanual curve manipulation. In *GI '05: Proceedings of the 2005 conference on Graphics interface*, pages 17–24, School of Computer Science, University of Waterloo, Waterloo, Ontario, Canada, 2005. Canadian Human-Computer Communications Society.

[171] Dynal Patel, Gary Marsden, Steve Jones, and Matt Jones. An evaluation of techniques for browsing photograph collections on small displays. In *Mobile HCI*, pages 132–143, 2004.

[172] Ken Perlin and David Fox. Pad: an alternative approach to the computer interface. In *SIGGRAPH '93: Proceedings of the 20th annual conference on Computer graphics and interactive techniques*, pages 57–64, New York, NY, USA, 1993. ACM Press.

[173] Ken Perlin and Jon Meyer. Nested user interface components. In *UIST '99: Proceedings of the 12th annual ACM symposium on User interface software and technology*, pages 11–18, New York, NY, USA, 1999. ACM Press.

[174] Richard Phillips and Liza Noyes. An investigation of visual clutter in the topographic base of a geological map. *Cartographic Journal*, 19(2):122–132, 1982.

[175] Catherine Plaisant, David Carr, and Ben Shneiderman. Image-browser taxonomy and guidelines for designers. *IEEE Softw.*, 12(2):21–32, 1995.

[176] Matthew D. Plumlee and Colin Ware. Zooming versus multiple window interfaces: Cognitive costs of visual comparisons. *ACM Trans. Comput.-Hum. Interact.*, 13(2):179–209, 2006.

[177] Stuart Pook. *Interaction and Context in Zoomable User Interfaces*. PhD thesis, École Nationale Supérieure des Télécommunications Paris, 2001.

[178] Stuart Pook, Eric Lecolinet, Guy Vaysseix, and Emmanuel Barillot. Context and interaction in zoomable user interfaces. In *AVI '00: Proceedings of the working conference on Advanced visual interfaces*, pages 227–231, New York, NY, USA, 2000. ACM Press.

[179] Roope Raisamo. Evaluating different touched-based interaction techniques in a public information kiosk. In *Conference of the CHI Special Interest Group of the Ergonomics Society of Australia*, 1999.

[180] Gonzalo Ramos and Ravin Balakrishnan. Fluid interaction techniques for the control and annotation of digital video. In *UIST '03: Proceedings of the 16th annual ACM symposium on User interface software and technology*, pages 105–114, New York, NY, USA, 2003. ACM Press.

[181] Gonzalo Ramos and Ravin Balakrishnan. Zliding: fluid zooming and sliding for high precision parameter manipulation. In *UIST '05: Proceedings of the 18th annual ACM symposium on User interface software and technology*, pages 143–152, New York, NY, USA, 2005. ACM Press.

[182] Gonzalo Ramos, Matthew Boulos, and Ravin Balakrishnan. Pressure widgets. In *CHI '04: Proceedings of the SIGCHI conference on Human factors in computing systems*, pages 487–494, New York, NY, USA, 2004. ACM Press.

[183] Ramana Rao and Stuart K. Card. The table lens: merging graphical and symbolic representations in an interactive focus+context visualization for tabular information. In *CHI '94: Conference companion on Human factors in computing systems*, page 222, New York, NY, USA, 1994. ACM Press.

[184] Ramana Rao and Stuart K. Card. Exploring large tables with the table lens. In *CHI '95: Conference companion on Human factors in computing systems*, pages 403–404, New York, NY, USA, 1995. ACM Press.

[185] Jef Raskin. *The Humane Interface. New Directions for Designing Interactive Systems*. Addison-Wesley, 2000.

[186] Uwe Rauschenbach, Stefan Jeschke, and Heidrun Schumann. General rectangular fisheye views for 2d graphics. *Computers & Graphics*, 25(4):609–617, 2001.

[187] Uwe Rauschenbach, Tino Weinkauf, and Heidrun Schumann. Interactive focus and context display of large raster images. In *WSCG*, 2000.

[188] Jun Rekimoto. Tilting operations for small screen interfaces. In *UIST '96: Proceedings of the 9th annual ACM symposium on User interface software and technology*, pages 167–168, New York, NY, USA, 1996. ACM Press.

[189] Jun Rekimoto. Pick-and-drop: a direct manipulation technique for multiple computer environments. In *UIST '97: Proceedings of the 10th annual ACM symposium on User interface software and technology*, pages 31–39, New York, NY, USA, 1997. ACM Press.

[190] Theresa-Marie Rhyne, Panelist-Bill Hibbard, Panelist-Chris Johnson, Panelist-Chaomei Chen, and Panelist-Steve Eick. Panel 1: Can we determine the top unresolved problems of visualization? In *VIS '04: Proceedings of the conference on Visualization '04*, pages 563–566, Washington, DC, USA, 2004. IEEE Computer Society.

[191] Daniel C. Robbins, Edward Cutrell, Raman Sarin, and Eric Horvitz. Zonezoom: map navigation for smartphones with recursive view segmentation. In *AVI '04: Proceedings of the working conference on Advanced visual interfaces*, pages 231–234, New York, NY, USA, 2004. ACM Press.

[192] George Robertson, Mary Czerwinski, Kevin Larson, Daniel C. Robbins, David Thiel, and Maarten van Dantzich. Data mountain: using spatial memory for document management. In *UIST '98: Proceedings of the 11th annual ACM symposium on User interface software and technology*, pages 153–162, New York, NY, USA, 1998. ACM Press.

[193] George Robertson, Maarten van Dantzich, Daniel Robbins, Mary Czerwinski, Ken Hinckley, Kirsten Risden, David Thiel, and Vadim Gorokhovsky. The task gallery: a 3d window manager. In *CHI '00: Proceedings of the SIGCHI conference on Human factors in computing systems*, pages 494–501, New York, NY, USA, 2000. ACM Press.

[194] George G. Robertson and Jock D. Mackinlay. The document lens. In *UIST '93: Proceedings of the 6th annual ACM symposium on User interface software and technology*, pages 101–108, New York, NY, USA, 1993. ACM Press.

[195] George G. Robertson, Jock D. Mackinlay, and Stuart K. Card. Cone trees: animated 3d visualizations of hierarchical information. In *CHI '91: Proceedings of the SIGCHI conference on Human factors in computing systems*, pages 189–194, New York, NY, USA, 1991. ACM Press.

[196] René Rosenbaum and Heidrun Schumann. Remote raster image browsing based on fast content reduction formobile environments. In N. Correia, J. Jorge, T. Chambel, and Z. Pan, editors, *EG Multimedia Workshop*, pages 13–19, Nanjing, China, 2004. Eurographics Association.

[197] René Rosenbaum and Heidrun Schumann. Grid-based interaction for effective image browsing on mobile devices. In *Proceedings SPIE - Electronic Imaging 2005*, pages 16–20, 2005.

[198] Virpi Roto and Anne Kaikkonen. Perception of narrow web pages on a mobile phone. In *19th International Symposium on Human Factors in Telecommunication*, 2003.

[199] Virpi Roto, Andrei Popescu, Antti Koivisto, and Elina Vartiainen. Minimap: a web page visualization method for mobile phones. In *CHI '06: Proceedings of the SIGCHI conference on Human Factors in computing systems*, pages 35–44, New York, NY, USA, 2006. ACM Press.

[200] Manojit Sarkar and Marc H. Brown. Graphical fisheye views of graphs. In *CHI '92: Proceedings of the SIGCHI conference on Human factors in computing systems*, pages 83–91, New York, NY, USA, 1992. ACM Press.

[201] Manojit Sarkar, Scott S. Snibbe, Oren J. Tversky, and Steven P. Reiss. Stretching the rubber sheet: a metaphor for viewing large layouts on small screens. In *UIST '93: Proceedings of the 6th annual ACM symposium on User interface software and technology*, pages 81–91, New York, NY, USA, 1993. ACM Press.

[202] Joshua Savage and Andy Cockburn. Comparing automatic and manual zooming methods for acquiring off-screen targets. In *People and Computers XIX: British Computer Society Conference on Human Computer Interaction*, pages 439–454, 2005.

[203] Doug Schaffer, Zhengping Zuo, Saul Greenberg, Lyn Bartram, John Dill, Shelli Dubs, and Mark Roseman. Navigating hierarchically clustered networks through fisheye and full-zoom methods. *ACM Trans. Comput.-Hum. Interact.*, 3(2):162–188, 1996.

[204] Jörn Schneidewind, Mike Sips, and Daniel Keim. Pixnostics: Towards measuring the value of visualization. In *Proceedings of the 2006 IEEE Symposium on Visual Analytics And Technology*, pages 199–206. IEEE Computer Society, 2006.

[205] B. Shneiderman. Direct manipulation: A step beyond programming languages. pages 461–467, 1987.

[206] Ben Shneiderman. The future of interactive systems and the emergence of direct manipulation. In *Proc. of the NYU symposium on user interfaces on Human factors*

and interactive computer systems, pages 1–28, Norwood, NJ, USA, 1984. Ablex Publishing Corp.

[207] Ben Shneiderman. The eyes have it: A task by data type taxonomy for information visualizations. In *VL '96: Proceedings of the 1996 IEEE Symposium on Visual Languages*, pages 336–343. IEEE Computer Society, 1996.

[208] Ben Shneiderman and Catherine Plaisant. *Designing the user interface.* Pearson/Addison-Wesley, 4. ed edition, 2005.

[209] Amy Skopic and Carl Gutwin. Finding things in fisheyes: memorability in distorted spaces. In *GI '03: Proceedings of the Graphics Interface conference*, pages 67–75, New York, NY, USA, 2003. ACM Press.

[210] Amy Skopik and Carl Gutwin. Improving revisitation in fisheye views with visit wear. In *CHI '05: Proceedings of the SIGCHI conference on Human factors in computing systems*, pages 771–780, New York, NY, USA, 2005. ACM Press.

[211] David Small and Hiroshi Ishii. Design of spatially aware graspable displays. In *CHI '97: CHI '97 extended abstracts on Human factors in computing systems*, pages 367–368, New York, NY, USA, 1997. ACM Press.

[212] Robert Spence. *Information Visualization.* Pearson Education, 2 edition, 2007.

[213] Robert Spence and Martin Apperley. Data base navigation: an office environment for the professional. *Behaviour and Information Technology*, 1(1):43–54, 1982.

[214] Carla J. Springer. Retrieval of information from complex alphanumeric displays: Screen formatting variables' effects on target identification time. In *HCI (2)*, pages 375–382, 1987.

[215] Kay M. Stanney and Gavriel Salvendy. Information visualization: Assisting low spatial individuals with information access tasks through the use of visual mediators. *Ergonomics*, 38(6):1184–1198, 1995.

[216] Monica Tavanti and Mats Lind. 2d vs 3d, implications on spatial memory. In *IN-FOVIS '01: Proceedings of the IEEE Symposium on Information Visualization 2001 (INFOVIS'01)*, page 139, Washington, DC, USA, 2001. IEEE Computer Society.

[217] L. L. Thurstone and T. G. Thurstone. Primary mental abilities. *Psychometric Monographs*, 1, 1938.

[218] Anne Treisman. Preattentive processing in vision. *Comput. Vision Graph. Image Process.*, 31(2):156–177, 1985.

[219] Marjan Trutschl, Georges Grinstein, and Urska Cvek. Intelligently resolving point occlusion. *infovis*, 00:17, 2003.

[220] Edward Tufte. *The Visual Display of Quantitative Information.* Graphics Press, 1983.

[221] Jarke J. van Wijk and Wim A. A. Nuij. Smooth and efficient zooming and panning. In *INFOVIS*, 2003.

[222] K. J. Vicente and R. C. Williges. Accommodating individual differences in searching a hierarchical file system. *Int. J. Man-Mach. Stud.*, 29(6):647–668, 1988.

[223] Kim J. Vicente, Brian C. Hayes, and Robert C. Williges. Assaying and isolating individual differences in searching a hierarchical file system. *Hum. Factors*, 29(3):349–359, 1987.

[224] Carsten Waldeck and Dirk Balfanz. Mobile liquid 2d scatter space (ml2dss). In *IV '04: Proceedings of the Information Visualisation, Eighth International Conference on (IV'04)*, pages 494–498. IEEE Computer Society, 2004.

[225] Colin Ware. *Information Visualization: Perception for Design*. Morgan Kaufmann Publishers, 2 edition, 2004.

[226] Christopher Williamson and Ben Shneiderman. The dynamic homefinder: evaluating dynamic queries in a real-estate information exploration system. In *SIGIR '92: Proceedings of the 15th annual international ACM SIGIR conference on Research and development in information retrieval*, pages 338–346, New York, NY, USA, 1992. ACM Press.

[227] Graham J. Wills. An interactive view for hierarchical clustering. In *INFOVIS '98: Proceedings of the 1998 IEEE Symposium on Information Visualization*, page 26, Washington, DC, USA, 1998. IEEE Computer Society.

[228] Jacob O. Wobbrock, Jodi Forlizzi, Scott E. Hudson, and Brad A. Myers. Webthumb: interaction techniques for small-screen browsers. In *UIST '02: Proceedings of the 15th annual ACM symposium on User interface software and technology*, pages 205–208, New York, NY, USA, 2002. ACM Press.

[229] Allison Woodruff, Andrew Faulring, Ruth Rosenholtz, Julie Morrsion, and Peter Pirolli. Using thumbnails to search the web. In *CHI '01: Proceedings of the SIGCHI conference on Human factors in computing systems*, pages 198–205, New York, NY, USA, 2001. ACM Press.

[230] Allison Woodruff, James Landay, and Michael Stonebraker. Constant density visualizations of non-uniform distributions of data. In *UIST '98: Proceedings of the 11th annual ACM symposium on User interface software and technology*, pages 19–28, New York, NY, USA, 1998. ACM Press.

[231] Allison Woodruff, James Landay, and Michael Stonebraker. Constant information density in zoomable interfaces. In *AVI '98: Proceedings of the working conference on Advanced visual interfaces*, pages 57–65, New York, NY, USA, 1998. ACM Press.

[232] Allison Woodruff, James Landay, and Michael Stonebraker. Goal-directed zoom. In *CHI 98: conference summary on Human factors in computing systems*, pages 305–306, New York, NY, USA, 1998. ACM Press.

[233] Allison Woodruff, James Landay, and Michael Stonebraker. Vida: (visual information density adjuster). In *CHI '99: CHI '99 extended abstracts on Human factors in computing systems*, pages 19–20, New York, NY, USA, 1999. ACM Press.

[234] Allison Woodruff, Alan Su, Michael Stonebraker, Caroline Paxson, Jolly Chen, Alexander Aiken, Peter Wisnovsky, and Cimarron Taylor. Navigation and coordination primitives for multidimensional visual browsers. In *Proceedings of the third IFIP WG2.6 working conference on Visual database systems 3 (VDB-3)*, pages 360–371, London, UK, UK, 1995. Chapman & Hall, Ltd.

[235] Ka-Ping Yee. Peephole displays: pen interaction on spatially aware handheld computers. In *CHI '03: Proceedings of the SIGCHI conference on Human factors in computing systems*, pages 1–8, New York, NY, USA, 2003. ACM Press.

[236] Ka-Ping Yee. Two-handed interaction on a tablet display. In *CHI '04: CHI '04 extended abstracts on Human factors in computing systems*, pages 1493–1496, New York, NY, USA, 2004. ACM Press.

[237] Robert Zeleznik and Timothy Miller. Fluid inking: augmenting the medium of free-form inking with gestures. In *GI '06: Proceedings of the 2006 conference on Graphics interface*, pages 155–162, Toronto, Ont., Canada, Canada, 2006. Canadian Information Processing Society.

[238] Polle T. Zellweger, Jock D. Mackinlay, Lance Good, Mark Stefik, and Patrick Baudisch. City lights: contextual views in minimal space. In *CHI '03: CHI '03 extended abstracts on Human factors in computing systems*, pages 838–839, New York, NY, USA, 2003. ACM Press.

[239] S. Zhai and B. A. Smith. Multistream input: an experimental study of document scrolling methods. *IBM Syst. J.*, 38(4):642–651, 1999.

[240] Shumin Zhai, Barton A. Smith, and Ted Selker. Improving browsing performance: A study of four input devices for scrolling and pointing tasks. In *INTERACT '97: Proceedings of the IFIP TC13 Interantional Conference on Human-Computer Interaction*, pages 286–293, London, UK, UK, 1997. Chapman & Hall, Ltd.

www.ingramcontent.com/pod-product-compliance
Lightning Source LLC
LaVergne TN
LVHW062315060326
832902LV00013B/2238